THE BEST AMERICAN RECIPES 2002–2003

The Year's Top Picks

From Books, Magazines,

Newspapers, and the Internet

THE BEST AMERICAN RECIPES

2002–2003

Fran McCullough

SERIES EDITOR

With

Molly Stevens

With a foreword by

Anthony Bourdain

Houghton Mifflin Company
Boston   New York
2002

ISSN: 1525-1101
ISBN: 0-618-19137-2

Designed by Anne Chalmers
Cover photograph by Anna Williams
Food styling by Rori Trovato
Prop styling by Joelle Hoverson

Printed in the United States of America

DOW 10 9 8 7 6 5 4 3 2 1

contents

foreword

THE DESIRE, THE URGE TO COOK well is a noble one. There is, of course, the laudable instinct to nourish, to provide sustenance and pleasure to others — and whether it is a talented amateur or a hardened professional doing the cooking, there is also the desire to dazzle, to impress, either with the technical proficiency or creativity of one's efforts or simply with the seriousness and generosity of one's intent. There is in the heart of every cook the need to share. We share by cooking for other people. We share through our appreciation of a fresh ingredient, the glory of the seasons, a regional specialty of which we're proud, a beloved family tradition, and ethnic identity, or the knowledge the cook has acquired of a particular dish or preparation and the recognition that it is good. If you stumble across a tiny mom-and-pop Italian restaurant in a neglected part of town and discover a simple dessert of fresh strawberries tossed with balsamic vinegar, sugar, and mint, a dessert that makes your head nearly explode with the flavor of the first bite — and if you are a foodie — your first thought is to tell others about the restaurant. If you're a cook, your first impulse is to buy some impeccable wild strawberries, a bunch of mint, some superfine sugar, and a nice bottle of balsamic vinegar and get busy in the kitchen.

No one knows more intimately — and with more certainty — that food can be magical than world-weary professionals who spend most waking hours cooking. Twenty years of drilling out plates of food for a hungry public does nothing to diminish our appreciation of the sheer mystical power of a slowly braised hunk of meat just removed from the oven, its raw, sharp, tough edges gone soft and rich and multidimensional through the passage of time and the controlled application of heat. And how can one not gaze in wonder at a loaf of freshly baked bread, once pale and nearly shapeless, now firm and deeply hued in browns and golds, smelling of some sudden and intensely remembered moment past? Cooks are alchemists, and they like to practice their magic in front of an audience. It is deeply and almost instantaneously gratifying to prepare a meal for others, to show them how good, how different, how easy, or how amazing food can be.

The Best American Recipes 2002–2003 is a collection of recipes from people who fully understand the strange and fabulous powers that a well-prepared meal can have. Professional or not, the creators of the dishes in these pages share the trait that cooks of every variety and from every culture and background have always had in common: a familiarity with the hows, whats, and whys of the kitchen — what happens when an egg is agitated in a hot pan, why cakes rise and soufflés fall, that (for reasons understood explicitly or instinctively) peeled potatoes turn dark when exposed to air, soups and stews seem to get better overnight, and almost everything tastes better on the bone. They share a need to make people happy, to please and delight others. Regardless of their motivations, the desired reactions are always smiles, glassy looks, moans of pleasure. They understand the importance of the seasons and the imperative that food come from a specific place. Food is not solely chemistry, however literally one reads and follows recipes. It is also geography, history, anthropology, and ethnography, with a dash of the visual arts. At its heart, a good recipe and the ability to prepare it well require an understanding of human nature: the undefined, unmeasured, unprintable ingredients like sense memory, nostalgia, love, and emotional need, and others even less quantifiable, such as my personal favorite, Weltschmerz, defined best as "a sense of homesickness for a place one has never been."

Case in point: the shrewd and wonderful recipe for Smoked Salmon Croque Monsieur with Baby Watercress Salad (page 134) from four-star chef Eric Ripert of New York's Le Bernardin. Eric is a battle-hardened veteran of the Manhattan restaurant trenches, a former protégé of Joël Robuchon. He's a smooth, slick, sophisticated chef at the top of his game, a man used to catering to the caprices of maybe the most jaded yet demanding palates on the planet. I know Eric. He spends a lot of time in limousines, dresses way too well for a cook, and has had all the excuses necessary to become a hard-case cynic, getting by on dazzling technical proficiency and a repertoire of big-league preparations stretching back to Methuselah. But what is this? A simple fried cheese and ham (in this case, salmon) sandwich, the old standby quick lunch for generations of Frenchmen and millions of visitors. A dish that summons up memories of places we've been or want to have been or feel as if we've been: a tiny café, one of thousands like it in Paris and elsewhere. A small, round table that wobbles slightly, a not particularly nice waiter, perhaps a cold drizzle outside. A glass of Stella, an ashtray that says Ricard, Serge Gainsbourg and Jane Birkin on the stereo, and a cloud of Gitane smoke from the horseplayers at the tiny zinc bar. It's an easy recipe, a seeming lay-up from a man with such an accomplished résumé. (The preserved lemon is a tease, a Moroccan element — a touch of the exotic, perhaps reminding you not to get so comfortable that you think you're actually at that table in Paris.) But that's my point — and Eric's, I'm guessing. Many of the real ingredients are nowhere to be found, in either recipe or finished product; they're thousands of miles away and years past.

Or there's the thing itself, direct from the source, like Clem and Ursie Silva's Sea Clam Pie (page 118), from their eponymous clam bar in a former Dairy Queen in Provincetown, Massachusetts. This is a dish completely and triumphantly without irony. The recipe is a straight-ahead, honest reflection of what Clem and Ursie do best: a reflection of its Cape Cod surroundings, traditional

Portuguese ingredients, and the very real needs and expectations of the community. Their restaurant is about as far away from Le Bernardin as any place could be, yet both recipes reflect food at its very best.

Tom Douglas is one of Seattle's hottest chefs, a man for whom current trends and the latest ingredients hold no mystery, but his Spice-Rubbed Turkey with Sage Gravy and Wild Mushroom Stuffing (page 150) reveals the same kind of empathy and understanding for the human soul and its needs as the others. Look at the recipe. Quickly. You know it's going to be good, don't you? It makes immediate sense. Maybe your grandmother didn't use hazelnuts or dried porcini mushrooms in her Thanksgiving turkey, but you can taste it, you can picture it, just scanning the recipe. My stomach is growling as I write these words.

From Nigella Lawson, a cook with an absolutely bred-in-the-bone sense of what's good, a frighteningly talented amateur who is immediately recognizable (if you watch her on TV) as what professional ballplayers enviously refer to as a "natural," comes Green Pea Risotto (page 216) — exactly the kind of dish I'd select if facing imminent execution. Simple, beautiful, lush, a little sinful, it should serve as convincing evidence that yes, you can cook well. Fortunately, Nigella has provided us mere mortals with concept, preparations, and measurements.

I waxed philosophical earlier about the pleasures of slowly braised meat, such as Braised Short Ribs of Beef (page 168) from Gray Kunz and Todd Humphries. The dish comes from Kunz's time at Lespinasse, about

as fine and as fancy a restaurant as you could expect to find anywhere on earth. But take a deep breath, scan the recipe, and what do you see? Looking past the shock of the new — the coriander seeds and allspice berries, the cumin seeds and Szechwan peppers, the scary and unfamiliar (but good) tamarind paste — there remains an unpretentious preparation of slowly braised beef short ribs, a four-star chef's take on something people have been doing at home for centuries. It's innovative and exciting, yet wonderfully familiar, an expression of what all of us who love good food know to be magic.

A final note: It serves no one to be a slave to recipes. Unless we're talking about pastry and baked goods, which require more exacting directions than "a little of this, a little of that," you should be encouraged, as soon as reasonably possible (meaning when you feel comfortable with a recipe and your way of handling it), to unchain yourself from the directions. Food, like a horse, senses fear. A hollandaise made a thousand times will break when you absolutely need it. Approached with confidence, a pure heart, and casual, well-meaning intent, most food will behave. Treated tenuously, as a potential enemy, it will not. Anticipate having fun and sharing that fun with others. A poker player who needs to break the bank rarely does. The player who sits down looking only to enjoy, to learn, to experience, is the one who goes home richer than he came.

Cook free or die.

ANTHONY BOURDAIN
March 2002

introduction

We're always asked how we manage to find the recipes in this series of Bests. The process begins in January of each new year, as we troll through hundreds of cookbooks, magazines, newspapers, newsletters, and websites. We narrow it down to about 700 likely contenders and start cooking our way to the best of them.

We've been thinking a lot this year about what a good recipe really is, partly in response to the question we're always asked: How do you know one when you see it? We're mildly embarrassed to say we don't always know, even though we're pretty good at scoping out the ingredients and directions so we can imagine what the dish will taste like.

The trouble is that what's on the page isn't always a good indication of what it will taste like in your mouth. Usually our instincts are reliable, but sometimes we're just dumbfounded by the proof of the pudding — and sometimes the finished dish goes straight into the garbage, even if it has a great pedigree.

So what are we looking for? First of all, it has to taste great and be a dish we'd want to make again. It needs to be useful; we don't think you're looking for a recipe for homemade egg noodles, however foolproof. If you can make it out of pantry staples, if it keeps well and can be used in a number of different ways, so much the better. If it's a really good recipe, it makes anyone a good cook, even a tenderfoot in the kitchen. That kind of recipe works because it has an inner logic that allows a little imprecision or improvisation. Russ Parsons's foolproof Oven-Steamed Salmon with Cucumber Salad (page 130) and Faith Willinger's Anarchy Cake (page 268) are good examples.

Those are the basics, but there are also recipes that get bonus points. They might come from an unlikely source (like the supermarket handout at the Palace Market in tiny Point Reyes, California) or teach us a new way of doing something that's been written in stone for decades or more (such as the "backwards" German Potato Salad on page 62) or show us how to use a new ingredient or be the best version we've seen yet of a classic. There's a reason these classics are classic — everyone loves them, and they have a kind of built-in comfort-food factor that always makes them warmly greeted at the table. Pam Anderson's stunningly good Light Crisp Waffles (page 80) is a fine example — so very good that you really ought to buy a waffle iron if you don't have one already just so you can make these waffles on a lazy Sunday.

On the opposite end of the scale from the exemplary classic recipe is the thrilling new recipe, preferably one that's incredibly simple. John Ash's wonderful Laksa (page 32) is one of those — new to us, but old to Indonesia and Australia, where it's wildly popular. It takes a few minutes, and possibly a trip to the Asian market, to put together Laksa, but once you've got the paste (and you can buy a good commercial one) you've got the makings of a sensational soup.

Probably the best example in this collection of our dream recipes is a real showstopper, the Heirloom Tomato and Watermelon Salad (page 56) from Geoffrey Zakarian, the chef at Town in New York City. The dramatically new (and brilliant) idea of combining watermelon and tomato — and this was one of several recipes featuring this odd couple we found this year — is taken to another level by adding cracked coriander seeds and a bit of dill. The salt is key here, to bring up the flavors of the fruits (tomato's a fruit, remember?). There's no acid beyond the tomatoes and just a little olive oil to make it a salad. Nothing cheffy and complicated here: with just a few ingredients, no cooking, almost no prep, perhaps a total of five minutes in the kitchen, you have a gorgeous, exciting dish that will be the hit of any dinner party. That's an ultimate Best Recipe, one you have to tell everyone about and can't wait to make again.

There's another element as well, a sort of X factor, which is what tastes good to us right now. What's happening at any given moment is to some degree a question of trendiness, but it's also more than that. This year, for instance, we got all excited about hunting for a great meat loaf and some terrific blueberry muffins. We have no idea why, but suddenly that's what we wanted to find. In the course of putting the word out, we discovered we weren't alone in our quest; other people have the same craving. These are quintessential American specialties, and yet they're often disappointing.

We think we've actually found our meat loaf and blueberry muffins, the ones we'll make again and again. Blue Plate Meat Loaf (page 157) couldn't be simpler, and yet it's got soul; it just tastes right. The Jordan Marsh Blueberry Muffins (page 85) — well, ask any old-line Bostonian, and you'll hear raves about these muffins — are a lost-and-found recipe from the famous old Boston department store's bakery.

A Best Recipe is, in the end, a keeper. We hope you find some good keepers of your own in this year's collection. And, as we embark on next year's collection, we welcome your suggestions and comments. Write to us in care of our publisher, Houghton Mifflin Company, 222 Berkeley Street, Boston, Massachusetts 02116.

—FRAN MCCULLOUGH
and MOLLY STEVENS

the year in food

ONCE AGAIN, WE CAN'T HELP ourselves. From our unique perch, looking at all the recipes we can find in cookbooks, magazines, newspapers, the Internet, and anywhere else good cooks exchange their favorites, we see patterns of electricity gathering around certain foods, techniques, tools, and ideas. We can't resist sharing them with you, so here goes.

FAVORITE INGREDIENT
Butter

It's back, in every conceivable form, used every conceivable way. Butter isn't just butter anymore; there's superfatted butter, like Plugrá and the new Land O' Lakes high-fat butter, which are a bit more like European butter. But we want that too, that cultured butter from France which has a slight tang; there are now homegrown versions as well, and they're very good. To see this butter used as a main flavoring, try the French Butter Cookies (page 244), and you'll see what all the excitement is about.

Close on boutique butter's heels is crème fraîche, this year's chef's darling, which turns up everywhere from panna cotta to dessert topping in place of whipped cream. Just a few years ago, homegrown crème fraîche was likely to be spoiled before you even unpacked the groceries. Now there are several small companies producing an excellent product. By comparison, sour cream seems impossibly one-dimensional.

MUST-HAVE TASTE
Tart

It makes perfect sense that in the era of incredibly rich dairy products, tart foods are just what we want to be eating. Lemon was clearly the lead fruit this year, at least up until about October, when cranberries suddenly took over. We wanted to eat them, drink them, turn them into chutneys and have them raw or cooked or dried. We just can't get enough cranberries this year. Runners-up are also appealing: Key limes from Mexico and rhubarb.

COOKING TECHNIQUE
Grilling

We had a year or two off from grilling, but it's back with a vengeance. A number of grilling books have reignited this love affair, and we now want to grill everything, from fish to cabbage (truly: check out the Barbecued Stuffed Cabbage on page 196).

VEGETABLE
Cabbage

We're not kidding. This wallflower of a vegetable has been lucky that Americans like coleslaw, but this year it's hit the big time (see Barbecued Stuffed Cabbage, above). We even saw (and loved) a cabbage pesto. Cabbage goes into gratins, where its inherent sweetness and delicacy come through, and into sophisticated salads, like Fiesolana (page 68). Even coleslaw has some invigorating new flavors from Southeast Asia.

HERB
Sage

Why everyone suddenly fell in love with sage is inexplicable — except that it goes so well with pork, which is increasingly on the comeback trail, and turkey. Our turkey this year has a major sage component, and it's just wonderful. Sage is also one of those good old herbs you can grow easily and keep forever. A little goes a long way, but we seem to want more than a little lately.

CURIOSITY
Eggs over everything

Eggs themselves have only recently come out of rehab, and now they're being used to top everything from spaghetti to chickpeas. They make a lovely, rustic, simple sauce, and now that we have some good organic free-range eggs around, it's worth trying them this way. This year's egg-topped recipes are very homey and comforting. New York chef Gabrielle

Hamilton also figured out how to cook an egg to the perfect point for this phenomenon — a great public service.

SURPRISING INGREDIENT
Bread

We've had years in which bread was incredibly important on the table, but this year we notice it as an ingredient in its own right: in bread puddings, even in a bread lasagna, and in endless recipes where bread crumbs play a significant role. This thrifty peasant approach makes for some interesting dishes. It's not just for French toast and turkey stuffing anymore.

OBSESSION
Chocolate

Wasn't this last year's obsession? Isn't it always the obsession? Well, yes, but this year chocolate has outdone itself, in a number of cookbooks, to begin with, but also in a huge number of sophisticated new chocolate products with high cacao content. With the new top-quality chocolates, both imported and domestic, chocolate connoisseurs now really have something to sink their teeth into. They also have a new bible, Maricel Presilla's *The New Taste of Chocolate,* from Ten Speed Press.

DRINK
Port

Port is a magical ingredient (showcased in Ported Rhubarb on page 285 and Cranberry and Dried Cherry Relish on page 227) that seems finally to be coming into its own. It's also one of the world's great drinks, and we're just beginning to have an appreciation of its complexities.

Nonstick baking mats

This was a tough one. There were lots of great new tools this year, such as the gizmo that juliennes vegetables and looks like a potato peeler or the terrific enameled Mexican lime and lemon squeezers that look so cheery and work so well. Our runner-up, the endlessly useful and satisfying mortar and pestle is possibly the most ancient cooking utensil of all, except perhaps for stones, but it's a necessity these days for making your own garlicky aioli, grinding the huge number of fresh spices that appear in contemporary recipes, or making a quick uncooked sauce.

But the baking mats are truly useful, and a lot of cooks have yet to discover them, so we've given them the nod. They look like big place mats, but they're made of a space-age material that keeps everything from sticking to them. Cookies, sticky candied fruits, almost anything that's likely to give you problems with baking (see Cumin Apple Chips on page 225) requires these. They have various trade names, such as Silpat. One rinse, and they're ready to go again.

FINALLY, we have to mention the extraordinary change that's taken place in the American pantry. It used to be that recipes in cookbooks from the American South listed just the ingredients you needed to buy at the store to make something, with notes about basic pantry staples at the end — and there were maybe 20 basics. But now a well-stocked pantry will probably have five-spice powder, Szechwan peppercorns, polenta, sea salts, vanilla beans, capers, anchovies, canned chipotles in adobo sauce, Thai chile paste, and spices by the yard, everything from coriander seeds to cardamom pods. Recipes not only require such exotica these days, but they use them in simple, familiar ways. We love Russ Parsons's Asian take on the classic salmon with cucumber salad or the Greek version of macaroni and cheese from Nora Pouillon. These dishes are just exactly what we want to be eating now — and we hope their excitement catches on in your kitchen as well.

starters

SOURCE: *Fine Cooking*
COOK: **Barbara J. Witt**

spicy maple walnuts

THESE ARE CAN'T-STOP-EATING-THEM NUTS — buttery, spicy with ginger and Tabasco, and lightly sweetened with maple syrup. The roasted nuts are crisp and crunchy and, if you leave the bits of fresh ginger in at the end, full of zingy little surprises. They're especially appropriate for holiday entertaining, or to serve with cocktails before an Asian meal.

makes 4 cups

- 4 tablespoons ($\frac{1}{2}$ stick) unsalted butter
- 6 quarter-sized slices fresh ginger, halved
- 1 teaspoon ground ginger
- 1 teaspoon salt

- $\frac{1}{3}$ cup pure maple syrup
- 1 tablespoon water
- $\frac{1}{4}$ teaspoon Tabasco sauce, or to taste
- 1 pound (4 cups) walnut halves

Preheat the oven to 300 degrees. In a small saucepan, combine all the ingredients except the walnuts and slowly simmer over low heat for 2 to 3 minutes. Put the walnuts in a large bowl, pour the glaze over them, and stir and toss to coat.

Line a rimmed baking sheet with foil and spread the walnuts on it in a single layer. Bake for 30 to 40 minutes, stirring and scooping up the glaze to cover the walnuts again at least every 10 minutes. When the walnuts look almost dry, they're done. Don't touch them; the syrup is extremely hot. Slide the walnuts, still on the foil, onto a wire rack and let them cool completely.

Store in airtight containers or plastic freezer bags.

cook's notes

- When the walnuts come out of the oven, use a spatula to scoop any syrup that's left on the foil onto them.
- Taste the walnuts when they've cooled — they may need more salt.

starters

SOURCE: *Asian Vegetables*
by Sara Deseran
COOK: Jennifer Cox after Barbara Tropp

edamame with szechwan pepper-salt

WE LIKE EATING EDAMAME (steamed soybeans in their pods) at Asian restaurants, but they don't seem to work too well at home — they're either soggy or oily or tasteless. Because they stump us, we tend to ignore them. But now that we have this incredibly easy recipe for roasting them, we plan to keep a steady supply in the freezer.

These soybeans are roasted, not boiled or steamed, in their pods without any oil at all. Instead, they're liberally dusted with fragrant Szechwan pepper-salt, which you make yourself in just a few minutes. Once you have the pepper-salt, you can make the edamame in just five minutes.

Leftover pepper-salt, and there will be plenty, is a good thing to keep around for seasoning stir-fries, roasted meats, and almost any Asian-style dish. It keeps for months.

serves 4

SZECHWAN PEPPER-SALT
½ cup kosher salt
¼ cup Szechwan peppercorns

1 pound fresh or frozen soybeans in their pods, thawed in the refrigerator if frozen

TO MAKE THE PEPPER-SALT:

In a medium heavy skillet, toast the salt and peppercorns over medium-low heat for about 5 minutes, or until the mixture smells aromatic and the salt takes on the color of the peppercorns.

Remove from the heat and let cool. Grind the cooled pepper-salt to a fine powder in a food processor. Pass through a strainer to remove any husks. (The pepper-salt can be stored for months in a sealed glass jar.)

Preheat the oven to 450 degrees. Place the soybean pods on a rimmed baking sheet and sprinkle them with about 2 tablespoons of the pepper-salt.

Roast the soybeans for 5 to 7 minutes, or until tender but toothsome. Serve warm or at room temperature.

cook's notes

♋ Not all of the hard little Szechwan peppercorns will be ground by the food processor blade. Just discard the whole ones.

♋ If you can't find whole Szechwan peppercorns, it may be easier to find the ground version at an Asian market. Just mix it with an equal amount of kosher salt and skip the pan-roasting.

to drink

Asian beer
or warm sake

SOURCE: **Calraisins.org**
COOK: **Robert Del Grande**

spicy margarita raisins

SUPER SIMPLE AND JUST PLAIN WONDERFUL, these south-of-the-border raisins are a perfect combination of spicy, sweet, and salty. There's a hint of buttery flavor, the zing of chile, red pepper, and all the elements of a good margarita — tequila, Cointreau, lime, and salt. Be sure to cook the raisins slowly so that they begin to puff up and soften; too much heat will toughen them so that they won't soak up all of the seasonings.

Once you start munching these little guys, you can't stop. We love snacking on them, either on their own or mixed with roasted salted peanuts, especially with a beer or cocktail. They'd also be good tossed into a Waldorf salad.

makes about 1 ½ cups

1 tablespoon butter

½ teaspoon crushed red pepper flakes

1½ cups California raisins

2 tablespoons silver tequila

2 teaspoons Cointreau

2 teaspoons fresh lime juice

1 teaspoon kosher or coarse salt

In a large skillet, melt the butter until foaming over medium heat. Add the red pepper flakes and sauté for about 1 minute. Add the raisins and stir to coat with the butter. Cook slowly until the raisins begin to puff slightly. Carefully add the tequila and Cointreau and cook just until the liquid evaporates. Stir in the lime juice. Remove from the heat and let cool.

When the raisins have cooled, add the salt and toss until evenly distributed. Serve at room temperature.

cook's notes

- If you don't have pricey silver tequila in the liquor cabinet, any tequila will do. We used standard margarita tequila and liked it just fine.
- Likewise, you may use Grand Marnier or Triple Sec in place of Cointreau.

to drink

Watermelon Punch (page 299)
or Mexican beer

SOURCE: *Williams-Sonoma Taste*
COOK: Marimar Torres

bacon-wrapped dates with almonds

THIS IS A GREAT SWEET-SALTY PAIRING with a little crunch from the almond in the middle. You can make these tapas ahead and serve them at room temperature — but don't chill them. And there are a couple of other important elements: the bacon has to be thinly sliced, or it won't cook right and will mask the other elements, and be sure to toast the almonds, which brings out their flavor and crunch.

serves 8

24 blanched whole almonds
24 Medjool dates, pitted

8 thin bacon slices, cut crosswise into thirds

Preheat the oven to 350 degrees. Place the almonds on a baking sheet and toast until lightly golden, about 10 minutes. Let cool. Leave the oven on.

Stuff each date with an almond, then wrap with a piece of the bacon. Secure the package with a toothpick. Place the stuffed dates on a large baking sheet.

Bake until the bacon is crisp, 20 to 30 minutes. Transfer to paper towels to drain. Let cool briefly and serve warm.

cook's notes

❧ Pitted dates sometimes contain pits, left inadvertently by whatever machine pits them. Feel for them when you're stuffing the almonds in to avoid any unpleasant surprises.

❧ Smoky hickory bacon will be fine here, even though it's not very Spanish.

serve with

An assortment of tapas, such as Manchego cheese,
peppers, and caper berries or green olives

❧

to drink

Sparkling Spanish Cava
or rosé Bandol

SOURCE: *Gourmet*
COOK: Katy Massam

vodka-spiked cherry tomatoes with pepper-salt

PEELING CHERRY TOMATOES MIGHT SEEM to be in the category of peeling grapes — i.e., life is too short — but it's such a cinch and the results are so astoundingly good that we beg you to indulge us and give these a try. It's a good mindless job you can do while watching TV or get the kids to do it, because it's actually kind of fun. If peeling little tomatoes is out of the question, see the tip on the next page for a simpler variation with no nude tomatoes.

Vodka brings out a new flavor dimension in tomatoes, an indescribable zing with a sweet, lemony kick. One guest we served these tomatoes to called four days later to say she couldn't get them out of her mind. We can't either.

serves 12

3 pints firm small red and yellow cherry tomatoes
½ cup vodka
3 tablespoons white wine vinegar
1 tablespoon superfine sugar

1 teaspoon finely grated lemon zest
3 tablespoons kosher salt
1½ tablespoons coarsely ground black pepper

Cut a small X in the skin of the blossom end of each tomato. Have ready a bowl of ice water. Drop the tomatoes, 5 at a time, into a saucepan of boiling water for 3 seconds, then immediately scoop them out and transfer them to the bowl of ice water so they don't cook. Drain and peel the tomatoes. Place the tomatoes in a large shallow dish.

In a small bowl, stir together the vodka, vinegar, sugar, and lemon zest until the sugar is dissolved. Pour over the tomatoes, gently tossing to coat. Marinate, covered and chilled, for at least 30 minutes and up to 1 hour.

In a small bowl, stir together the salt and pepper. Serve with the tomatoes for dipping on toothpicks.

❧ You can prepare the tomatoes and the vodka marinade the day before you plan to serve them and combine them before serving. Place the vodka mixture in a screw-top jar, cover the tomatoes with plastic wrap, and store both in the refrigerator.

❧ Be sure the tomatoes are firm and not too ripe, or they'll be mushy.

tip

For those who refuse to peel cherry tomatoes, make James Beard's Drunken Cherry Tomatoes, which Arthur Schwartz resurrected this year in the *New York Times Magazine*. All you need is a bowl of cherry tomatoes, some small bowls of vodka or gin, and some even smaller bowls of salt, pepper, and ground cumin or cayenne pepper — with some toothpicks, of course. Guests dip the tomatoes in the vodka or gin, then into the seasonings as they please.

SOURCE: Marian Burros, *New York Times*
COOK: Ann Amernick, Palena Restaurant

almond cheese straws

THESE SUPERLATIVE CHEESE STRAWS are from master baker Ann Amernick, one of the brightest culinary stars in Washington, D.C. When she sends out these little treats at Palena restaurant (where she is the pastry chef), eager diners lunge for them. Here's a way to make them at home with store-bought puff pastry. They really are a welcome change from standard cheese straws. It's the combination of cheeses that makes them so savory, bold, and intense — and the sweet crunch of toasted almonds that makes them hard to stop eating. Bonus: these cheese straws freeze well, so you can have an easy and distinctive cocktail snack at a moment's notice.

Be sure to read through the entire recipe before you start baking. You'll need two same-sized baking sheets so you can neatly perform the little "flip" halfway through baking that makes these cheese straws crisp on both sides.

makes 7 to 9 dozen straws

2 cups blanched sliced almonds

2 cups grated Parmigiano-Reggiano and aged Gouda cheese (see note)

1 pound frozen puff pastry, thawed (see note)

1 large egg, beaten

In a large bowl, stir together the almonds and cheeses.

Line a 14-x-17- or 12-x-18-inch baking sheet with parchment paper. Place the pastry dough on a well-floured board. Flour the top and turn the dough over. Flour a rolling pin and roll out the dough to fit the baking sheet. Roll the dough loosely onto the rolling pin, then unroll it onto the parchment. Brush the dough with the beaten egg. Sprinkle the almond-cheese mixture evenly over the dough and press down lightly to make the topping stick.

Cut the dough crosswise into three or four even-sized pieces. Cut each piece into 1/2-inch-wide strips (see notes below). Refrigerate for 30 minutes.

Preheat the oven to 325 degrees, with a rack in the bottom third. Bake the dough strips for 20 to 25 minutes. Remove from the oven. Place a second baking sheet of the same size over the baking sheet filled with the strips, and carefully flip the two sheets so that the parchment paper is on top. Remove the paper carefully. Reduce the oven temperature to 275 degrees and bake the strips for 20 to 25 minutes more, or until golden brown. Do not let the almonds burn. Let cool on a wire rack, then use a serrated knife to separate the cheese straws. The straws can be frozen; reheat in a 350-degree oven until warm.

cook's notes

- If you are using a brand of frozen puff pastry that comes in two sheets, ignore the dimensions specified in the recipe. Instead, use the sheets as they are, first rolling out each lightly to eliminate the creases, and bake on two baking sheets, dividing the topping evenly between the two.

- When you're cutting the dough pastry into strips, don't be too worried about cutting all the way through the pastry. If you only manage to score it in places, that's fine. In fact, it's a bit easier to flip if all of the strips aren't separate and sliding around. You will need to separate the strips with a serrated knife after they are baked anyway.

- The straws will keep for several days in an airtight container.

- If you can find a brand of puff pastry made with all butter (such as Dufour Pastry Kitchen, (212) 929-2800 or dufourpk@aol.com), by all means buy it.

- Don't feel obliged to use aged Gouda and Parmigiano cheeses. Aged goat cheese and Manchego work too, as does any hard or semihard grating cheese with an assertive flavor. Use the cheese in whatever proportions you want or happen to have on hand.

to drink

Cranberry Martinis (page 304)

SOURCE: *Cook & Tell* by Karyl Bannister
COOK: Karyl Bannister

party cheese crackers

YOU CAN'T STOP EATING THESE CRACKERS, we promise. They're cheesy, buttery, and delicious, with little bits of pistachio making them very pretty as well. Blue cheese and chili powder are used judiciously to elevate the flavors and add depth. They're also a cinch to make, fortunately, since once you make them everyone will be begging you to bring them to the next party. They're icebox crackers, made just like icebox cookies.

If there are any leftovers after the party, they go very well with soup or salad.

makes 6½ dozen crackers

1½ cups grated Cheddar cheese (about 6 ounces), at room temperature

1 cup (2 sticks) butter, at room temperature

½ cup crumbled blue cheese (about 2 ounces), at room temperature

1 teaspoon chili powder

½ cup chopped salted pistachios

2 cups all-purpose flour

In a medium bowl using a wooden spoon, cream the Cheddar, butter, blue cheese, and chili powder. Stir in the pistachios. Sift the flour into the cheese mixture and work it in with the spoon until well blended. Form the dough into three 9-inch-long logs. Wrap the logs in waxed paper or plastic wrap and chill for 2 hours, or until firm.

Preheat the oven to 350 degrees. Slice the logs into ³⁄₈-inch-thick rounds. Place the rounds 1 inch apart on ungreased baking sheets. Bake for 10 to 14 minutes, or until barely browned on the edges. Serve warm or at room temperature. Store the crackers in an airtight container for up to 2 weeks.

cook's notes

- If you can only find shell-on salted pistachios, discard any loose bits of papery skin as you shell the nuts.
- You can use a pinch of cayenne pepper in place of the chili powder for similar effect.
- If the ingredients are not truly at room temperature, blending the dough is a real chore. Once the cheeses and butter have softened, however, it's a breeze.

tip

We all know that it's not easy to shape dough into perfectly cylindrical logs, so we were happy to find this tip for shaping perfect icebox cookies on foodweb.com. Use scissors to cut down the length of a cardboard tube (such as a paper-towel tube). Line the inside of the tube with waxed paper. Pack the dough into the tube, close it, wrap a rubber band around each end, and refrigerate. After the dough is chilled, unwrap and you're all set to slice and bake.

SOURCE: *Metropolitan Home*
COOK: Victoria Spencer

curried almond shortbread

THESE SAVORY SHORTBREADS CAN BE A LIFESAVER during a busy holiday season. You can make them up to a week ahead — in fact we liked them even better the second day — and keep them on hand to serve with cocktails, or with soup and salad for a light lunch. They're also great with afternoon tea.

"Curried" in this case means gently warming and mellow, not a big hit of spice. The almonds contribute a nice little crunch and some sweetness to the shortbread, while the cream cheese keeps it tender. These are buttery, crumbly, and a bit on the dry side, as a proper shortbread should be.

Add these simple homemade nibbles to a sampling of olives, cured meats, and cheeses and you've got a great hors d'oeuvres feast.

makes about 20 squares

6 tablespoons (³/₄ stick) butter, at room temperature

2 ounces cream cheese, softened

¹/₄ cup finely chopped almonds or cashews

1 cup all-purpose flour

¹/₄ cup rice flour (available at natural food stores)

1 teaspoon curry powder

¹/₄ teaspoon salt

Preheat the oven to 350 degrees. Grease an 8-inch-square baking pan and set aside.

In an electric mixer with a paddle attachment, cream the butter and cream cheese until soft and light, scraping down the sides of the bowl. Mix in the almonds or cashews. Add the all-purpose flour, rice flour, curry powder, and salt; stir to combine. The mixture should look like fine bread crumbs.

Use the back of a large spoon to press the shortbread mixture into the prepared pan. Bake for 35 minutes. Cut the shortbread into 1¹/₂-inch squares while it is still hot. Let the squares cool on a wire rack. Serve immediately or store in an airtight container for up to a week.

olive shortbread: Follow the recipe above, omitting the nuts, curry powder, and salt. Stir in ¹/₄ cup finely chopped oil-cured olives (about 12 pitted olives) after the flour. Proceed as directed.

cheese shortbread: Cream the butter as in the recipe above, omitting the cream cheese. Mix in 1 cup grated Pecorino or Parmesan cheese instead of the nuts. Then add ⁵/₈ cup (which is ¹/₂ cup plus ¹/₈ cup) all-purpose flour and ¹/₈ cup rice flour. Omit the curry powder and salt. Proceed as directed.

cook's notes

- You can press the dough into the pan with your fingers if you'd rather not dirty another utensil.
- Be sure to cut the squares while the shortbread is still hot; otherwise you'll end up with a pan full of crumbles.

SOURCE: *The Art of the Tart*
by Tamasin Day-Lewis
COOK: Tamasin Day-Lewis

porcini mushroom and red onion tart

THREE-QUARTERS OF A CUP OF DRIED PORCINI is indeed a lot (and pricey), but it makes this tart heady and wonderful. The mascarpone-based filling doesn't set up firm, but, instead, remains creamy and soft — perhaps not as neat to serve but delicious and luxurious to eat. Using the porcini-soaking liquid to stew the onions deepens the flavor of the filling. While thyme is nice, we love the way fresh sage marries with the woodsy mushroom taste of this tart.

This is a rich, earthy winter tart. Serve as a starter to a bigger meal or as a vegetarian main dish.

**serves 6 as a main dish
or 10 as a starter (makes one 9-inch tart)**

TART SHELL
- 1 cup all-purpose flour (see note)
  Salt
- 4 tablespoons (½ stick) cold unsalted butter
- 2–2½ tablespoons ice water
  Lightly beaten large egg, for brushing the tart shell

FILLING
- ¾ cup dried porcini mushrooms
- 2 tablespoons unsalted butter
- 2 medium red onions, thinly sliced into rings
- 1 cup plus 2 tablespoons mascarpone cheese
- 1 large egg
- 3 large egg yolks
- 8–10 fresh sage leaves or 2–3 sprigs fresh thyme, chopped
  Salt and freshly ground black pepper

TO MAKE THE TART SHELL:

Sift the flour and a pinch of salt into the workbowl of the food processor, and cut the butter into small pieces on top of it. Process for 20 to 30 seconds, then add the ice water, 1 tablespoon at a time, with the machine running. If the pastry is still in crumbly bits after 1 to 2 minutes, add 1 tablespoon more water, being careful not to add too much water or the crust will shrink when you bake it. The moment the dough forms a ball, stop the processor. Shape the dough into a disk, wrap it in plastic, and refrigerate for at least 30 minutes.

Grease a 9-inch round or 5-x-14-inch rectangular tart pan. Roll out the dough on a floured surface. Line the pan with the dough — taking care not to stretch or tug it. Chill the tart shell for 30 minutes more.

Preheat the oven to 400 degrees. Line the tart shell with waxed paper or parchment so the edges of the paper overhang the sides. Fill the shell with a layer of dried beans; the idea is to prevent the shell from rising up in the oven. Bake the tart shell for 10 minutes, then remove the beans and the paper, prick the bottom with a fork, and bake for 5 minutes more. Remove the tart shell from the oven and brush it with a little beaten egg. Set the tart shell aside to cool. Reduce the oven temperature to 350 degrees.

MEANWHILE, TO MAKE THE FILLING:

In a small bowl, soak the porcini mushrooms in $1\frac{1}{2}$ cups warm water for about 1 hour, turning them when you remember, until they are completely rehydrated.

Strain the mushrooms into a small bowl, pressing gently; reserve the liquid. In a large skillet, melt the butter over medium heat. Add the onions and sauté gently for a few minutes until softened. Coarsely chop the mushrooms, add them to the onions, and sauté for a few minutes more. Strain the mushroom-soaking liquid into the skillet and cook, stirring occasionally, until it reduces completely; expect this to take some time. Transfer the onion mixture to a medium bowl and set aside to cool. (You can complete the cooking to this stage several hours in advance.)

In a medium bowl, whip together the mascarpone, egg, and egg yolks, then add the chopped sage or thyme. Stir in the mushroom and onion mixture, and season with salt and pepper. Spread the filling over the bottom of the cooled tart shell.

Bake for 10 minutes. Reduce the oven temperature to 325 degrees and cook for 25 to 30 minutes more. Check the tart after 25 minutes to see how loose the filling is. Remove from the oven when it is still quite obviously shuddery in the center, and let cool for 10 minutes before serving. Cut into pieces and serve warm.

❧ For the crust, you may substitute whole wheat flour for some or all of the all-purpose flour. Its heartier taste goes well with the mushroom filling.

❧ For a richer crust, add one egg yolk before you add the water. In this case, you'll need only 1 to 1½ teaspoons ice water.

serve with

Curried Almond Shortbread (page 12), with drinks
Roasted Winter Squash (page 194)
Simple spinach salad
Ported Rhubarb (page 285) over vanilla ice cream

❧

to drink

Sangiovese
or Merlot

SOURCE: *Santé*

COOK: Alex Duran

beef tenderloin tapas

TAPAS, THE WONDERFUL BAR NIBBLES that get eaten all through the day and night in Spain, are a great choice for casual entertaining. This especially delicious recipe comes from the chef at Málaga Tapas & Bar in Austin, Texas, and it's destined to be the star of any tapas collection. Just add some good Spanish ham, olives, cheese, and roasted nuts for a cocktail spread. The beef also makes a good starter on its own — or even a main course — but be warned, it's very rich.

You don't immediately think of beef, cream, and whiskey when you think of tapas, but that's part of the surprise of this dish. It's the little bit of pimiento and sweet Spanish paprika that provides the Spanish accent. Serve with bread to soak up the sauce.

serves 6 to 8

1 pound beef tenderloin, thinly sliced

1½ teaspoons cracked black pepper

2 tablespoons extra-virgin olive oil

1 medium yellow onion, thinly sliced

1 tablespoon minced garlic

½ cup whiskey

½ cup chicken stock

½ cup whipping cream

Salt

1½ teaspoons chopped fresh parsley

1½ teaspoons chopped red pimiento

1½ teaspoons sweet Spanish paprika

Season the sliced tenderloin with the pepper. In a large skillet, heat 1 tablespoon of the olive oil over medium-high heat. Add the beef and sear it for 30 seconds per side. Remove the beef from the pan.

Add the remaining 1 tablespoon olive oil and the onion to the skillet, and cook for 1 to 2 minutes. Add the garlic and stir for 1 minute. Add the whiskey and boil to reduce by about two-thirds. Stir in the stock and cream, reduce the heat to medium, and simmer for 3 to 4 minutes. Season with salt to taste. Return the beef with all its juices to the skillet, stir to coat with the sauce, and reheat.

Sprinkle the beef with the parsley, pimiento, and paprika. Serve immediately with bread to soak up the sauce.

ℒ Make sure the tenderloin is very cold when you slice it, and slice across the grain, as if you were slicing it to serve. Make the slices $1/4$ to $1/3$ inch thick, no thinner, or they'll dry out.

ℒ Don't use a nonstick pan when you sear the meat, since you want the pan drippings to become the base of the sauce. Sear the meat in batches; if you crowd the pan, you'll steam the meat into a very unappetizing grayness.

ℒ You can use canned roasted red peppers in place of the pimiento — and if you can find jarred piquillo peppers from Spain, so much the better. The garnish is minimal, but a few strips of pepper make the dish even more attractive.

serve with

Sliced crusty bread for sopping up sauce

ℒ

to drink

Amontillado
or *palo cortado* sherry

SOURCE: Garlic package, Cody Creek Farm
COOK: Vivian Beatrice

garlicky sun-dried tomato spread

CODY CREEK FARM IS IN SAUGERTIES, NEW YORK, where they grow some awesome hardneck garlic — the garlic equivalent of heirloom tomatoes. On our package, we discovered this simple but memorable recipe, and we've already passed it along to several enthusiastic samplers who insisted on having it.

This spread is earthy, sweet, and intensely garlicky, even when made with supermarket garlic. If that's inappropriate for your party (if it's Valentine's Day or you expect vampires), make it with roasted garlic instead for a milder version. The spread needs a sturdy companion, such as whole-grain bread or hearty crackers. It's also very good spread on bread and toasted briefly in a toaster oven or under the broiler.

makes about ¾ cup

12 sun-dried tomatoes (*not* packed in oil)
¼ cup almonds

¼ cup grated Parmesan cheese
4 garlic cloves
¼ cup olive oil

In a small bowl, soak the sun-dried tomatoes in warm water until they're soft and flexible, about 10 minutes.

Drain the tomatoes and place them in a blender or food processor along with the almonds, Parmesan, garlic, and oil. Process to blend, but not for too long — the spread should be a little chunky.

Serve the spread in a small crock or in a hollowed-out green or yellow bell pepper.

cook's note

❦ For a less pungent spread, use roasted garlic cloves. To roast a whole head of garlic, preheat the oven to 400 degrees. Place the garlic on a square of aluminum foil. Separate the cloves a bit and drizzle a little olive oil over the top. Pull the foil up over the garlic and seal loosely. Roast for 30 to 45 minutes, or until the cloves are soft. Squeeze the roasted garlic out of the cloves.

starters

SOURCE: *Cook's Illustrated*
COOK: Julia Collin

bacon, scallion, and caramelized onion dip

THIS IS WHAT ONION DIP SHOULD TASTE LIKE. It's more work than the standard soup-mix onion dip, but the results are far superior in flavor and consistency. It's got sweetness from the caramelized onions, a subtle bacon flavor, and a fresh lift from the scallions — altogether very yummy. The dip has a higher vegetable-to-sour-cream ratio than usual, but that's part of what makes it so good. Serve it with raw vegetables or crackers.

makes about 1¹/₂ cups

CARAMELIZED ONIONS
1 tablespoon unsalted butter
1 tablespoon vegetable oil
1 teaspoon light brown sugar
¹/₂ teaspoon salt, or to taste
2 pounds onions, peeled and cut into ¹/₄-inch-thick slices
    Freshly ground black pepper

3 slices (about 3 ounces) bacon, cut into ¹/₄-inch pieces
2 scallions, minced
³/₄ cup sour cream
¹/₂ teaspoon cider vinegar
    Salt and freshly ground black pepper

TO MAKE THE CARAMELIZED ONIONS:

In a large nonstick skillet, heat the butter and oil over high heat. When the foam subsides, stir in the sugar and salt. Add the onions and stir to coat; cook, stirring occasionally, until the onions begin to soften and release some moisture, about 5 minutes. Reduce the heat to medium and cook, stirring frequently, until the onions are deeply browned and slightly sticky, about 40 minutes more. (If the onions are sizzling or scorching, reduce the heat. If the onions are not browning after 15 to 20 minutes, increase the heat.) Remove from the heat. Stir in 1 tablespoon water and season to taste with pepper. You should have about 1 cup onions. Set aside to cool. The onions can be refrigerated in an airtight container for up to a week.

In a small skillet, fry the bacon until crisp, about 5 minutes. Transfer to a paper-towel-lined plate with a slotted spoon and set aside.

In a medium bowl, combine ½ cup of the caramelized onions (save the rest for another use) with the scallions, sour cream, vinegar, and cooked bacon. Season with salt and pepper to taste and serve. The dip can be refrigerated in an airtight container for up to 3 days.

cook's notes

- The caramelized onions do take some time — about 45 minutes — and then you need to let them cool. So be sure to start these well ahead of time. They keep for days, so you can prepare them in advance.

- The recipe makes twice the amount of caramelized onions that you need for the dip, but they are useful to have around (try them in omelettes, scrambled eggs, grilled cheese sandwiches, pasta, salads, bruschetta). If you want to make only what you need for the dip, be sure to use a smaller skillet so the onions don't scorch.

- We like to use Spanish onions for this, but almost any onion will do, although red onions tend to get very "jammy."

- You may want to chop up the caramelized onions a bit so they won't dangle off the vegetables or crackers when dipped.

tip

There are a few ways to slice an onion. This is how the folks at *Cook's Illustrated* tell us to do it, and it speeds things up when you've got two pounds of onions in front of you. First, cut off the root end of the onion. Halve the onion from pole to pole and then peel it. Place the onion halves flat side down on a cutting board and cut into ¼-inch-thick slices across the grain.

to drink
Minted Vodka Tonic (page 302)

SOURCE: *Food & Wine*
COOK: Grace Parisi

roasted artichoke, lemon, and garlic dip

We're not at all embarrassed to say that we adore that tired old cocktail party warhorse, the fifties artichoke dip, so we were really excited to see it reinvented this year. The update is a knockout, the first item in a cocktail spread to disappear. The secret is to roast the artichokes at high temperature with chunks of lemon and garlic cloves until caramelized and tender. A bit of mayonnaise and cream cheese makes the dip familiar, but you'll be amazed by how much more depth and character this dip has over the original.

The roasting adds a step, but you can do it days in advance and then bake the dip just before your party. Serve it with any crackers or toast — we notice Triscuits always seem to disappear first.

Here's the best news of all: frozen artichoke hearts work equally well in the recipe. If you're one of those aficionados who enjoy trimming fresh artichokes down to the heart (or if they happen to be on sale), by all means buy them — otherwise, do what we do and look for boxes of frozen artichoke hearts in the freezer case.

serves 10

1 small lemon (or ½ lemon, if using frozen artichokes)

9 large artichokes (about 5½ pounds), or four 9-ounce packages frozen artichoke hearts, thawed

8 large garlic cloves, unpeeled

2 thyme sprigs

¼ cup extra-virgin olive oil
Salt and freshly ground black pepper

1 cup mayonnaise

4 tablespoons cream cheese, at room temperature

3 tablespoons fine dry bread crumbs

2 teaspoons unsalted butter, melted

Crackers or bagel chips, for serving

If using fresh artichokes, squeeze a lemon half into a large bowl of cold water and then drop the lemon half into the water. Working with one artichoke at a time, trim the stem to 1 inch and snap off all of the tough outer leaves. Using a sharp knife, cut off the top two-thirds of the artichoke. Peel the artichoke, removing all the dark green skin and tough leaves. With a teaspoon, scoop out the furry choke. Place the artichoke heart in the bowl of acidulated water. Repeat with the remaining artichokes. (If using frozen artichoke hearts, simply squeeze them dry after thawing and proceed.)

Preheat the oven to 425 degrees. If using fresh artichokes, drain them, pat dry, and cut each into eighths (frozen are already cut up). Quarter the remaining lemon half and remove the seeds. In a large bowl, toss the artichokes with the lemon quarters, garlic, thyme, and olive oil. Season with salt and pepper to taste and spread on a large nonstick rimmed baking sheet. Roast, stirring occasionally, until the artichokes are golden and tender, about 40 minutes. Let cool slightly. Discard the thyme. Reduce the oven temperature to 375 degrees.

Coarsely chop 8 of the roasted artichoke pieces and set aside. Peel the garlic and place it in a food processor. Add the remaining roasted artichokes and the lemon pieces. Pulse until finely chopped. Add the mayonnaise and cream cheese and process until smooth. Season with salt and pepper to taste. Add the reserved chopped artichoke and pulse just until combined. Spread the dip in an even layer in a small shallow baking dish. At this point, the dip may be covered and refrigerated for up to 3 days.

In a small bowl, combine the bread crumbs and butter; sprinkle over the dip. Bake until heated through and the topping is golden, about 20 minutes. Serve warm with the crackers or bagel chips.

cook's notes

- If the dip has been refrigerated before baking, expect it to take a little longer to bake.
- Bake the dip in the dish you plan to serve it in — a small soufflé or ceramic baking dish works well.
- Thaw frozen artichokes in the microwave or just leave them in the refrigerator for a day or two. Running water over them makes them soggy.

to drink

Chardonnay

SOURCE: Avocado.org
COOK: Unknown

guacamole with lemon and roasted corn

NEW RIFFS ON GUACAMOLE SEEM TO SPRING UP every year, and sometimes we're impressed by the sheer inventiveness of the cook. In this case, we don't know if it's the little bits of lemon or the roasted corn niblets that make this guacamole so special — maybe it's both. You dice up half a lemon, peel and all, and mix it right in. It adds a nice tang to the dip, and the texture is a good contrast to the creamy avocado. The other novelty here is the roasted corn. If that's new to your kitchen, be sure to roast some extra corn, because it's so delicious that we guarantee you'll end up munching it out of hand.

This guacamole is the ultimate Super Bowl treat — an all-time favorite taken to exciting new heights.

makes about 1³/₄ cups

2 ripe Hass avocados (about 1 pound), pitted and peeled

¹/₂ cup roasted corn kernels (see tip)

¹/₂ lemon, thinly sliced (with peel on), seeded, and cut into small dice

2 garlic cloves, minced

1 medium jalapeño pepper (or to taste), finely chopped

¹/₂ teaspoon ground cumin, or to taste

¹/₂ teaspoon salt, plus more to taste

Tortilla chips, for serving

In a medium bowl, mash the avocados into a coarse paste with a wooden spoon, pestle, or fork. Stir in the remaining ingredients, except the tortilla chips. Taste and adjust the seasonings with salt and cumin. Scrape the guacamole into a serving bowl and serve with tortilla chips.

Guacamole is best made right before serving, but for short-term storage, scrape it into an airtight container, lay a piece of plastic wrap against the surface of the dip, and refrigerate for a few hours.

cook's notes

🦂 Control the heat of this dip by removing the seeds from the jalapeño. If you leave the seeds in (we took them out), the guacamole will be quite fiery.

♔ For those blessed with sweet Meyer lemons, use them here — their soft skin and sweet flesh will make this dip even more tasty.

tip

Here are the directions for roasting corn from the California Avocado Commission: For $1/2$ cup roasted corn, soak 1 ear corn in water for 1 hour. Preheat the oven to 375 degrees. Remove the husks and silk and roast the ear directly on the oven rack, turning occasionally, until the kernels appear slightly shriveled. Cut the corn off the cob as closely as possible.

If corn is not in season, we use frozen shoepeg corn: Thaw the kernels, then lightly oil a baking sheet and spread the corn kernels on it in a single layer. Roast at 375 degrees, turning with a spatula once or twice, until shriveled and beginning to brown, about 15 minutes.

serve with

Tortilla chips

♔

to drink

Margaritas
or Serrano Bloody Marys (page 303)

soups

Black Bean and Chorizo Soup   27

Pureed Sweet Potato Soup   28

Creamy Carrot Parsnip Soup   30

Laksa (Malaysian Noodle Soup)   32

Roasted Onion and Saffron Soup with Sautéed Shrimp   34

One-of-Each Soup   36

Chilled Tomato Soup, Gazpacho Style   38

Chilled Melon Soup with Almonds and Grapes   40

Ecuadorian Shrimp Ceviche   42

Vatapa (Brazilian Fish Soup)   44

SOURCE: *Gourmet*
COOK: Shelton Wiseman

black bean and chorizo soup

WHEN THERE'S A NIP IN THE AIR, nothing seems quite so appealing as a bowl of this deeply flavored black bean soup. It's full of spice from the chorizo sausage and crushed red pepper flakes, but not so much that it will take your head off. The finishing touch is elegant: a garnish of thin lemon slices plus the surprise of chopped cilantro. But perhaps the best thing about this soup is that it's made with canned black beans, an excellent product that cuts your time in the kitchen to a minimum.

serves 4

2 tablespoons olive oil
1 3-to-4-ounce link Spanish chorizo (spicy cured pork sausage), coarsely chopped
1 medium onion, chopped
1/2 green bell pepper, chopped
1 large garlic clove, minced
1/2 teaspoon ground cumin

1/4 teaspoon crushed red pepper flakes
1/4 teaspoon salt
2 1/2–3 cups chicken stock
2 15- or 19-ounce cans black beans, rinsed and drained

Thin lemon slices and chopped fresh cilantro leaves, for garnish

In a large heavy saucepan, heat the oil over medium heat. Add the chorizo, onion, bell pepper, garlic, cumin, red pepper flakes, and salt and sauté until the vegetables are softened, about 10 minutes. Add the stock (2 1/2 cups if using 15-ounce cans of beans or 3 cups for 19-ounce cans) and beans and simmer, partially covered, for 15 minutes. Lightly mash the beans with a potato masher to slightly thicken the soup. Serve hot in warmed soup bowls garnished with the lemon slices and cilantro. The soup will keep, covered, in the refrigerator for 2 days.

serve with

Avocado and tomato salad
Corn bread or warm flour tortillas
Fruit and cheese

℮

to drink

A young, medium-bodied Rioja

soups

SOURCE: *Saveur*
COOK: Bob Anderson

pureed sweet potato soup

IT'S VIRTUALLY IMPOSSIBLE TO SCORE an invitation to the famous annual Bracebridge Dinner Christmas pageant at the Ahwahnee Hotel in Yosemite National Park unless you've signed up years in advance. But if you manage it, this lovely soup will be your first course. The hotel kitchen estimates that it serves 45 gallons at each seating. We like it because it makes a big batch and is a perfect starter for a holiday meal, though you could easily cut the recipe in half for a less grand gathering.

This sweet, mellow soup is not too rich, but creamy, smooth, and delicate. Cooking the sweet potatoes in their skins before adding them to the soup helps them retain their sweet flavor and bright color. The soup doesn't need the final swirl of cranberry oil, but it does add a festive touch.

serves 10 to 12

5 medium orange-fleshed sweet potatoes, unpeeled
Salt
3 tablespoons olive oil
1 large yellow onion, chopped
1 large leek (white part only), cleaned and chopped
2 medium carrots, peeled and chopped

1 celery rib, chopped
2 garlic cloves, chopped
1 cup dry white wine
10 cups chicken stock
1 cup heavy cream
Freshly ground white pepper

¼ cup cranberry oil (recipe follows; optional)

Place the sweet potatoes into a large pot, add cold water to cover and 2 large pinches of salt. Bring to a boil over high heat, reduce the heat to medium, and simmer until the sweet potatoes are soft when pierced with the tip of a knife, 30 to 40 minutes. Drain and set aside until cool enough to handle. Peel and quarter the sweet potatoes; set aside.

Meanwhile, in a large heavy soup pot, heat the oil over medium-high heat. Add the onion, leek, carrots, celery, and garlic and cook, stirring often with a wooden spoon, until the vegetables begin to soften, about 5 minutes. Add the wine, scraping up any brown bits stuck to the bottom of the pot, and cook until the alcohol has evaporated, about 2 minutes.

Add the stock and reserved sweet potatoes to the pot, increase the heat to high, and bring to a boil. Reduce the heat to medium and simmer until all the vegetables are very soft, about 30 minutes.

Working in batches, puree the soup until smooth in a food processor or blender, and return it to the pot. Stir in the cream, season with salt and white pepper to taste, and bring to a simmer over medium heat. Ladle into bowls or cups to serve, and drizzle some of the cranberry oil over each serving, if desired.

cranberry oil

Put 1 cup fresh cranberries into a mortar and finely crush with a pestle. (Or you could use a food processor to grind the berries to a pulp.) Transfer to a small bowl, add ½ cup extra-virgin olive oil, and stir to combine. Cover and refrigerate overnight. The following day, strain the cranberry mixture through a wire-mesh strainer set over a small bowl, pressing gently on the solids with a rubber spatula or wooden spoon to extract the red, pulpy cranberry oil. Discard the solids. Season to taste with salt and pepper. Whisk the oil before using. Makes ½ cup

cook's note

If you do make the cranberry oil, it really is best to use fresh cranberries. For some reason, frozen berries that have been thawed seem to make the oil less vibrant in both taste and color. There are a world of uses for leftover cranberry oil: use it as a dressing on simple greens or drizzle it over steamed green beans, boiled potatoes, baked fish, or roasted chicken. It keeps, refrigerated, for several days.

serve with

Green Onion Buttermilk Biscuits (page 23)

℘

to drink

A light, dry Riesling
or Chardonnay

SOURCE: *Country Living*
COOK: *Country Living* staff

creamy carrot parsnip soup

THIS VERY TASTY, PRETTY SOUP brings a lot of flavor and a lovely Popsicle orange color to a wintertime dinner table. It's deeply sweet from the parsnips and carrots and tangy from the buttermilk. Horseradish and ginger add some zing.

It's a versatile soup. If you don't add the cream garnish, it's low-fat. If you use vegetable stock, it's vegetarian. And you can make it a day in advance.

serves 6

2 pounds carrots, peeled and coarsely chopped (about 8 cups)

2 pounds parsnips, peeled and coarsely chopped (about 8 cups)

3 cups low-sodium chicken stock

2 teaspoons sugar

1 teaspoon salt

3 tablespoons butter

1 medium onion, finely chopped (about 1 cup)

4 garlic cloves, crushed

2 cups buttermilk

1 teaspoon freshly grated horseradish

1 teaspoon freshly grated ginger

1 tablespoon crème fraîche or sour cream (optional)

1 tablespoon chopped fresh dill (optional)

In a large soup pot, combine the carrots, parsnips, 3 cups water, stock, sugar, and salt and bring to a boil. Reduce the heat and simmer until the vegetables are tender, about 15 minutes.

In a medium skillet, melt the butter over medium heat. Add the onion and sauté until translucent, about 5 minutes. Add the garlic and cook for 2 to 3 minutes more.

Using a slotted spoon, remove the carrots and parsnips from the pot. Working in batches, puree the carrots and parsnips in a food processor or blender. Add the onion mixture and puree until smooth. Return the mixture to the pot, add the buttermilk, and heat until warm but not boiling.

When ready to serve, stir in the horseradish and ginger. Divide among soup bowls and garnish with the crème fraîche or sour cream and a sprinkling of dill, if desired.

cook's notes

- If you can't find fresh horseradish, just use the bottled variety, but drain it well first.
- You can simplify this soup by making it all in one pot: Start by sautéing the onion in the soup pot, and then add the vegetables and stock and puree everything later.
- If the soup seems too sweet (root vegetables vary a lot in their sweetness), you can add more ginger and/or horseradish to taste.

serve with

Hoosier Ham and Cheese Biscuits (page 231)

SOURCE: **Handout at Ramekins Sonoma Valley Culinary School, Sonoma, California**
COOK: **John Ash**

laksa (malaysian noodle soup)

WE TASTED OUR FIRST LAKSA only two years ago, but it's unforgettable. This heady, delectable Malaysian soup has no definitive recipe, but there are several constants, whether you eat it in Singapore or Australia or even in America. There's a fragrant spice paste, full of chile, garlic, lime, macadamia nuts (candlenuts in Malaysia), coriander seeds, ginger, fish sauce, and lots of coconut milk. The broth has even more coconut milk and ends up a creamy apricot color, luscious and slightly sweet.

Several things go into the soup bowl before you add the broth: chicken, as in this recipe, or shrimp, cooked rice noodles, maybe a vegetable or two. Add the fragrant broth and top the soup bowls with cilantro, scallions, and perhaps a little mint. If the seasoning's just right, one bowl won't be enough — this is an addictive soup, so you might as well make a lot of laksa paste (or acquire some, see note), since it freezes well.

serves 4 to 6

LAKSA PASTE

1/3 cup chopped shallots

1/3 cup chopped toasted macadamia nuts or blanched almonds

1/4 cup peeled finely chopped ginger

2 tablespoons coriander seeds, crushed

2 teaspoons sugar
   Zest and juice of 2 limes

2 tablespoons fish sauce (nam pla)

2 tablespoons chili garlic sauce, or to taste (Lee Kum Kee is a good brand that's widely available)

2 tablespoons vegetable oil

1 teaspoon toasted sesame oil

1/2 cup unsweetened coconut milk

SOUP

1 pound boneless, skinless chicken breasts

2 tablespoons soy sauce

2 tablespoons rice wine or sake

3 1/2 cups unsweetened coconut milk, well stirred

3 cups chicken broth

1 cup laksa paste, or to taste

2 cups peeled and diced butternut or other hard squash

2 tablespoons vegetable oil

2 small zucchini, cut in long julienne

4 ounces thin rice vermicelli or somen, cooked
   Fresh lime juice
   Salt and freshly ground black pepper

   Cilantro leaves and scallions, sliced on the bias, for garnish

TO MAKE THE LAKSA PASTE:

In a blender, combine all the ingredients except the coconut milk and blend for 1 to 2 minutes, or until very smooth. Transfer the paste to a small saucepan and cook over medium heat for 4 to 5 minutes, stirring constantly. The paste will be very fragrant. Stir in the coconut milk and cook for 2 to 3 minutes more. Store, covered, in the refrigerator for up to 1 week or in the freezer for up to 3 months.

TO MAKE THE SOUP:

Trim any fat from the chicken breasts and cut in half lengthwise. At a steep angle, cut the chicken crosswise into ⅛-inch-thick slices. In a medium bowl, combine the soy sauce and rice wine or sake, add the chicken and toss to coat lightly. Set aside to marinate for up to 30 minutes.

In a large saucepan, heat the coconut milk and broth over medium-high heat. Whisk in the laksa paste. Add the squash and simmer for 5 minutes, or until the squash is just tender.

Meanwhile, in a wok or large skillet, heat the oil over high heat. Add the chicken and stir-fry until just cooked through and the slices separate. Transfer the chicken to a plate.

Divide the zucchini and noodles among warm bowls and top with the chicken. Taste the broth and add lime juice and salt and pepper to taste. Ladle the hot soup into the bowls and garnish with the cilantro and scallions. Serve hot.

cook's notes

- If you're as crazy about laksa as we are, you can make it almost instantly if you have some of Charmaine Solomon's excellent laksa paste in your pantry. Order it from www.charmainesolomon.com.
- Play around with this soup: try adding bean sprouts, fresh green chiles, or even diced cucumber. John Ash's version of laksa is gorgeous, but this is the sort of soup you make with what's on hand in the Asian kitchen.
- And what would you do with leftover laksa? John Ash uses it as a base for a vinaigrette or as a marinade for chicken, fish, or pork.

SOURCE: *San Jose Mercury News*
COOK: Mark Dommen

roasted onion and saffron soup with sautéed shrimp

THIS IS THE SORT OF POLISHED, deeply flavored soup you'd expect at a first-class restaurant, but it's so simple you can easily make it at home. It was served at the opening of Copia, the American Center for Wine, Food, and the Arts in Napa Valley, where Mark Dommen is the chef at Julia's Kitchen — named in honor of *the* Julia. It's a dazzling and innovative soup: elegant, rich, smooth, and delicious. The color is a lovely buttery deep ivory, almost a pale yellow.

There are several flavor secrets here. One is roasting onions slowly in olive oil and salt, sealed inside a foil pouch. Another is the tarragon- and saffron-infused vegetable broth. Finally, there are sautéed shrimp in each soup bowl and the finished soup is enriched with a little butter.

This is a good starter for an extravagant full-course dinner — or it can be a casual meal in itself along with a salad and good bread. You can make it a day ahead.

serves 6

2 medium onions
1 tablespoon olive oil
Sea salt
5 tablespoons (¹/₂ stick plus 1 tablespoon) cold butter
1 leek (white part only), cleaned and chopped
4 cups vegetable stock, chicken stock, or shellfish stock

1 bunch tarragon, tied with string
1 large pinch saffron
1 tablespoon Pastis or Pernod Cayenne pepper
6 ounces fresh rock shrimp or other small shrimp, peeled and deveined
6 fresh chervil sprigs
1 bunch chives, snipped

Preheat the oven to 300 degrees. Peel the onions and place them on a large piece of aluminum foil. Drizzle with the oil and sprinkle with a large pinch of salt. Seal the onions in the foil and place them in a baking dish. Bake for 2¹/₂ hours, or until very soft.

Meanwhile, in a large saucepan, melt 1 tablespoon of the butter over medium heat. Add the leek and sauté until very tender but not browned. Add the stock and bring to a boil. Turn off the heat and add the tarragon and saffron. Cover the pan and let steep for 30 minutes. Discard the tarragon. Transfer the stock to a large bowl.

When the onions are ready, working in two batches, puree 1 onion, half of the liquid and half of the stock in a blender until very smooth. Stop the blender and add 1^1/$_2$ teaspoons of the Pastis or Pernod, 2 tablespoons of the butter (cut into 2 pieces), and salt and cayenne pepper to taste. Blend until the butter is incorporated. Transfer the soup back to the pan. Repeat with the remaining onion, liquid, stock, Pastis or Pernod, butter, and seasonings. Transfer the remaining soup to the pan and reheat.

To serve, sauté the shrimp (see the note below) and divide among 6 bowls. Divide the soup among the bowls, garnish with the chervil and chives, and serve hot.

cook's note

To sauté the shrimp, in a medium skillet, heat a little butter and vegetable oil together over medium-high heat. Add the shrimp, season with salt and pepper, and sauté just until they turn pink on both sides. Set aside. Seared scallops or bits of sautéed lobster tail would be nice here, too.

SOURCE: *Gourmet*
COOK: Leslie Charteris

one-of-each soup

IT WAS THE BANANA THAT THREW US. This recipe has an odd-looking list of ingredients, and it's so insanely simple that we were a bit skeptical — but it really delivers. The soup has been around in various incarnations since at least the 1950s. It turned up twice this year that we know of, and it very much deserves its long life. It relies on ordinary ingredients you probably have on hand and takes very little time to make — other than a bit of chopping, you just simmer it for 15 minutes, blend, and voilà.

But what about that banana? It's the secret ingredient, the one you don't taste that pulls this semi-vichyssoise together. The flavor is faintly sweet with a hint of heat from the curry powder.

Serve this soup hot in the winter and cold in the summer — it satisfies all year long. Or serve it hot when you first make it, then enjoy the leftovers chilled for lunch the next day.

serves 4 to 6

1 large boiling potato (about 8 ounces), peeled and coarsely chopped

1 large apple (preferably Granny Smith), peeled and coarsely chopped

1 medium onion, coarsely chopped

1 firm-ripe banana, peeled and coarsely chopped

1 celery heart (inner pale stalks with leaves), coarsely chopped (about ½ cup)

2 cups chicken stock

1 cup heavy cream or milk

1 tablespoon unsalted butter

1 heaping teaspoon curry powder

1 teaspoon salt

1 tablespoon snipped fresh chives, for garnish

In a large heavy saucepan, combine the potato, apple, onion, banana, celery, and stock over medium-high heat. Bring to a boil, cover, reduce the heat to a simmer, and cook until the vegetables and fruits are very tender, about 15 minutes. Stir in the cream or milk, butter, curry powder, and salt and heat just until hot (do not boil).

Working in batches, puree the soup in a blender until smooth. Serve hot or cold, sprinkled with the chives. The soup can be made 2 days ahead and chilled, covered.

cook's notes

- Cream is the smoother choice here, but we find that the soup is plenty rich made with milk.
- When pureeing hot liquid in a blender, use caution. Do not fill the blender jar more than two thirds full and be sure to vent the lid. This prevents the hot liquid from erupting and splattering your kitchen and yourself.
- Use a good-quality curry powder, such as Madras, since it plays a starring role.
- Finely chopped scallions can be used in place of the chives if you're chiveless.

SOURCE: *Saveur*

COOKS: **David Tanis and Russell Moore**

chilled tomato soup, gazpacho style

THIS SUMMER SOUP, SERVED AT THE ANNIVERSARY BLOWOUT of the legendary Berkeley restaurant Chez Panisse this year, is what Chez Panisse is all about. Start by getting the best tomatoes you can find, preferably organic, and then do very little to them. There's no cooking, no heating, no pureeing, and not even much chopping. It's all very basic and produces one of the most delicious tastes of summer you can imagine.

The soup base is made by extracting the pulp from five pounds of red, ripe tomatoes (in a very low-tech way — by grating them on a box grater). The tomato pulp is then just slightly thickened with a few handfuls of soaked bread and seasoned with a mash of ancho chile and garlic — just enough to add some depth. A bit of extra-virgin olive oil adds body as well as flavor.

To serve, you spoon a salsalike relish of different-colored tomatoes, cucumber, yellow bell pepper, onion, and herbs into the center of each bowl. Lean a garlicky slice of toast along the rim, and it's summer's perfect soup.

serves 6

SOUP

1 dried ancho chile, stemmed and seeded

1½ cups crustless cubes day-old country white bread

2–3 garlic cloves
Kosher salt

5 pounds best available vine-ripened red tomatoes, halved

⅓ cup extra-virgin olive oil

RELISH

½ pound small vine-ripened tomatoes (mixed varieties and colors), quartered

1 small cucumber, peeled, seeded, and diced

1 small yellow bell pepper, cored, seeded, and diced

½ small red onion, diced
Leaves from ½ bunch fresh chervil, chopped
Leaves from ½ bunch fresh basil, chopped

¼ cup extra-virgin olive oil

2 tablespoons red wine vinegar
Salt and freshly ground black pepper

6 slices country white bread, brushed with extra-virgin olive oil, toasted, and rubbed with a peeled garlic clove

TO MAKE THE SOUP:

In a small bowl, soak the chile in hot water until soft, about 30 minutes. Drain, peel, and crush the chile to a paste with a mortar and pestle (or on a cutting board with the flat of a knife); set aside. In a medium bowl, soak the bread cubes in cold water until soft, about 5 minutes. Drain, squeeze out the excess water, and set aside. Crush the garlic to a paste with 2 tablespoons salt as you did with the chile. Add the soaked bread and grind until smooth; set aside.

Set a wire-mesh strainer over a large bowl. Grate the tomatoes on the large holes of a box grater into the strainer, starting with the cut sides and grating just until you reach the skin. Strain out the seeds, pressing as much pulp as possible through the strainer with a wooden spoon. Discard the skins and seeds. Stir in the reserved chile, garlic-bread paste, and olive oil and season with salt to taste. Cover and refrigerate until chilled.

TO MAKE THE RELISH:

In a medium bowl, combine the tomatoes, cucumber, bell pepper, onion, chervil, basil, oil, vinegar, and salt and pepper to taste.

Divide the soup among 6 bowls. Add a generous spoonful of relish and a slice of toast to each bowl. Serve immediately.

cook's notes

- For the relish, a mix of yellow and red cherry tomatoes works well.
- If you can't find chervil, you might use a pinch of tarragon — but not too much, since it is stronger. Or add a splash of tarragon vinegar to the red wine vinegar.
- Don't use too fine a strainer — you want a rather open-mesh strainer so that you can push the pulp through but not the seeds.
- If you truly can't bear to hand-grate the tomatoes, peel them (by cutting an X in the skin of their bottoms and dropping them very briefly into boiling water), cut them in half, and remove the seed sacs to a strainer over a bowl. Cut the tomato shells roughly and put them in the food processor. Carefully pulse them — you don't want to end up with a puree. Push the seeds against the strainer with a wooden spoon to release as much of the jelly around them as possible, and add to the tomatoes.

to drink

Sauvignon Blanc

SOURCE: *BayWolf Restaurant Cookbook*
by Michael Wild
COOK: Michael Wild

chilled melon soup
with almonds and grapes

WHEN YOU MAKE THIS STUNNING SUMMER SOUP, you can't believe that you have the entire ingredient list. It's like one of those stump-the-cook tests: What do you make if all you have in your kitchen is a honeydew melon, some grapes, a loaf of bread, some almonds, and a lemon? That's it, plus some salt and white pepper. Out of these humble ingredients, in about five minutes, you can make this creamy (with no cream — the creaminess comes from ground almonds and bread), soothing, refreshing blender soup. There's no cooking at all, so it's not only perfect for those at the table on a hot day but perfect for the cook, too.

This is one of those soups you'll make at least once every summer.

serves 6 to 8

3/4 cup whole blanched almonds

1/4–1/2 cup fresh lemon juice

2 small honeydew or Sharlyn melons, peeled, seeded, and cut into large chunks (6–7 cups)

1 cup white bread pieces, crusts removed

Salt

Freshly ground white pepper

1 cup seedless grapes, halved

1/4 cup almonds, toasted and cut into slivers (see note)

Crème fraîche

Puree the blanched almonds and 1/4 cup of the lemon juice in a blender until totally smooth. Add the melon and bread and puree again. If the melon needs more liquid to puree properly, add a little water. (You will most likely need to puree the melon in batches. After pureeing one batch, pour out all but 1 cup of the liquid and then add the next batch.) Transfer the soup to a large bowl. Season well with salt and white pepper to taste. If the soup needs more acid, add the remaining 1/4 cup lemon juice. If the soup is too thick, you can add a little water, but if the melons are really ripe this shouldn't be a problem. Serve slightly chilled, garnished with the grapes, toasted almonds, and a swirl of crème fraîche.

cook's notes

❧ We confess that we didn't toast whole almonds and cut them into slivers. We toasted sliced almonds, and they were just fine.

❧ The crème fraîche is lovely with the soup, but you don't really need it.

to drink

Prosecco
or other light, dry sparkling wine

SOURCE: *¡Gusto!*
COOK: **Douglas Rodriguez**

ecuadorian shrimp ceviche

WE HAD TROUBLE DECIDING WHAT CHAPTER this recipe belongs in, because it falls somewhere between a fancy shrimp cocktail and a bright bowl of gazpacho. The ceviche is zesty and lively, but not spicy-hot, so it's perfect for anyone who enjoys good shrimp. It's also gorgeous, so we agree with the chef's suggestion to serve it in a stemmed martini glass to show it off.

The "soup" base gets its complex flavor from combining roasted onions, jalapeños, red pepper, and tomato with fresh citrus juice (lime and orange), tomato juice, and a bit of hot sauce.

We like the couldn't-be-simpler shrimp-cooking method of dropping them into the boiling water, turning off the heat, and letting them sit for just 1½ minutes to avoid overcooking. The shrimp go right onto the ice and then into the juicy marinade for four hours. The results: perfect texture and a great fresh flavor. Don't skimp and use small shrimp — look for shrimp with some heft to them — like 16 to 20 shrimp per pound at least — which allows for 4 or 5 nice-sized shrimp per serving.

Since all the work is done four hours ahead, this ceviche is a great party dish. Oh, and there's a surprise: a crunchy topping of popcorn and Cornnuts. We were frankly skeptical, but the Cornnuts provide a delightful saltiness — and the popcorn, well, it's just plain fun.

serves 4

- 1 red bell pepper
- 2 jalapeño peppers
- 1 large tomato
- 1 small onion, peeled and halved
- ¾ cup fresh lime juice (about 3 limes)
- ½ cup fresh orange juice (about 1 orange)
- ¼ cup tomato juice
- 1 tablespoon sugar
- ¼ teaspoon salt

- ¼ teaspoon hot sauce
- 1 pound extra-large or jumbo shrimp, peeled and deveined
- 1 cup vertically sliced red onion
- ¼ cup chopped fresh cilantro
- 2 tablespoons snipped fresh chives
- 2 tablespoons sliced scallions
- ½ cup popcorn (popped without salt or fat)
- ½ cup nutlike toasted-corn snacks (such as Cornnuts)

Preheat the oven to 400 degrees. Cut the bell pepper and jalapeños in half lengthwise; discard the seeds and membranes. Place the peppers skin side up on a foil-lined baking sheet and flatten the peppers with your hand. Add the tomato and onion to the baking sheet. Bake for 30 minutes. Remove from the oven and place the bell pepper in a sealed zip-top plastic bag; let stand for 15 minutes, then peel the bell pepper.

Roughly chop the bell pepper, jalapeños, tomato, and onion and drop them all in a food processor. Pulse a few times to make a rough paste, then add the lime juice, orange juice, tomato juice, sugar, salt, and hot sauce and process until smooth. Set aside.

In a large saucepan, bring 6 cups water to a boil. Have ready a large bowl filled with ice. Add the shrimp to the boiling water and remove from the heat. Let stand for 1½ minutes. Drain and transfer the shrimp to the ice-filled bowl. Once the shrimp are well chilled, transfer them to a glass bowl. Pour the pepper-tomato-citrus mixture over the top and toss to coat. Cover and refrigerate for 4 hours, stirring occasionally.

To serve, add the red onion, cilantro, chives, and scallions and toss gently. Taste for seasoning. Spoon about 1 cup of the ceviche into each of 4 serving bowls or glasses. Top each serving with 2 tablespoons popcorn and 2 tablespoons corn snacks. Serve immediately.

cook's notes

- If you don't have an air-pop popcorn maker, use just enough oil to very thinly coat a heavy pan.
- The marinated shrimp by themselves would be great for a cocktail party — just spear them with toothpicks.

tip

In *Fine Cooking*, we found a good popcorn tip: instead of using a lid on the pot, use a splatter screen. It makes the popcorn crisper and you can keep track of what's happening inside.

SOURCE: *Splendid Soups* by James Peterson
COOK: James Peterson

vatapa (brazilian fish soup)

CHANCES ARE YOU'VE NEVER HEARD OF THIS Brazilian soup, which tastes as though it grew up in Thailand, with its coconut milk, chiles, and dried shrimp (an optional ingredient). But we urge you to try it because it's sublime, truly one of the great soups of the world. Vatapa is usually more of a stew than a soup, so it can easily be a main course, especially if you add a bit more fish and shrimp.

If you'd like a bolder soup, you could use half again as much ginger and also increase the lime. If you have leftover soup, gently reheat it and taste carefully — it may need more ginger and lime as well as more spice.

serves 6

2 pounds fish fillets, bones and skin removed

1 pound large shrimp, peeled and deveined

1/2 cup shelled raw peanuts or cashews, or 1/3 cup peanut butter or cashew butter

3 tablespoons safflower oil

1 large onion, finely chopped

3 garlic cloves, minced

3 Thai chiles or 6 jalapeño peppers, halved, seeded, and finely chopped

1 1/2-inch slice fresh ginger, peeled and finely chopped

6 medium tomatoes, peeled, seeded, and coarsely chopped, or 3 cups canned tomatoes, seeded and drained

Juice of 2 limes

1/4 cup dried shrimp, ground to a powder (about 2 tablespoons; optional)

4 cups chicken stock

2 cups unsweetened coconut milk

2 tablespoons finely chopped fresh cilantro leaves

Salt and freshly ground black pepper

Cut the fish fillets into 1- or 2-inch cubes. Keep the fish and shrimp refrigerated until just before serving.

If you're using whole nuts, grind them in a food processor until they have the consistency of smooth peanut butter. This takes about 3 minutes, and you may have to scrape the sides of the bowl with a rubber spatula once or twice to get the mixture moving. Set aside.

In a soup pot, heat the oil over medium heat. Add the onion, garlic, chiles or jalapeños, and ginger and sauté until the vegetables shine and the kitchen fills with their aroma, about 10 minutes. Add the tomatoes, lime juice, ground dried shrimp, if using, and pureed nuts or nut butter. Whisk in the stock 1 cup at a time to keep the mixture smooth. Whisk in the coconut milk and cilantro.

Just before you're ready to serve the soup, arrange the fish cubes in a straight-sided sauté pan just large enough to hold them in a single layer. Place the shrimp in a medium saucepan. Pour half of the soup over the fish and half over the shrimp, making sure both the fish and the shrimp are completely covered. Slowly bring the fish and shrimp to a simmer and cook until they are done — the fish will take about 8 minutes per inch of thickness and the shrimp about 3 minutes. The shrimp are done as soon as they turn completely pink.

Distribute the fish and shrimp among hot soup bowls. Season the broth with salt and pepper to taste and pour it into the bowls. Serve immediately.

cook's note

Dried shrimp are sold in cellophane packets and can be found in Asian or Mexican markets.

tip

In *Lemongrass and Lime*, chef Mark Read explains how to remove the seeds from a skinny chile without cutting into it, so you can cut it into thin rings. Cut off the top and the tail, then rub the chile between your palms. The seeds will fall out, and any remaining can be easily removed from the rings.

salads

SOURCE: *Insalate* by Susan Simon
COOK: **Marina Prada Danieli**

christmas salad

THIS DELIGHTFUL ITALIAN SALAD is simply gorgeous — as Susan Simon points out, it looks like a deconstructed wreath and tastes like a holiday. And there's a secret ingredient that makes this salad out of the ordinary: pomegranate seeds.

This salad isn't just a pretty holiday face: you can serve it anytime in pomegranate season, which is fall/winter — and even longer if you freeze the pomegranate seeds.

serves 4 to 6

2 ripe avocados, pitted, peeled, and cut into 1-inch chunks

2 tablespoons fresh lemon juice

3 cups tightly packed torn arugula leaves

2 tablespoons olive oil

1/4 pound Emmenthaler cheese, cut into 1-inch-long matchsticks

1/2 cup pomegranate seeds

1/2 teaspoon salt

In a large bowl, toss the avocados with the lemon juice. Toss to coat the avocado. Add the remaining ingredients and toss thoroughly to combine. Serve immediately.

cook's notes

- We tried this salad with Parmesan curls (just shaved with a vegetable peeler) instead of Emmenthaler, and with extra-virgin olive oil — lovely.

- To get into a pomegranate (and we hope you've chosen the worst-looking, most battered one, which will be the tastiest), cut it in half crosswise and dig into the seed pockets gently with a spoon, trying not to break the seed sacs. Don't wear your best shirt when doing this, since the juice does stain. The seeds will freeze perfectly if you have some left over.

- To get the maximum visual effect, serve the salad in a wide shallow bowl. Scatter the pomegranate seeds wreath fashion around the outer edge and place the avocado and cheese over the arugula in the middle. Toss the salad at the table just before serving.

SOURCE: *Joanne Weir's*
More Cooking in the Wine Country
COOK: Joanne Weir

layered salad of bulgur, fennel, pine nuts, dill, and mint

IT SEEMS THAT WE'RE ALWAYS AGREEING to bring a big salad to an informal dinner party only to discover, too late, that there's no time to make a last-minute salad. No one would guess that this wonderfully fresh salad started its journey to dinner two days earlier — in fact, it requires that extra time to mellow its flavors. It's a very portable salad that can sit for hours at room temperature with no ill effects.

The salad is a brighter, greener, subtler version of tabouli, the Middle Eastern salad made with bulgur. Lots of crunchy green vegetables replace the usual tomatoes. Joanne Weir says this salad captures all the freshness of the season, and we imagine she means spring. But we made it for the first time in December, and it was a great treat then, too.

serves 6 to 8

1 cup medium-fine bulgur or cracked wheat (see note)
1 cup fresh lemon juice, plus more to taste
½ cup extra-virgin olive oil
4 garlic cloves, minced
Salt
8 scallions (white and green parts), thinly sliced

1 cup chopped fresh flat-leaf parsley
½ cup chopped fresh dill
⅓ cup chopped fresh mint
2 English cucumbers, peeled, seeded, and cut into ½-inch dice
Freshly ground black pepper
1 large fennel bulb
⅓ cup toasted pine nuts

Place the bulgur or cracked wheat in a large salad bowl. In a small bowl, whisk together 1 cup lemon juice, the olive oil, garlic, and 1 teaspoon salt; drizzle this dressing over the bulgur. Layer on the scallions, parsley, dill, mint, and cucumbers. Sprinkle 1 teaspoon salt and ¼ teaspoon pepper over the top. Cover with plastic wrap and refrigerate for at least 24 hours or up to 48 hours.

Bring the salad to room temperature.

Meanwhile, cut the fennel bulb in half from top to bottom. Cut the halves into paper-thin slices crosswise. Add the fennel and pine nuts to the salad and toss. Season with salt, pepper, and lemon juice to taste and serve.

cook's notes

- This dressing is very lemony and light on olive oil compared with traditional dressings. If your lemons are very tart, you might want to substitute a little water for some of the lemon juice and add grated lemon zest at the end instead of more juice. Or make the salad as written and add more olive oil at the end if needed.

- Be sure to get medium-fine bulgur. A larger grain will be overly chewy.

- If you don't have pine nuts or don't like them, you can use chopped pecans instead.

SOURCE: **Formaggiokitchen.com**
COOK: **Ana Sortun**

carrot, parsley, and pine nut salad with fried goat cheese

THIS VERY BRIGHT AND TASTY SALAD is simple but delivers a lot of bang for the buck, in terms of both taste and presentation. It makes a nice first course or light lunch salad — especially when summer's star vegetables are gone but you can still get good carrots and parsley. Serve it on individual salad plates to really show it off; it's a pretty creamy orange flecked with green, with luscious brown buttons of fried goat cheese, which melts onto the crunchy salad as you eat it.

serves 4

2 2-to-3-ounce goat cheese buttons (see note)

1/3 cup all-purpose flour, for dredging

1 egg beaten with 1 tablespoon milk

2 garlic cloves, minced

1 teaspoon sugar

1 tablespoon fresh lemon juice

1 tablespoon good-quality white wine vinegar

1/2 cup plain whole-milk yogurt, preferably sheep's milk (see note)

1/4 cup extra-virgin olive oil
Salt and freshly ground black pepper

2 cups shredded carrots (2 large or 3 medium)

1/4 cup finely chopped fresh parsley

1/4 cup toasted pine nuts

3–4 tablespoons vegetable oil, for frying

Slice the goat cheese into four 3/4-to-1-inch-thick disks. Place the flour and the egg mixture into separate small bowls. Lightly coat each piece of goat cheese with flour, shaking off any excess. Dip into the egg mixture and coat again with flour. Set aside on a plate.

In a medium bowl, combine the garlic, sugar, lemon juice, and vinegar. Let stand for 5 minutes. Whisk in the yogurt, olive oil, and salt and pepper to taste. Add the carrots, parsley, and pine nuts and toss to coat. Taste and season again. Divide the salad among 4 salad plates.

Heat a medium heavy or nonstick skillet over medium-high heat. Add enough vegetable oil to lightly coat the skillet. Fry the goat cheese, turning only once, until browned on both sides. The center of the cheese should be warm so that it will melt over the salad, but don't cook it so long that it loses its shape. Place a piece of goat cheese on top of each salad and serve immediately.

cook's notes

- The carrots can be grated (shredded) on a box grater, with a mouli, or in a food processor, using the shredding disk.
- Flat-leaf parsley is nicest here.
- If you can't find sheep's-milk yogurt, go for any good-quality whole-milk yogurt. Low-fat yogurt is too thin and won't work very well.
- For the goat cheese, you want something relatively fresh and mild so that it will have a bit of creaminess inside when fried. If you can't find small buttons (crottin), just get a log of chevre, like Montrachet, and cut it into four pieces ($^3/_4$-to-1-inch-thick disks). You'll need 4 to 6 ounces total.
- When coating the cheese, you can minimize the mess if you use one hand for the flour bowl and one hand for the egg wash.

to drink

A bright, dry Sancerre
or Pinot Bianco

SOURCE: *Recipes from Home*
by David Page and Barbara Shinn
COOKS: **David Page and Barbara Shinn**

radish salad

RADISH SALAD? We remember a radish and sour cream salad from the fifties that was pretty tasty, but this one is really special. The radishes keep their spunk and their crunch, but they also get mellowed a bit by a dressing that has both lemon juice and vinegar. And the radishes look terrific, with their bright red borders and rosy cheeks, just right alongside a ham for a Christmas party.

You can slice the radishes and onion and make the dressing ahead. Just toss the salad with the chives half an hour before you plan to serve it.

serves 4

1 bunch radishes (about 8), thinly sliced
1 small red onion, thinly sliced
1/4 cup extra-virgin olive oil
1 tablespoon red wine vinegar
1 tablespoon fresh lemon juice
2 tablespoons snipped fresh chives
Kosher salt and freshly ground black pepper to taste

In a medium bowl, combine the radishes and onion.

In a small bowl, whisk the remaining ingredients together. Pour the dressing over the radishes and onion and toss. Let stand for 30 minutes before serving.

SOURCE: **Rei.com**
COOK: **Sujata P. Halarnkar**

zesty coleslaw with peanuts

WHEN REI, THE OUTDOOR EXPERTS, held a cooking contest — the first-ever "Camp Stove Cook-Off" — they had strict rules: no more than eight ingredients, easy to transport, and a short cooking time. This big-flavor salad was submitted at their Berkeley store, and it more than fulfills the criteria. It's bright, pretty, and so good we could've eaten the whole bowl ourselves. It's not goopy or oily as so many slaws are, so it's perfect with a big juicy steak or grilled chicken or ribs. It's also a good choice for hot weather, when light, clean flavors are especially appealing.

There are lots of peanuts here — the better to sustain hikers on the trail — but you could easily cut the amount in half.

serves 4

- 3 cups finely shredded green cabbage
- 1/2 cup chopped dry-roasted peanuts
- 1 chopped green chile pepper (optional)
- 2 tablespoons olive oil
- 1/2 teaspoon mustard **seeds**
- 1/2 teaspoon cumin seeds
- 3 tablespoons fresh lime juice
- Salt
- 1/4 cup chopped fresh cilantro

In a large salad bowl, lightly mix the cabbage, peanuts, and green chile, if using.

In a small skillet, heat the oil over medium heat. Add the mustard seeds. As soon as the mustard seeds begin to pop, add the cumin seeds and let them crackle for 3 to 4 seconds. Remove from the heat and immediately add the oil-spice mixture to the salad bowl. Add the lime juice and salt to taste and mix well. Garnish with the cilantro. Serve immediately.

cook's notes

- For a little bit of heat, use a jalapeño chile pepper; for more, use a skinny serrano.
- Savoy cabbage is a good choice here, because it's more tender than ordinary green cabbage.

SOURCE: *Food & Wine*
COOK: **Gabrielle Hamilton**

chickpea salad with four-minute eggs

YOU'VE PROBABLY NEVER SEEN ANYTHING quite like this salad — at least, we hadn't — but we find it completely delightful. It's the work of Gabrielle Hamilton, a rules-breaking young Manhattan chef. There's a rustic base of roughly mashed chickpeas and whole chickpeas, which creates a nice texture for the bottom layer of this salad — not a gloppy puree — and you aren't chasing chickpeas around the plate with your fork either, as so many chickpea salads require you to do. Next comes a sharp salad of parsley leaves, radishes, scallions, and green olives. Finally — the best part — a soft-cooked egg sits on top of it all. When you break the egg open with your fork, it spills its yolk and completes the dressing. In fact, without the richness of the runny yolk, the parsley salad is too sharp, but once the yolk mixes with the lemony dressing everything comes together in perfect balance.

If you follow Hamilton's instructions exactly, you'll be able to peel the eggs while still warm (running cold water over them just cools the outside), leaving you with a just-warm wobbly ovoid that will sit neatly atop the salad. Each guest gets the fun of breaking open an egg.

serves 4

3 tablespoons fresh lemon juice
5 tablespoons extra-virgin olive oil
   Salt and freshly ground black
      pepper
1 19-ounce can chickpeas, drained
   and rinsed (see note)
2 cups fresh flat-leaf parsley leaves

10 small radishes, quartered
2/3 cup small green olives, pitted
3 scallions (white and light green
   parts), finely chopped
4 large eggs, at room temperature
1 teaspoon white vinegar (if
   poaching the eggs)

In a medium bowl, whisk the lemon juice with 4 tablespoons of the oil and salt and pepper to taste. In a separate medium bowl, lightly crush half the chickpeas; mix in the whole chickpeas. Add half the dressing to the chickpeas and toss. Add the parsley, radishes, olives, and scallions to the remaining dressing and toss. Spoon the chickpeas onto 4 salad plates and top with the parsley salad.

Bring a medium saucepan of water to a boil. Lower the eggs into the water one at a time and boil over medium-high heat for 4 minutes. Drain, then rinse the eggs under cool water for 1 minute. Using the back of a spoon, gently crack the eggs all over and peel off the shells. Alternatively, if you prefer poached eggs, fill a large skillet two thirds full of water. Add the vinegar and bring to a simmer. One at a time, crack the eggs into the simmering water and poach until the whites are set but the yolks are still soft, 3 to 4 minutes. Remove the eggs with a slotted spoon.

Place an egg on each salad and drizzle with the remaining 1 tablespoon oil. Sprinkle the salads with salt and pepper to taste and serve immediately.

cook's notes

- If you can't find a 19-ounce can of chickpeas, use 2 smaller cans and measure out about 2 cups (drained). Toss the extras with a green salad the next night, or mash with a little olive oil and lemon zest to make crostini for lunch or a cook's snack.
- Having the eggs at room temperature means less risk of their cracking when they hit the boiling water. Using a large spoon to lower them into the water also helps soften their landing.
- If you're not a fan of soft-cooked eggs or just don't want to bother with peeling the warm eggs, one by one, make poached eggs instead. You'll get much the same results.
- If you have trouble visually dividing the dressing in half, figure that you want to put about 3½ tablespoons on the chickpeas and save the rest for the parsley salad.

serve with

Chewy, airy ciabatta bread
Blood orange and grapefruit segments
macerated with mint and a little sugar

to drink

Orvieto Classico Secco
or a light-style Chardonnay

salads

55

SOURCE: *New York*
COOK: Geoffrey Zakarian

heirloom tomato and watermelon salad

OF ALL THE WATERMELON-TOMATO COMBINATIONS we've seen this year — and there are plenty — this is the one we liked best. We couldn't stop making it, even though we first tried it in January, with indifferent watermelon and low-wattage cherry tomatoes. This salad is just stunning, and stunningly simple. It's a great jumble of different-sized tomatoes and different-sized cubes of watermelon tossed with very little olive oil, salt and pepper, dill, and a big surprise: cracked coriander seeds. Because the salad is made with heirloom tomatoes — yellow, striped green, pink, whatever color you fancy — and both red and yellow watermelon, it's completely gorgeous as well.

This is the perfect summer salad for grilled dishes or a Fourth of July picnic or Labor Day barbecue.

serves 6 to 8

6–8 heirloom tomatoes, varying in size, at room temperature

1 small to medium yellow watermelon (cantaloupe size)

1 small to medium red watermelon (cantaloupe size)

2 tablespoons extra-virgin olive oil

1 teaspoon cracked coriander seeds (see note)

Sea salt (preferably Maldon) and cracked black pepper

$1\frac{1}{2}$ teaspoons finely chopped fresh dill

$1\frac{1}{2}$ teaspoons finely chopped flat-leaf parsley

Cut the tomatoes into chunks of varying sizes (1 to $1\frac{1}{2}$ inches). Chop the watermelon flesh into cubes of varying sizes (1 to $1\frac{1}{2}$ inches).

In a large bowl, combine the tomatoes, watermelon, oil, coriander, and salt and pepper to taste and gently toss, taking care not to bruise the fruit. Sprinkle with the dill and parsley and serve immediately.

cook's notes

🍃 Like Geoffrey Zakarian (chef at Town in Manhattan), we love Maldon salt (from England, available in specialty shops and some supermarkets here) and think it's even tastier in this salad if you sprinkle it on the tomatoes and watermelon separately before you mix them together. Let them stand for up to half an hour to bring out the flavors.

- Because this is such a simple dish, every ingredient really counts, so use a very good extra-virgin olive oil.
- To crack the coriander seeds, you can either put them in a kitchen towel and smack them with a meat mallet or some other heavy object or crush them using a small mortar and pestle.

tip

In *Food Arts* magazine, we found another tasty way to pair watermelon cubes and cherry tomatoes from chef José Andrés of Jaleo restaurant in Washington, D.C. He stacks the two together on toothpicks or little cocktail skewers to serve as a refreshing and colorful tapa. Each skewer gets a 1-inch cube of watermelon (seedless, please) and then a cherry tomato half. Line up the picks or skewers on a tray, drizzle them with a quick vinaigrette of sherry vinegar and extra-virgin olive oil, scatter on some shredded fresh mint, and you're good to go. We don't need to remind you that watermelon and cherry tomatoes both come in red and yellow, so you can play around with the colors. If there's no good watermelon available, use cantaloupe. And, if you think of it, sprinkle the tomatoes and melon separately with a little sea salt and let them stand for up to half an hour before you build the skewers — the flavor will be even better. You might want to add a little sliver of serrano ham to the assemblage, too.

SOURCE: *Soup Makes the Meal* by Ken Haedrich
COOK: Ken Haedrich

broccoli salad
with creamy mustard dressing

THIS SALAD TASTES A BIT LIKE an unusual potato salad that's lost its potatoes. It uses both broccoli florets and the sweet nutty-tasting stalks (which some chefs prefer to the florets) and combines them with surprising elements: two kinds of mustard, chickpeas, fresh basil, and Parmesan cheese. If there are any around, Ken Haedrich throws in some croutons as well.

You get new tastes with every bite of this hearty salad, which could also be a vegetarian main course. It travels well, so it's good for a picnic or a potluck supper. It's even good the next day, if there are any leftovers.

serves 6

1 large head broccoli
½ cup plain yogurt
½ cup mayonnaise
2 tablespoons chopped fresh parsley, plus more for garnish
1 tablespoon chopped fresh basil, or 1 teaspoon dried
1½ tablespoons Dijon mustard
1 teaspoon dry mustard
1 tablespoon tarragon vinegar or white wine vinegar

1 cup canned chickpeas, drained and rinsed
1 celery rib, finely chopped
½ cup finely chopped red onion
½ cup freshly grated Parmesan cheese
Freshly ground black pepper
1 cup croutons (optional)

Bring a medium pot of salted water to a boil. Meanwhile, cut the broccoli into bite-sized florets and peel and dice the stalks. When the water boils, add the broccoli and boil just until crisp-tender, 3 to 4 minutes. Drain; immediately spread on a baking sheet or platter to cool. Transfer the broccoli to a bowl, cover with plastic wrap, and refrigerate.

In a large bowl, whisk together the yogurt, mayonnaise, parsley, basil, Dijon mustard, dry mustard, and vinegar. Add the chickpeas, celery, onion, cheese, broccoli, and pepper to taste and toss well. Cover the salad with plastic wrap and refrigerate for at least 30 minutes before serving.

Just before serving, toss again, with the croutons, if using. Sprinkle with more parsley, if you like.

cook's note

🍃 If you're using good whole-milk yogurt with a cream top, spoon off the cream before adding the yogurt to the dressing or it will be too rich.

serve with

Cumin Apple Chips (page 225)

SOURCE: *The Joy of Cooking:*
All about Salads and Dressings
COOK: **Anonymous**

georgian bean salad

THIS ZINGY SALAD COMES NOT FROM the American South but from the former Soviet Republic of Georgia, famous for its wonderful food. It's spicy, hot, sweet, and subtle all at the same time. We can't think of any other canned-bean salad that tastes this good — and we can scarcely think of another salad that has no oil. And certainly no other salad we've ever met features plum jam. The first bite is a surprise, but once you start, you definitely want more.

The flavor is so intense that this salad probably works best as an appetizer, but we also like it as a sort of relish or a side salad—great on a buffet table.

serves 6 to 8

1 19-ounce can kidney beans, rinsed and drained
2 tablespoons–1/3 cup plum jam (see note)
2 tablespoons red wine vinegar
1 tablespoon fresh lemon juice
1–2 tablespoons minced fresh cilantro

1/2 small jalapeño pepper or other small chile pepper, seeded and minced
1 garlic clove, minced
1/2 teaspoon salt
1/4 teaspoon ground coriander
Freshly ground black pepper to taste

Place the beans in a medium bowl. Stir in the remaining ingredients. Taste and adjust the seasonings. Serve at room temperature.

cook's notes

❧ This is quite a bit of plum jam, so we suggest that you add half of it to start, then taste your way toward a balance you think works.

❧ Perfectionists may want to cook their own beans from scratch. To do that, pick over, rinse, and soak overnight 1/2 pound of dried kidney beans. Drain, transfer the beans to a medium saucepan and add water to cover by 2 inches. Add a small onion, peeled and halved, a whole peeled garlic clove, and a bay leaf. Bring to a boil over high heat, reduce the heat to low, and simmer, covered, until the beans are tender but not mushy, about 1 hour. Drain and discard the onion, garlic, and bay leaf.

SOURCE: *Food & Wine*
COOK: Joanne Weir

sugar snap pea and prosciutto salad

THIS IS ONE OF THOSE VANISHING SALADS that people can't stop eating. The sweet crunch of snap peas is punched up by the salty, earthy prosciutto, then given a fresh zing with lemon zest and mint. In less than 20 minutes, you have an irresistible dish that also works well as a starter.

The salad won't wilt, but the snap peas will discolor slightly if they sit around in the dressing for a long time. The solution is to prepare the elements separately and combine them at the last minute.

serves 4

3/4 pound sugar snap peas

3 tablespoons extra-virgin olive oil

1 teaspoon finely grated lemon zest

1½ tablespoons fresh lemon juice

3 tablespoons finely chopped fresh mint

3 ounces thinly sliced prosciutto, cut into thin strips

Salt and freshly ground black pepper

Have ready a large bowl of ice water. Drop the peas into a medium saucepan of boiling salted water and boil until crisp-tender, about 1 minute. Drain the peas and plunge them into the ice bath. Pat the peas dry with a kitchen towel.

In a medium bowl, whisk together the oil, lemon zest, lemon juice, and mint. Add the peas, prosciutto, and salt and pepper to taste and toss. Arrange the salad on a platter and serve.

cook's note

Once the peas have been patted dry, you may want to cut them in half on the diagonal, so they'll be easier to eat.

SOURCE: *The Atlantic Monthly*
COOK: Corby Kummer after Heike Tubbesing

german potato salad

WE'RE ESPECIALLY FOND OF THE inquiring-palates-want-to-know genre, those culinary adventurers who track down the perfect version of this or that dish. No one is better at this than Corby Kummer, the Italophile food critic at *The Atlantic Monthly*. So when he turned his sights to the humble German potato salad, we couldn't wait to see what he'd find.

He's found something wonderful, a sort of backwards potato salad from our American point of view. The boiled potatoes here are cool, the better to slice them, and the oil-and-vinegar dressing is hot. The key to this salad's flavor is to let it sit for six hours or more before you serve it. Then you have perfection indeed: an extremely simple, intensely flavored, light, subtly sweet, pure potato salad. Even the salt and pepper ratios here are perfect.

As Kummer points out, this salad is safer at a picnic or on a buffet than heavy, creamy, mayo-rich American potato salads. But that's just a bonus; the reason to make this is that it tastes so good.

serves 8

3 pounds Yukon Gold potatoes, peeled or not

DRESSING

1/4 cup white wine vinegar

3 tablespoons mild-flavored olive oil

1 tablespoon sugar

2 teaspoons kosher salt, or 1 1/2 teaspoons fine sea salt, preferably Maldon

1/2 teaspoon white pepper

1/2 cup minced white onion

2 tablespoons chopped fresh parsley

Boil the potatoes until just tender. Drain and let cool.

MEANWHILE, TO MAKE THE DRESSING:

In a small saucepan, combine 1 1/2 cups water, the vinegar, and oil and bring to a simmer. Stir in the sugar, salt, and white pepper. Simmer for about 1 minute to emulsify the oil, then add the onion. Return the mixture to a simmer, then remove from the heat. You don't want the onion to cook through, but the brief heating will tame its bite.

Peel (if you didn't before cooking) and slice the potatoes and put them in a large bowl. Toss the potatoes with the hot dressing, cover, and let stand for at least 6 hours and preferably overnight. If the weather is cool, leave the salad out overnight; if it's warm, refrigerate it, but bring it back to room temperature before serving. Toss the salad with the parsley just before serving.

cook's note

 Even after their long, thirsty nap, the potatoes won't have absorbed every little bit of dressing. Not to worry; diners will mop it up, it's so tasty.

tip

A good trick for cooling boiled potatoes is to spoon them gently onto a wire rack over the sink to drain. This avoids both the breakage you get when you dump them into a colander and the oversteaming of the potatoes in the bottom of the colander, which continue to cook during the draining process. From *One Potato, Two Potato*, by Roy Finamore and Molly Stevens.

SOURCE: *Boston Globe Magazine*
COOK: **Seta Keshishian after Angel Yapoudjian**

fattoush (middle eastern bread salad)

THIS LEBANESE-ARMENIAN RECIPE comes from Seta's Gourmet World, a takeout shop in Newton Centre, Massachusetts. Everyone in Seta's family, including her 75-year-old mother, Angel, works in the business. This favorite salad is always on the Christmas menu, and it looks very festive with its brilliant reds and greens.

Fattoush is a chopped vegetable salad with little bits of toasted bread to lend a chewy quality and soak up the delicious vegetable juices. What's special about this fattoush is two ingredients that have recently caught the attention of adventurous American cooks: sumac and Aleppo pepper. Sumac has a delightful lemony taste that perks up almost everything it touches; Aleppo pepper is sweetly spicy. You can leave out the sumac and substitute for the Aleppo pepper, but if you can find them, they'll make a truly memorable dish.

serves 8 generously

- 2 pints cherry tomatoes, quartered
- 2 cucumbers, peeled and finely chopped
- 2 bunches fresh flat-leaf parsley, finely chopped
- 1 red bell pepper, seeded and finely chopped
- 1 bunch scallions (including the firm greens), chopped
- 1/2 bunch fresh mint, finely chopped
- 2 tablespoons sumac (optional)
- 2 teaspoons ground Aleppo pepper (or Turkish pepper or a combination of hot and sweet Hungarian paprika)
- Salt to taste
- 2/3 cup olive oil
- 1/2 cup fresh lemon juice
- 1 1/2 large pita bread rounds, torn into small pieces (about 1 1/2 inches) and toasted until golden

In a large bowl, combine everything but the pita bread and toss well. Just before serving, add the toasted pita pieces and mix well. Serve at once.

cook's notes

- If you prefer green bell pepper, by all means use it.
- Sumac and Aleppo pepper can be found at Middle Eastern markets or by mail order and from Kalustyan's Online Store (www.kalustyans.com).

SOURCE: *The Naked Chef Takes Off*
by Jamie Oliver
COOK: Jamie Oliver

"squash and smash" tomato-olive salad

WE LOVE EVERYTHING about this rustic salad. It's made in moments with just a few ingredients, it tastes terrific, and it's a huge amount of fun to pummel defenseless little cherry tomatoes and olives.

It's such a minimal recipe, in fact, that brash British TV chef Jamie Oliver just tells you about it, doesn't actually write it up as a recipe. So this is our version, for which we ask his forgiveness, to make things a bit clearer. But you don't really need a recipe if you just remember to use four parts cherry tomatoes to one part olives, plus some vinegar, black pepper, and a few glugs of good olive oil. Some basil, some arugula, and you're done. If this sounds like pasta sauce, you're on: toss leftovers with hot spaghetti.

serves 6

2 pints cherry tomatoes

⅓ cup unpitted olives (any kind)

Red wine vinegar to taste

Freshly ground black pepper to taste

Extra-virgin olive oil to taste

1 handful torn fresh basil leaves

1 handful torn arugula leaves

In the serving bowl you plan to use, squash the cherry tomatoes with one hand while holding the other over them so they don't splatter all over everything. Put the olives on a cutting board and gently smash them with a rolling pin, a cup, or even your thumb. Remove the pits and add the olives to the salad bowl.

Drizzle in a little vinegar and grind some pepper on top. Add oil and toss. Just before serving, rip in, as Oliver says, the basil and arugula and toss well.

cook's notes

- Oliver encourages us to use different colors of cherry tomatoes — yellow, green, striped, whatever we can find.
- You can use pitted olives, but you won't have the fun of squashing out the pits.

salads

SOURCE: *Food & Wine*
COOK: **Paula Wolfert**

sicilian slow-roasted onion salad

THIS DISH FROM THE ANCIENT CITY of Siracusa is an onion salad unlike any other. Instead of cooking the onions whole, as they do in Sicily, Mediterranean cooking guru Paula Wolfert cuts them into slices, paints the slices with olive oil and slowly roasts them into caramelized deliciousness. Then they get a simple dressing, not too concentrated because it's diluted with water, with tiny bits of fresh garlic and the occasional hot bite of crushed red pepper.

The salad is wonderful with grilled meats or fish, great on a buffet, and a good trick to have up your sleeve because it's so easy and unusual.

serves 4

Olive oil for brushing the pan and the onions

3 large onions (about 2 pounds total)

2 tablespoons olive oil

1 garlic clove, minced

1 tablespoon minced fresh flat-leaf parsley

½ teaspoon red or white wine vinegar

½ teaspoon salt

¼ teaspoon freshly ground black pepper

¼ teaspoon crushed red pepper flakes

Preheat the oven to 300 degrees. Brush a heavy baking sheet with oil. Cut off and discard the ends of the onions. Leaving the outer skin intact, slice the onions crosswise ½ inch thick. Lay the slices on the prepared baking sheet and brush them lightly with oil.

Bake the onions for 1 hour, or until just tender. Turn the slices and bake for 30 minutes more, or until deeply browned. Transfer to a large shallow serving dish and let cool to room temperature. Discard the onion skins and any dried-out rings.

In a small bowl, whisk together the 2 tablespoons oil, 2 tablespoons water, and the remaining ingredients. Spoon the vinaigrette over the onions and serve.

cook's notes

❧ If you make the onions and dressing a day ahead, refrigerate them separately and bring to room temperature before combining and serving.

❧ You can take the salad in another direction by skipping the dressing and just drizzling balsamic vinegar over the onion slices after they're turned, crumbling a little oregano or thyme on top, and adding salt and pepper to taste. When the onions are golden brown and soft, remove them from the oven. Discard the skins and any dried-out onion rings. Serve as a side dish, warm or at room temperature.

❧ For easier cleanup, line the baking sheet with foil and brush the foil with oil before adding the onion slices.

tip

Leave it to Martha Stewart to come up with the most romantic kitchen tip of the year. When you're working with onions, you can avoid tears by lighting a votive candle and keeping it next to your chopping board. Amazingly, this really works, though you may feel a bit like Liberace in the kitchen.

SOURCE: *New York Times Magazine*
COOK: Stefano Lascialfari,
adapted from Valdino West Restaurant

fiesolana (italian cabbage salad with ham and fontina)

THIS SALAD IS NOT ONLY SUPER-SIMPLE and tasty, it also looks great. It's a fresh, crunchy, mild salad with an innovative presentation. And it solves a problem, or so the chef claims: The acid in the light olive oil–lemon juice vinaigrette neutralizes cabbage's annoying digestive repercussions — or gastric irritation, as the text describes it.

The combination of Virginia ham, fontina cheese, and thinly sliced cabbage works really nicely, and the fun part is the putting it all together — cabbage has never looked so elegant. You pack individual portions of the salad into a small bowl and then turn them out onto salad plates, so you end up with little domes of salad that are then covered with shredded cheese and decorated with parsley and cherry tomatoes. Bravo, cabbage!

serves 4

VINAIGRETTE
1 cup extra-virgin olive oil
1/3 cup fresh lemon juice

SALAD
1 small head green cabbage (about 1 1/2 pounds), cored and very thinly julienned (about 6 cups)
6 thin slices Virginia ham, rind trimmed, thinly julienned
1/4 cup chopped fresh parsley, plus more for garnish

3/4 teaspoon salt
1/2 teaspoon freshly ground black pepper
2 ounces fontina cheese, refrigerated so that it's easy to shred
16 cherry tomatoes, cut almost in quarters but still attached at the stem end
1 lemon, quartered and rolled in chopped parsley

TO MAKE THE VINAIGRETTE:

In a medium bowl, whisk together the oil and lemon juice. Set aside.

TO MAKE THE SALAD:

In a large bowl, toss the cabbage, ham, parsley, salt, and pepper with your fingers until combined. Sprinkle with 6 tablespoons of the vinaigrette and toss lightly with your fingers until coated.

Working with one portion at a time, lightly pack about 1¹/₂ cups of the salad in a bowl just large enough to contain it, then invert the bowl onto a salad plate. Shred one fourth of the cheese on the medium side of a cheese grater onto each serving so that the cheese covers the salad. Sprinkle decoratively with parsley and arrange the tomatoes at 12, 3, 6, and 9 o'clock — or at any other times of day you fancy. Serve with a parsleyed lemon quarter.

cook's notes

- Take the time to cut the cabbage into a fine julienne, because the texture of the fine ribbons is much of the pleasure of this salad.

- The vinaigrette makes more than three times the amount you'll actually need for the salad. You can either make the full amount and refrigerate any leftovers — just add salt and pepper for salad dressing — or make much less. The basic rule is three parts oil to one part lemon juice, so 4 teaspoons of lemon juice and 4 tablespoons (¹/₄ cup) of olive oil should be enough.

to drink

Pinot Grigio
or Sancerre

breakfast and brunch

OTHER IDEAS FOR BRUNCH

Roasted Apricots with Cardamom (page 286) and yogurt

Smoked Salmon Croque Monsieur
with Baby Watercress Salad (page 134)

Honey-Bourbon Ham Steaks (page 182)

Sardinian Old Bread and Tomato Casserole (page 218)
topped with eggs fried in olive oil

Double Corn Polenta (page 222)

Sweet Potato Spoon Bread (page 224)

Pecan Whiskey Cake (page 266)

Cinnamon-Caramel Hot Chocolate (page 295)

Serrano Bloody Marys (page 303)

Watermelon Punch (page 299)

Fragolas (Sparkling Strawberry Cocktails) (page 301)

SOURCE: *Back to the Table* by Art Smith
COOK: Art Smith

sesame-orange granola

WE'VE NOTICED A MINI RESURGENCE in granola recipes this year, not to mention a bit more panache. This one, from Oprah's highly touted chef, Art Smith, is our favorite. This isn't one of those rugged granolas, although it will carry you from breakfast right through lunchtime. It's sophisticated, with its tropical elements — coconut, cashews, sesame seeds — and orange zest, which gives it a special quality. "Fabulous," our notes say, and we're sticking with that opinion.

Smith suggests serving it over yogurt with fresh fruit, which is great. But it's also good enough to eat out of hand, so it makes a fine healthy snack for kids. The only question here is what fruit to use. After making several batches, the one we like best is dried cranberries.

makes about 8 cups

1 cup shredded sweetened coconut	1/3 cup sesame seeds
1/2 cup vegetable oil	2 teaspoons ground cinnamon
1/3 cup pure maple syrup	1/2 teaspoon freshly grated nutmeg
Grated zest of 2 large oranges	1/3 cup honey
4 cups old-fashioned rolled oats	1 cup chopped dried fruit, such as apples, dates, apricots, cranberries, or a combination
1 cup sliced almonds	
1 cup coarsely chopped unsalted cashews	

Preheat the oven to 375 degrees, with racks in the center and top third. Spread the coconut on a baking sheet. Bake on the center rack, stirring often, until the coconut is lightly toasted, about 10 minutes. Set the baking sheet on a wire rack to cool.

In a medium saucepan, combine the oil, maple syrup, and orange zest and bring to a boil over medium heat. Meanwhile, place the remaining ingredients, except for the dried fruit, in the bowl of a heavy-duty mixer and mix on low speed with the paddle attachment until combined, about 1 minute (or mix well with your hands in a large bowl). Add the syrup mixture and mix (or toss with 2 large spoons) until well coated. Spread in 1/2-inch-thick layers on 2 large baking sheets.

Bake, stirring often and switching the positions of the baking sheets from top to bottom and front to back halfway through baking, until the granola is golden brown, about 15 minutes.

Remove from the oven and let cool. In a large bowl, mix together the granola, toasted coconut, and dried fruit. The granola can be stored at room temperature in an airtight container for up to 1 month.

cook's notes

- Be careful when toasting the coconut — it overbrowns easily.
- Although it will fit on one baking sheet, the granola won't be crunchy unless you use two.
- We like the stronger-tasting, cheaper grade B maple syrup here. You can play with the oil element too, using half nut oil, such as almond or hazelnut.

SOURCE: *Backpacker*
COOK: Dorcas Miller

lemon-raisin breakfast bars

PEOPLE GO CRAZY FOR THESE BARS, which have a crunchy nut crust and lots of lemony flavor. They're not the usual compromise backpacking food — these are just as good in a lunch box, at a tea party, as a snack, or even as dessert for a picnic. Because they're loaded with raisins, you might think they'd be too sweet, but they're well balanced.

Try these bars on kids who hate to eat breakfast.

makes 12 bars

2 cups raisins
1 14-ounce can sweetened condensed milk
1 tablespoon grated fresh lemon zest
1 tablespoon fresh lemon juice
16 tablespoons (2 sticks) butter, at room temperature

$1\frac{1}{3}$ cups light brown sugar
$1\frac{1}{2}$ teaspoons pure vanilla extract
1 cup all-purpose flour
$\frac{1}{2}$ teaspoon baking soda
$\frac{1}{2}$ teaspoon salt
$1\frac{1}{2}$ cups old-fashioned rolled oats
1 cup chopped walnuts

Preheat the oven to 350 degrees. Grease a 9-x-13-inch baking pan. In a medium saucepan, combine the raisins, milk, lemon zest, and lemon juice and cook, stirring, over medium heat until bubbling. Remove from the heat and let cool slightly.

In a large bowl, beat the butter, brown sugar, and vanilla until well combined. Stir in the flour, baking soda, and salt, then the oats and walnuts.

Press all but 2 cups of the batter into the prepared pan. Spread the raisin mixture on top to within $\frac{1}{2}$ inch of the edges. Top the raisin mixture with dollops of the reserved batter and press down lightly.

Bake for 25 to 30 minutes, or until golden. Let cool. Cut into 12 bars.

cook's note

Instead of raisins, you could use currants or golden raisins, or a mixture.

SOURCE: *New Orleans Times-Picayune*
COOK: Marcelle Bienvenu

double-boiler scrambled eggs

THESE TENDER SCRAMBLED EGGS with large fluffy curds take more patience than standard skillet-scrambled eggs, but they're worlds better. This is the French way of making scrambled eggs — very slowly over low heat. The double boiler ensures that you keep them over low, even heat because it insulates the eggs from the direct heat of the stove. The scrambling process can take from 8 to 20 minutes, depending on the size of the batch, the shape of your double boiler, and the temperature of the water. You can do other things in the meantime, such as turn the bacon, butter the toast, and squeeze the oranges — and have everything ready all at once

serves 6

12 large eggs

1/2 cup milk

3/4 teaspoon salt

1/4 teaspoon freshly ground black
    pepper

Hot sauce

3 tablespoons butter

2 tablespoons snipped fresh chives

Break the eggs into a medium bowl. Add the milk, salt, pepper, and hot sauce to taste, and beat with a wire whisk.

In the top of a double boiler, melt the butter over gently boiling water. Add the eggs and cover. Stir occasionally until the eggs thicken. Remove from the heat and stir until the eggs set. Garnish with the chives and serve.

cook's note

℘ If you don't have a double boiler large enough to hold a dozen eggs, improvise with a stainless-steel bowl set over a pan of simmering water. As with any double boiler, be sure that the bottom of the bowl is above the level of the water.

serve with

Sausage Links with Apricot-Mustard Glaze (page 76)
Toasted slices of Orange-Rum Sweet Bread (page 236)

℘

to drink

Serrano Bloody Marys (page 303)

breakfast and brunch

SOURCE: *Bon Appétit*
COOK: Betty Rosbottom

sausage links with apricot-mustard glaze

BEST-QUALITY COMMERCIAL SAUSAGES are an excellent product, but that's not to say they can't be dressed up for a special occasion. Apricot-mustard does that good sweet-spicy thing, and rosemary adds a pleasant piquant touch. The sausages end up with an appealing spicy glaze that makes them a step above the ordinary. Use sweet or hot links according to your preference.

For a brunch buffet, transfer the browned sausages to a baking dish, pour the glaze over them, toss to coat, cover, and reheat in a medium oven.

serves 8

- 1/2 cup apricot preserves
- 1/4 cup sweet-hot mustard
- 2 teaspoons chopped fresh rosemary
- Salt and freshly ground black pepper

- 2 tablespoons vegetable oil
- 18 ounces (about 20 links) breakfast sausage links (such as pork links or hot and sweet links)

In a medium heavy saucepan, whisk the apricot preserves over medium heat until melted and smooth, about 1 minute. Add the mustard and whisk until mixture begins to simmer, about 30 seconds. Remove from the heat. Stir in the rosemary and salt and pepper to taste. (The glaze can be made ahead. Cover and refrigerate. Stir over medium heat until heated through before using.)

In a large heavy skillet, heat the oil over medium-high heat. Add the sausages and sauté until browned and cooked through, about 10 minutes. Transfer to the saucepan with the glaze. Stir over medium heat until all the sausages are glazed, about 1 minute. Transfer to a platter and serve hot.

cook's note

℮ You can use any spicy mustard, and if you want this dish less sweet use Dijon mustard in place of sweet-hot.

SOURCE: *Gourmet*
COOK: Amy Mastrangelo

three-cheese baked egg puff with roasted peppers and sweet spicy bacon

THIS BRUNCH DISH — a crustless quiche — was designed to be part of a holiday menu, and indeed it looks gorgeously festive, full of bright red and green vegetables against a creamy egg-cheese background. It's served with Sweet Spicy Bacon (recipe follows), a wonderfully crisp bacon that's a great foil for the eggs. It would also make a good lunch or a late-night supper. The first time we made it, we served it in thin slices on a holiday party buffet, and it worked perfectly as a small bite. Leave off the bacon, and it's vegetarian.

If you're making the eggs and the bacon at the same time and you have only one oven, start the eggs in the bottom third and the bacon in the top third and switch positions halfway through the cooking.

serves 6

3 medium red bell peppers

1/4 cup plus 2 tablespoons all-purpose flour

1 teaspoon salt

3/4 teaspoon baking powder

9 large eggs

3 tablespoons unsalted butter, melted

1 1/2 cups coarsely grated extra-sharp Cheddar cheese

1 cup whole-milk ricotta cheese

1 cup grated Parmigiano-Reggiano cheese

3 scallions, finely chopped

Thin slivers of scallion greens, for garnish

Roast the peppers on the racks of gas stovetop burners over high heat, turning with tongs, until the skins are blackened, 10 to 12 minutes. (Or broil the peppers on a broiler pan about 5 inches from the heat, turning occasionally, about 15 minutes.) Transfer to a bowl, cover tightly with plastic wrap, and let stand for 20 minutes.

When cool enough to handle, peel the peppers, discarding the stems and seeds, and cut into 1/3-inch dice.

Preheat the oven to 350 degrees. Butter a 10-inch (6 cup) glass pie dish. Into a small bowl, sift together the flour, salt, and baking powder; set aside. In a large bowl, beat the eggs with an electric mixer on medium-high speed until doubled in volume, about 3 minutes. Add the flour mixture, butter, and cheeses and mix well on low speed, then stir in the roasted peppers and chopped scallions.

Pour the mixture into the prepared pie dish and bake in the middle of the oven (or in the bottom third of the oven if baking with the bacon) until the top is golden brown and a tester inserted in the center comes out clean, 30 to 35 minutes. Let stand for 5 minutes before serving, garnished with the scallion greens.

cook's notes

- You can make the peppers and grate the cheeses the night before, which will make putting the dish together in the morning much faster. Seal them in plastic bags and refrigerate overnight.
- Leftovers can be stored in the refrigerator and reheated in a toaster oven.

sweet spicy bacon

makes about 12 slices

1½ tablespoons packed light brown sugar

¼ heaping teaspoon cayenne pepper

¼ heaping teaspoon freshly ground black pepper

1 pound thick-cut bacon (about 12 slices)

Preheat the oven to 350 degrees. In a small bowl, stir together the sugar and spices.

Arrange the bacon slices in a single layer on a large broiler pan and bake in the middle of the oven (or in the top third if you're also baking the eggs) for 20 minutes. Turn the slices over and sprinkle evenly with the spiced sugar. Continue baking until the bacon is crisp and brown, 15 to 20 minutes more, then transfer to paper towels to drain. Serve hot.

❦ We think hickory-smoked bacon is the most delicious choice here.

❦ If you use regular-cut bacon instead of thick-cut, it will cook faster — start checking it 5 minutes after you sprinkle on the spiced sugar.

serve with

Toasted herbed focaccia or stacks of toast

❦

to drink

Fragolas (Sparkling Strawberry Cocktails) (page 301)

SOURCE: *Fine Cooking*
COOK: Pam Anderson

light crisp waffles

IF YOU'RE USED TO BIG, bready, gummy waffles, you'll be amazed by these charmers. We'll go out on a limb here: they are so incredibly good that you ought to run out and buy a waffle iron if you don't have one already (see note). Just one bite and our editor's grandmother said, "These waffles are so good they make me want to open a waffle joint."

Why are they so good? There are several little tricks embedded in this recipe that make all the difference. One is using cornstarch for crispness; both buttermilk (for flavor) and milk (for texture); a little vanilla for taste; a whipped egg white mixed with sugar for lightness; and a final oven crisping. Nothing here is the least bit complicated, although you might feel a bit silly whipping up a single egg white (just use a medium stainless-steel bowl and have the egg white at room temperature).

We probably don't need to remind you that waffles are just as good for dinner as they are for breakfast.

serves 4

¾ cup bleached all-purpose flour
¼ cup cornstarch
½ teaspoon salt
½ teaspoon baking powder
¼ teaspoon baking soda
¾ cup buttermilk

¼ cup milk
6 tablespoons vegetable oil
1 large egg, separated, at room temperature
1 tablespoon sugar
½ teaspoon pure vanilla extract

Preheat the oven to 200 degrees and preheat the waffle iron. In a medium bowl, mix together the flour, cornstarch, salt, baking powder, and baking soda. In a Pyrex measuring cup, mix together the buttermilk, milk, and oil. Mix in the egg yolk and set aside.

In a separate medium bowl, beat the egg white almost to soft peaks. Sprinkle in the sugar and continue to beat until the peaks are firm and glossy. Beat in the vanilla.

Pour the buttermilk mixture into the dry ingredients and whisk until just mixed. Drop the whipped egg white onto the batter in dollops and fold in with a spatula until just incorporated.

Pour $1/2$ to $2/3$ cup of the batter onto the hot waffle iron and cook until the waffle is crisp and nutty brown. Set the cooked waffle directly on the oven rack to keep it warm and crisp. Repeat with the remaining batter, holding the waffles in the oven — but don't stack them or they'll lose their crispness. When all the waffles are cooked, serve immediately.

VARIATIONS

cornmeal waffles: Substitute cornmeal for $1/2$ cup of the flour.

cranberry-orange waffles: Stir 2 teaspoons finely grated fresh orange zest and $1/2$ cup coarsely chopped dried cranberries into the batter.

cook's note

🌙 *Fine Cooking* tested waffle irons this year and liked the low-end Toastmaster — it costs only $13 and can be stored on its side.

serve with

Whipped sweet butter and warmed maple syrup
Sweet Spicy Bacon (page 78)

SOURCE: *Los Angeles Times*
COOK: Unknown

sow's ear baked apple pancake

WE DON'T KNOW WHETHER the Sow's Ear is a restaurant or whether the title simply refers to the magical thing, a sort of culinary silk purse, that happens when these ordinary ingredients go into the oven. This baked apple pancake is a close relative of the Dutch baby, an oven pancake that is itself a sweet version of Yorkshire pudding. It puffs up gorgeously to form golden brown hills and valleys inside the skillet, and a few apple slices escape around the edges to give you a hint of what's inside. This is a simple, homey dish, one that's brought straight to the table from the oven and cut right in the skillet.

serves 6

¾ cup milk

3 large eggs, lightly beaten

5 tablespoons butter, melted

½ teaspoon pure vanilla extract

½ cup plus 1 tablespoon all-purpose flour

1 tablespoon sugar

¼ teaspoon ground cinnamon

¼ teaspoon salt

2 small tart apples, peeled, cored, and thinly sliced

3 tablespoons lightly packed light brown sugar

3 tablespoons powdered sugar

Preheat the oven to 450 degrees. In a medium bowl or a food processor, mix the milk, eggs, 2 tablespoons of the butter, the vanilla, flour, sugar, cinnamon, and salt. Set aside.

In a 10-inch ovenproof skillet, heat the remaining 3 tablespoons butter and the apple slices until the apples are sizzling and slightly cooked. Pour in the batter and sprinkle the top with the brown sugar. Bake until well browned and puffed, 20 to 25 minutes. Dust with powdered sugar, cut into wedges, and serve immediately.

cook's note

℘ If you don't have a 10-inch ovenproof skillet, just cook the apples in a medium skillet and transfer them to a 10-inch baking dish before adding the batter and baking.

SOURCE: *New York Times*
COOK: Amanda Hesser after Rhonda Hesser

morning bread pudding

IF YOU'VE BEEN LOOKING FOR THE PERFECT Christmas breakfast, here it is. Not only can you make it the night before and let it sit in the refrigerator overnight, but the pudding actually requires an overnight snooze so the bread can soak up the custard. This deliciously indulgent dish is like a cross between really good French toast and bread pudding. It's moist and tender, with a hint of almond and a buttery caramel topping. The caramel topping is made the same way you make crème caramel — the caramel sits on the bottom of the dish and becomes the top when you turn out the pudding. And as the pudding sits overnight, the caramel flavor gets infused throughout.

Serve the pudding with a citrusy fruit salad, some bacon or sausage, and lots of coffee. You won't need any syrup with it.

serves 6

3/4 cup plus 2 tablespoons sugar

6 tablespoons (3/4 stick) butter

12–15 slices brioche or challah bread, each about 1/2 inch thick and about 3 inches in diameter

8 large eggs

1/4 cup mascarpone cheese

1 cup milk

1/4 teaspoon almond extract

1/4 cup coarsely chopped toasted almonds

About 3/4 cup fromage frais or fromage blanc, for serving

In a small heavy saucepan, combine the 3/4 cup sugar with the butter over medium-low heat; the butter will melt and the sugar will dissolve. Boil for a few minutes, until the mixture begins to brown. Adjust the heat and stir occasionally with a wooden spoon so that the caramel browns evenly. When it reaches a dark brown, immediately remove from the heat and carefully pour into the bottom of a 9-inch ceramic or Pyrex deep-dish pie dish. Swirl the caramel around the base and 1 inch up the sides of the dish. Place the dish in the refrigerator and chill until the caramel is cold.

After chilling, place a heel of bread in the center of the dish (or two slices stacked on top of each other). Then arrange the bread slices, standing them against one another, around the center. They should fill the pie dish snugly.

In a large bowl, whisk together the eggs, the remaining 2 tablespoons sugar, and the mascarpone until very smooth. Whisk in the milk and almond extract. Pour the mixture over the bread, making sure to saturate all of it. Cover with plastic wrap and chill overnight.

In the morning, take the pie dish out of the refrigerator and discard the plastic wrap. Preheat the oven to 375 degrees. Bake the pudding for 15 minutes, then sprinkle the almonds over the top. Continue baking until moist but not wet in the center, 15 to 20 minutes more. Run a knife around the edge of the dish, loosening the bread from the sides. Place a serving plate over the top of the dish (bottom side up) and, using potholders, hold the pudding over the sink and in a single fluid motion, holding it away from your body, invert the plate. Lift off the pie dish. Scrape any extra caramel from the pie dish over the pudding. Serve, cutting into wedges at the table and spooning a healthy dollop of fromage frais or fromage blanc onto each plate.

cook's notes

℘ Be sure to read the entire directions for turning out the pudding before attempting it. It's a simple enough process; you just want to avoid spilling any hot caramel onto yourself and you don't want to stop halfway.

℘ This pudding would also be nice made with slices of panettone or plain country bread.

℘ Fromage frais or fromage blanc is a tangy, fresh French cheese sold in plastic tubs. If you can't find any, serve this with sour cream or whole milk yogurt, or au naturel.

serve with

Roasted Apricots with Cardamom (page 286) or a citrusy fruit salad
Little sausages

℘

to drink

Fresh-squeezed tangerine juice muddled with mint sprigs,
or mimosas

SOURCE: *Boston Herald*
COOK: **Linda McLaughlin**
after Jordan Marsh bakery

jordan marsh blueberry muffins

ANY OLD-TIME BOSTONIAN CAN TELL YOU that Jordan Marsh, the classic department store, used to make the best blueberry muffins imaginable. All we know is that we tested a heap of muffin recipes both last year and this year, including some titled "best ever" and "legendary," and all fell short — except this one. In the end, we returned to these simple and very delicious blueberry muffins.

They're exactly what you want a muffin to be: tender, sweet but not too sweet, fruit-filled, and with a crunchy, sugary top. The technique of smashing some of the blueberries before folding them into the batter seems to make the muffins extra moist.

makes 10 to 12 large muffins

8 tablespoons (1 stick) butter, at
   room temperature
1¼ cups sugar plus 2 teaspoons for
   the topping
2 large eggs

2 cups all-purpose flour
2 teaspoons baking powder
½ teaspoon salt
½ cup milk
2½ cups blueberries (see note)

Preheat the oven to 375 degrees. Grease a large muffin pan (be sure to grease the top of the pan, too).

In a large bowl, cream the butter with an electric mixer. Add the 1¼ cups sugar and continue creaming until light and fluffy. Add the eggs, one at a time, beating well after each addition.

In a medium bowl, sift together the flour, baking powder, and salt; add alternately with the milk to the butter-sugar mixture. Do not overmix.

In a small bowl, crush ½ cup of the blueberries with a fork and mix them into the batter by hand. Fold in the remaining berries. Fill the prepared muffin cups with batter. Sprinkle the tops with the remaining 2 teaspoons sugar. Bake until the tops are golden and spring back when lightly touched and a toothpick inserted into the center of a muffin comes out clean, about 30 minutes. Serve warm.

- If you want smaller muffins or don't own a large muffin pan, expect to get about 18 standard-sized muffins. Watch the baking time, too, since smaller muffins will be done about 5 minutes sooner than larger ones.

- Small wild blueberries are better in muffins than the pea-sized cultivated ones. If you can't find fresh, frozen will do — just let them sit in a colander for a few hours to thaw — or use them directly from the freezer.

- One reason we were looking for an exceptional muffin recipe is that we wanted an excuse to try the new flexible muffin pans — they're great.

tip

In *Cook's Illustrated*, we found a bright idea for making ginger- or lemon-glazed muffins. Omit the sprinkle of sugar before the muffins go into the oven, and while the muffins are baking, in a small bowl, mix 1 teaspoon grated fresh lemon zest or grated fresh ginger and $1/2$ cup sugar. In a small saucepan, bring $1/4$ cup lemon juice and $1/4$ cup sugar to a simmer over medium heat; simmer until the mixture is thick and syrupy and reduced to about $1/4$ cup. After the muffins have cooled, brush the tops with the glaze. Then, working one at a time, dip the tops of the muffins into the lemon sugar or ginger sugar. Set the muffins upright and serve.

SOURCE: *The Baker's Catalogue,*
King Arthur Flour Company
COOK: Unknown

apricot–cream cheese scones

THESE SCONES ARE TENDER, rich, and pretty, with bright bits of dried apricots. The cream cheese adds a nice tang and a rich texture. It also keeps them from being crumbly and dry, the scourge of scones; instead these are moist and delicate. Make them smaller than your standard giant coffee shop scone, since they're richer and more satisfying. Although the scones are best warm from the oven, they do keep for a day and even reheat quite happily.

makes about 18 scones

4¼ cups pastry flour or all-purpose flour

½ cup sugar

2½ teaspoons baking powder

½ teaspoon salt

1 8-ounce package cream cheese, chilled

8 tablespoons (1 stick) butter, chilled

1 cup diced or slivered dried apricots

1 large egg

¼ cup milk plus more for brushing

2 teaspoons pure vanilla extract or ½ teaspoon Fiori di Sicilia (see note)

Sparkling white or pearl sugar, for topping

Preheat the oven to 425 degrees. In a medium bowl, whisk together the flour, sugar, baking powder, and salt. Cut in the cream cheese and butter, using your fingers, a pastry blender, a fork or a mixer, until the mixture resembles coarse meal. Stir in the dried apricots. In a small bowl, whisk together the egg, ¼ cup milk, and the vanilla or Fiori di Sicilia. Combine the liquid and dry ingredients and stir until the dough becomes cohesive. Don't mix and mix and mix; the more you work the dough, the tougher it will get.

Turn the dough out onto a floured work surface and fold it over several times, until it holds together. Pat the dough into a ¾-inch-thick rectangle. Cut out scones with a round cookie cutter, gathering the scraps and rerolling the dough. Or simply cut the dough into square or diamond-shaped scones. Brush the tops lightly with milk and sprinkle with the sparkling white or pearl sugar.

Place the scones about 2 inches apart on an ungreased or parchment-lined baking sheet. Bake for 8 minutes. Turn the oven off, leave the door closed, and bake for 8 minutes more, or until the scones are light golden brown. Serve hot, with clotted cream or butter and jam or raspberry curd.

cook's notes

- Fiori di Sicilia is a combination of citrus and vanilla extracts that reminds us of the flavor of Creamsicles. It is used in traditional panettone and can be found at King Arthur Flour (www.bakerscatalogue.com).

- In order to get 18 scones, you'll want to make them rather small — about $2\frac{1}{2}$ inches across.

- If the dough appears too crumbly when you turn it out, just knead it gently by folding it over onto itself until it holds together.

- Since ovens do differ, if the scones are not done after the second 8 minutes, just leave them in the oven for an additional 4 minutes or so — they should be fine.

- If you have no fancy sugar to put on the scones, try sprinkling some Spiced Almond Powder (page 294) on them.

tip

If, like ours, your cookie cutter collection seems to look a little more tired each year, try this tip from Regan Daley, author of *In the Sweet Kitchen*. Choose only stainless-steel cookie cutters and dry them thoroughly after each use. Keep them in an aerated container and dust them with a little cornstarch before storing, to absorb any moisture and prevent rusting. Another trick is to store them with one or two silica gel packs or capsules, the sort that come in vitamin bottles. Just make sure the packets are intact and not leaking silica.

SOURCE: *Dierbergs Everybody Cooks*
(supermarket newsletter)
COOK: Staff of Dierbergs School of Cooking

cherry-almond twist pastry

THIS PASTRY IS A GREAT INVENTION that looks gorgeous and complicated but is a cinch to put together and tastes delicious. The combination of toasty almonds, tart dried cherries, and buttery pastry is addictive, like an almond croissant studded with dried cherries. Going into the oven, it looks atrocious, and you may think you've done something really wrong, because the pastry is going off in all directions. Once in the oven, however, everything smooths out into a bakery-perfect swirl of pastry.

The pastry would be perfect for Christmas breakfast, but it's so simple to make that it's good on any weekend morning. If you don't have time to make it in the morning, you can whip it up the night before, refrigerate it, and then glaze and bake it the next day.

serves 8 to 10

²/₃ cup (about 3 ounces) dried cherries

1 7-to-8-ounce package almond paste (not marzipan)

4 tablespoons (¹/₂ stick) butter, softened

1 17.3-ounce package frozen puff pastry, thawed

1 large egg beaten with 1 teaspoon water

¹/₄ cup sliced almonds (optional)

Preheat the oven to 400 degrees. In a small bowl, combine the dried cherries and just enough warm water to cover. Let stand for 3 to 5 minutes. Drain and set aside.

In a food processor, process the almond paste and butter until smooth. Add the cherries and pulse until they are evenly mixed — they'll still be chunky.

On a lightly floured surface, gently roll one of the pastry sheets to remove any creases. Place on a parchment-lined baking sheet. Using a sharp knife or pizza cutter, trim the corners of the pastry to form a circle about 11 inches in diameter. Spread the almond filling over the pastry, leaving a ¹/₂-inch border around the edge. Roll the second sheet of pastry to remove any creases and place over the filling. Trim to fit the bottom layer and press to seal the edges.

Lightly press a 1¹/₂-inch-wide biscuit cutter in the center of the pastry to form a guideline (without cutting through the pastry). Cut the pastry into 16 equal wedges, cutting just up to the edge of the center circle. (The wedges should be about 1¹/₂ inches wide at the outside edge.) Gently grasp the outside edge of each wedge and give it a double twist, forming a starburst pattern. Brush the egg wash over the pastry. Sprinkle the almonds over the top, if desired.

Bake until the pastry is golden brown and puffed, about 20 minutes. Cool slightly; the pastry is best served warm.

cook's notes

- Most supermarket puff pastry doesn't contain butter. The kind made with butter, such as the Dufour brand, is tastier, but the non-butter pastry is less finicky to work with.
- Several taste tests were conducted this year on almond paste. The Baker's Dozen, a Bay Area collective, liked canned almond paste better than the plastic-wrapped rolls. *Gourmet* magazine preferred the Odense canned brand.
- When you're sealing the edges of the two pieces of pastry, it helps to brush the outer perimeter of the first sheet with a little egg wash before you top it with the second sheet.
- If the pastry gets too warm and slouchy while you're fiddling with it, slip it into the refrigerator for a bit to let it firm up again. This can be a problem with butter pastry.
- Check the center of the pastry when you think it's done — it should be golden. If it's not, the pastry will be undercooked and may take as much as another 5 to 7 minutes.
- In our opinion, tart cherries are the ones for this pastry, and we wouldn't dream of leaving off the almonds.

SOURCE: *Caprial's Desserts*
by Caprial Pence and Melissa Carey
COOK: Caprial Pence and Melissa Carey

orange-caramel monkey bread

THIS BREAD IS TOTALLY OVER THE TOP — truly indulgent, caramel-y, buttery, tender and luscious. Remember the cheesy, pull-apart bread we used to call monkey bread (or monkey balls in some irreverent households)? Well, here's a breakfast version that far outshines its inspiration. The orange-caramel element is three-fold here — the dough, the caramel sauce, and the cinnamon-sugar topping.

You roll the soft yeasted dough into little balls, dip each one in melted butter, toss them in cinnamon-orange sugar, then pile them into the caramel-lined cake pan. The result: a glistening, towering ring of sweet, sticky pastry that you tear apart with your hands. Finger licking is encouraged. What could be more fun?

This is a great choice for a birthday breakfast, a lazy Sunday morning, or a brunch.

serves 12

DOUGH

1$\frac{1}{4}$ cups milk
8 tablespoons (1 stick) unsalted butter, cut into small pieces
$\frac{1}{3}$ cup sugar
1 teaspoon salt
1 tablespoon active dry yeast (or 1 package, which measures 2$\frac{1}{4}$ teaspoons)
Finely grated zest and juice of 2 oranges
2 large eggs, lightly beaten
5 cups all-purpose flour

ORANGE-CARAMEL SAUCE

8 tablespoons (1 stick) unsalted butter
$\frac{3}{4}$ cup firmly packed brown sugar
$\frac{1}{2}$ cup light corn syrup
Finely grated zest of 1 orange

TOPPING

1 cup sugar
Finely grated zest of 1 orange
1 teaspoon ground cinnamon
8 tablespoons (1 stick) unsalted butter, melted

TO MAKE THE DOUGH:

In a small saucepan, bring the milk just to a boil over medium heat. Meanwhile, in a large bowl, combine the butter, sugar, and salt. Pour the hot milk into the butter mixture. Let cool to 110 to 115 degrees; this won't take very long. Add the yeast, mix well, and let stand for about 10 minutes. Add the orange zest, orange juice, and eggs and mix well. Stir in the flour and mix until combined.

Transfer the dough to a well-floured work surface and knead until very smooth and elastic, about 10 minutes. Place the dough in a large, well-greased bowl, cover with plastic, and let rise until doubled in volume, about 1¹/₂ hours. While the dough is rising, generously butter a bundt pan or an angel food cake pan (you'll need at least a 12-cup pan to accommodate the bread).

TO MAKE THE ORANGE-CARAMEL SAUCE:

In a medium saucepan, melt the butter over medium-high heat. Add the brown sugar and whisk until well blended. Add the corn syrup and boil, whisking constantly, until the brown sugar has dissolved, about 1 minute. Stir in the orange zest. Pour the sauce into the prepared cake pan; set aside.

Punch down the dough, place it on a well-floured work surface, and form it into a log about 18 inches long. Cut the log in half lengthwise so you have 2 thinner logs, and then cut each half into 1-inch pieces to form about 36 pieces total. Roll each piece into a smooth ball.

TO MAKE THE TOPPING:

In a shallow bowl, combine the sugar, orange zest, and cinnamon.

Dip each ball of dough into the melted butter, then roll it in the sugar mixture until coated. Place the balls in the prepared pan, layering them evenly. Cover the pan with plastic wrap and let rise for about 30 minutes (don't let the bread rise until doubled, or it will spill out of the pan).

Meanwhile, preheat the oven to 350 degrees.

When the bread has risen, bake until it is golden brown and the bottom sounds hollow when tapped, 50 to 60 minutes. Let cool for 5 minutes, then invert the pan onto a large plate to release the bread; remove the pan carefully so you don't spill the hot caramel. Let cool for 15 minutes before serving. Serve warm.

❧ You can make this dough in an electric mixer. Start by putting the butter, sugar, and salt in the bowl of the mixer and continue accordingly. If the dough remains very sticky after kneading in the mixer, turn it out onto a well-floured board and give it a few turns by hand.

❧ You may need to add ½ cup or so more flour to the dough if it feels too sticky. You want it to be very soft, but smooth.

❧ Place a sheet of heavy-duty aluminum foil or a baking sheet on the oven rack beneath the bread to catch any drips during baking.

tip

Those handy Microplane rasps have made zesting citrus much easier, and Carol Field (of *The Baker's Dozen*) shares a tip for getting even more flavor from the zest: grate it right over the mixing bowl to catch the essential oils in the zest.

main dishes

SOURCE: *Enoteca* by Joyce Goldstein
COOK: Joyce Goldstein

baked eggplant parmesan

IF YOU THINK, AS WE ONCE DID, that there's nothing new to say about eggplant Parmesan, this version will be a revelation: lighter and more like a gratin than the heavy-breaded and gooey-cheesy southern Italian version so familiar in Italian-American restaurants.

The recipe, from the Enoteca Baldi in Panzano, Tuscany, eliminates the breading on the eggplant and loses the mozzarella. Instead, slices of eggplant are fried in olive oil, layered with a very small amount of a simple tomato sauce, covered with Parmesan and bread crumbs, and then baked. The resulting dish is meltingly tender and delectable and suffers no loss of satisfaction. It may seem as if you have not enough tomato sauce and way too much bread crumbs when you're assembling it, but don't change a thing — the combination works beautifully. Since there are so few ingredients, you must be sure to use good ones. If tomatoes are out of season, use a high-quality brand of canned whole tomatoes (such as San Marzano from Italy) and never, never use bread crumbs out of a box for this.

serves 6

3 medium (about ³/₄ pound each) eggplants
Salt
Olive oil, for frying
2 cups peeled, seeded, and diced tomatoes (see note)

2 garlic cloves, minced (optional)
Freshly ground black pepper
³/₄ cup freshly grated Parmesan cheese
1¹/₂ cups fine dry bread crumbs (see note)

Peel the eggplants and slice them into rounds about ¹/₃ inch thick. Place the slices in 1 or 2 colanders, sprinkling them with salt; this works best if the slices are just barely overlapping so they can drain. Let drain for 30 minutes. Rinse and pat dry.

Preheat the oven to 400 degrees. Oil a baking dish that will accommodate the eggplant slices in 2 layers. (A 9-x-13-inch baking dish works nicely.)

Heat ¹/₄ inch olive oil in a large preferably nonstick skillet over medium-high heat. Add the eggplant slices, in batches, and fry, turning once, until golden and tender, then transfer to paper towels to drain. Add oil to the skillet only as necessary to prevent sticking, or the porous eggplant will drink more than it needs. The frying should take about 6 minutes per batch.

Add the tomatoes to the oil remaining in the skillet and cook until they break down and acquire a saucelike consistency, about 10 minutes. Add the garlic, if using, during the last 2 minutes of cooking. Season with salt and pepper to taste.

Spread a thin layer of the tomato sauce in the prepared baking dish. Don't worry if the sauce doesn't cover the entire dish. Add half the eggplant slices, then half the remaining tomato sauce. Top with the remaining eggplant and then the remaining sauce. Scatter the Parmesan and then the bread crumbs evenly over the top.

Bake the eggplant until the top is golden, about 25 minutes. Let rest for 15 minutes before serving.

cook's notes

- Be sure to carefully rinse and dry the eggplant after salting. If not, the dish may end up too salty. Even so, go easy on the salt for the tomato sauce.
- If tomatoes are out of season, use a can of whole, peeled tomatoes. Squeeze the seeds out of the tomatoes and roughly chop them before adding them and the juice from the can to the skillet.
- In place of dry bread crumbs, you can make fresh bread crumbs and toast them in the oven.
- To make this more like the classic southern Italian version, add thin slices of mozzarella cheese between the layers of eggplant and sauce, but do not omit the bread crumbs or Parmesan.

serve with

Cybill's Greens (page 206)
Crusty Italian bread
Crème Fraîche Panna Cotta with Berry Puree (page 279)

to drink

Sangiovese
or Grenache

SOURCE: *Los Angeles Times*
COOK: **Marion Cunningham**

chile-cheese supper dish

THIS COMFORT-FOOD CASSEROLE could have appeared on the Brady Bunch dinner table. It's one of those nostalgic dishes that we never seem to grow out of — probably because in addition to being all cheesy and rich and tasty, it's a snap to make. Zipping it up a bit with mild green chiles (from a can, in keeping with the general theme) brings it somewhat up to date. It puffs up some in the oven and gets nicely browned on top. The little bit of cornmeal adds some texture and good corn flavor.

Because this vegetarian casserole is so simple, it makes a great weeknight meal with a sharp green salad and warm rolls or flour tortillas — and it's also a fine contribution to any potluck or buffet. This dish is a great place to tuck in a few carnivore leftovers, such as a cup or two of diced ham or shredded chicken.

serves 6

6 large eggs
1 cup milk
4 tablespoons ($\frac{1}{2}$ stick) butter, melted
1 pound Monterey Jack cheese, grated
1 cup cottage cheese

3 ounces cream cheese, cut into small pieces
1 7-ounce can chopped green chiles
$\frac{1}{2}$ cup cornmeal
$1\frac{1}{2}$ teaspoons baking powder
1 teaspoon salt

Preheat the oven to 350 degrees. Butter a $2\frac{1}{2}$-quart baking dish. In a large bowl, beat the eggs with a fork or an egg beater until well blended and all one color. Add the milk, butter, Monterey Jack, cottage cheese, cream cheese, green chiles, cornmeal, baking powder, and salt and briskly stir until well mixed.

Pour the mixture into the prepared baking dish. Bake the casserole until a skewer or table knife inserted in the center comes out clean and the top is puffed and golden, 35 to 45 minutes. Serve hot.

cook's notes

❧ One 7-ounce can of green chiles is about 1 cup, which is good to know since some markets sell only 4-ounce cans. We think whole canned green chiles are much nicer than the chopped ones. Just drain and chop them, discarding any seeds.

❧ Keeping the cream cheese chilled will make it easier to cut. The smaller the pieces, the more evenly it will be distributed in the casserole.

serve with

Guacamole with Lemon and Roasted Corn (page 24), with drinks

❧

Tossed green salad
Nadine's Onion and Black Pepper Rolls (page 229) or warm flour tortillas
The Best Chocolate Chip Cookies (page 242)

❧

to drink

Lightly chilled Beaujolais-Villages (for red)
or a Washington State Chenin Blanc (for white)

main dishes

SOURCE: *Fearless Baking* by Elinor Klivans
COOK: Elinor Klivans

roasted tomato, basil, and parmesan pie

ROASTED TOMATOES, BASIL, PARMESAN, fresh mozzarella, and olive oil — some of our favorite flavors made into a luscious pie — a very American take on some beloved Italian flavors.

We were also intrigued by the piecrust trick of blending soft butter and shortening and then freezing it into a stick so that you can grate it into perfect crumb-sized pieces. While it requires some planning ahead — the butter-shortening stick needs to freeze for at least five hours — it makes quick work of piecrust and the results are very flaky and tender. As we later learned, this is one of those old restaurant tricks we home cooks hardly ever hear about.

This savory pie makes a great light supper or fancy lunch, or put it out on a buffet at any time of day. While it's wonderful warm from the oven, it's just as good after several hours at room temperature.

makes one 9-inch pie

DOUGH

5 tablespoons unsalted butter, at room temperature

1/4 cup vegetable shortening, at room temperature

1 cup all-purpose flour

1/3 cup cake flour

1 tablespoon sugar

1/4 teaspoon salt

3 tablespoons plus 2–3 teaspoons ice water

ROASTED TOMATOES

5 large (at least 8-ounce) or 7 medium (at least 6-ounce) tomatoes, skinned and halved crosswise

1 teaspoon (about 2 cloves) finely chopped garlic, green center removed if any

1/4 teaspoon salt

15 whole fresh basil leaves

2 tablespoons olive oil

FILLING

1/2 cup freshly grated Parmesan cheese, preferably Parmigiano-Reggiano

4 ounces fresh mozzarella, cut into 1/2-inch pieces

Freshly ground black pepper

2 tablespoons tightly packed torn fresh basil (1/2-inch pieces)

15 black olives (preferably oil-cured), pitted

1 tablespoon extra-virgin olive oil

TO MAKE THE DOUGH:

In a medium bowl, beat the butter and shortening with an electric mixer on medium speed until smoothly blended, about 1 minute. Scrape the mixture onto a piece of plastic wrap and form it into a rectangle about 4 x 2½ inches and about 1 inch thick. (This shape is easy to hold for grating and can fit or be cut to fit into the feed tube of a food processor.) Wrap and freeze until firm, at least 5 hours or overnight.

In a large bowl, stir together the all-purpose flour, cake flour, sugar, and salt. Set aside.

Remove the frozen butter-shortening stick from the freezer. Holding one end with a clean kitchen towel so your hands won't melt it, grate the stick onto a piece of waxed paper using the large holes of a box grater. If there is a little piece left at the end, cut it into tiny pieces and add to the flour. Or grate the butter-shortening stick in a food processor fitted with the grating blade. Immediately add the grated butter-shortening to the flour mixture and stir with a fork until completely blended and crumbly-looking, about 40 strokes. Or mix with an electric mixer for about 15 seconds, until it forms crumbs. The largest of the crumbs should be about ¼ inch. Sprinkle 3 tablespoons of the ice water over the flour mixture and mix with the fork or electric mixer. Stir in more ice water, 1 teaspoon at a time, just until there is no loose flour and the dough holds together in clumps. The dough should feel cold.

Gather the dough together and turn it out onto a lightly floured work surface. With the heel of your hand, push the dough down and forward 3 or 4 times to form a smooth dough. A couple of additional strokes with the heel of your hand in order to form a smooth dough is fine. Gather the dough into a ball, then press it into a disk about 5 inches wide. The dough should feel soft and malleable, but not sticky. Wrap in plastic wrap and chill for at least 30 minutes or up to overnight.

TO ROAST THE TOMATOES:

Preheat the oven to 400 degrees with a rack in the middle. Line a shallow roasting pan or rimmed baking sheet with 2 layers of parchment paper. Put the tomato halves cut side up in the pan. Sprinkle with the garlic and salt, and top each with 1 or 2 basil leaves. Drizzle the olive oil over the basil. Bake for 1 hour and 15 minutes for large tomatoes or 1 hour for medium. The edges of the tomatoes may darken and the basil leaves turn dark and crispy, but they are not burned. Remove from the oven and set aside to cool. Reduce the oven temperature to 375 degrees.

TO FILL AND BAKE THE PIE:

Butter a 9-inch glass or ceramic pie dish. If the dough has been refrigerated for more than 30 minutes, you may need to let it sit at room temperature until it is easy to roll. Lightly flour the work surface and rolling pin. Roll the dough from the center out into a circle about 4 inches wider than the bottom of the pie dish. Roll up the dough circle loosely over the rolling pin and unroll it carefully into the pie dish. Press the dough into the pie dish without pulling or stretching. Trim the edge to a ³/₄-inch overhang. Press about ¹/₂ inch of the edge under and then crimp the edge all around. If the tomatoes are not ready, refrigerate the crust until ready to bake.

Sprinkle ¹/₄ cup of the Parmesan over the bottom of the crust. Spoon the roasted tomatoes and their basil topping, cut side up and close together, in an even layer over the Parmesan; press the tomatoes together to generously fill the crust. Discard any watery liquid from the tomatoes. Bake for about 40 minutes, or until the edge of the crust is lightly browned and the filling begins to bubble. Remove from the oven. Place the mozzarella pieces between the tomatoes evenly around the pie. Grind fresh pepper lightly over the top. In a small bowl, stir together the remaining ¹/₄ cup Parmesan and the basil and sprinkle over the top. Scatter the olives evenly over the top, and drizzle with the oil. Bake for 10 minutes more, or until the cheese melts. Let the pie rest for 10 minutes and serve warm, or serve at room temperature.

cook's notes

☙ Leftover pie can be refrigerated and brought to room temperature for serving.

☙ Skinning the tomatoes makes a big difference, so don't skip it. It's easy: Have a saucepan of boiling water ready and make a little X in the skin on the bottom of each tomato. Drop the tomato into the boiling water for just a few seconds, remove, and let drain. Peel back the skin from each corner of the X.

☙ The double layer of parchment keeps the tomatoes from sticking to the pan and makes cleanup a whole lot easier.

☙ The tomatoes may be roasted up to 8 hours ahead.

serve with

Arugula salad
Almond Crisps (page 253)
and fresh fruit

☙

to drink

Dolcetta d'Alba
or a light-style Zinfandel

SOURCE: *The Gastronomy of Italy*
by Anna del Conte
COOK: Anna del Conte

potato cake filled with mozzarella and prosciutto

POTATO CAKE IS A GREAT IDEA, and one we've seen previously only in an Italian-American version, which is a bit different. Here a potato puree is thickened with eggs, milk, and Parmesan, then baked in a cake pan with a layer of mozzarella, prosciutto, and mortadella or salami in the middle. The top of the cake is crisp with golden brown bread crumbs. As you cut into the cake, the cheese oozes out and you discover that the meats have flavored the potatoes.

We've listed this as a main dish, but you can also serve it as a starter at the beginning of a relatively light meal. It isn't at all hard to make, can be put together a few hours ahead and can be served hot or warm. People adore this potato cake, so it's well worth trying.

serves 4

2 pounds Idaho or russet potatoes, scrubbed

7 tablespoons milk (scant ½ cup)

5 tablespoons unsalted butter

½ cup freshly grated Parmesan cheese

Salt and freshly ground black pepper

A small grating of nutmeg

2 extra-large eggs (free-range, if possible)

1 extra-large egg yolk (free-range, if possible)

6 ounces fresh mozzarella cheese, cut into slices

2½ ounces prosciutto, not too thinly sliced

2½ ounces mortadella or salami

FOR THE PAN AND TOPPING

4 tablespoons unsalted butter

4–5 tablespoons dry bread crumbs

In a large saucepan of boiling water, cook the potatoes in their skins until you can easily pierce through to their middles with the blade of a small knife. Meanwhile, preheat the oven to 400 degrees.

Drain the potatoes and peel them as soon as they are cool enough to handle. Pass the potatoes through a food mill or potato ricer set over the pan in which they were cooked.

In a small saucepan, heat the milk and add to the potatoes with the butter. Beat well and add the Parmesan, $^1/_2$ teaspoon salt, pepper to taste, and the nutmeg. Mix well. Add the eggs and egg yolk and mix very thoroughly.

Butter an 8-inch springform cake pan and cover the buttered surface with some of the bread crumbs. Spoon half of the potato mixture into the pan and cover with the mozzarella, prosciutto, and mortadella or salami. Spoon the rest of the potatoes over the top. Dot with the remaining butter and sprinkle very lightly with the remaining bread crumbs.

Bake the potato cake for 20 to 30 minutes, or until it is brown on top and hot in the middle (test by inserting a small knife into the middle and then bringing it carefully to your lip — it should feel hot). If it is still a bit pale, flash it under the broiler.

Let the cake stand for 10 minutes before unmolding and serving.

serve with

Roasted Artichoke, Lemon, and Garlic Dip (page 20), with drinks
Steamed green beans tossed with olive oil and basil
Pecan Brittle with Black Pepper (page 254) and espresso

℘

to drink

Pinot Noir
or Dolcetto

SOURCE: *San Francisco Chronicle*
COOK: Robin Davis and Tara Duggan

moroccan root vegetable stew with charmoula

THIS VEGAN STEW GETS ITS FLAVOR from toasted spices and charmoula, a North African flavor-booster made from still more spices, fresh cilantro, lemon juice, and olive oil. The aroma of toasting spices alone is reason enough to make this. Use the recipe as a guideline — for instance, if you don't have parsnips (or don't care for them), just use a few more carrots. No celery root? Use branch celery. We suspect that even rutabaga would taste good in here. Just don't omit the sweet potatoes, which are chopped up smaller than the other vegetables so that they break down into the sauce and add body to the stew. As with most stews, this tastes even better the next day — it thickens up nicely as it sits, so you may need to add more water to thin it on day two.

The cooks tell us that besides being warming and comforting, this richly flavored dish is loaded with vitamins A and C, as well as potassium.

serves 5

SPICE MIXTURE
1½ teaspoons cumin seeds
1½ teaspoons coriander seeds
1 teaspoon sweet paprika
1 small dried red chile, or ½ teaspoon crushed red pepper flakes
4 whole cloves
1 cinnamon stick, snapped in half
1 bay leaf

VEGETABLE STEW
2 tablespoons vegetable oil
2 onions, cut into large dice
2 medium sweet potatoes (preferably red-skinned), peeled and cut into very small dice

2 garlic cloves, minced
3 parsnips, peeled and cut into large chunks
2 carrots, peeled and cut into large chunks
1 small celery root, peeled and cut into large dice (see note)
2 tablespoons tomato paste
1 teaspoon salt
Freshly ground black pepper
1 tablespoon fresh lemon juice

Charmoula (recipe follows)

In a small heavy pan, toast the spices and bay leaf over very low heat for about 10 minutes, stirring occasionally, until aromatic and toasty. Be careful that they don't scorch. Let cool, then grind to a fine powder. (Use a spice grinder or a coffee grinder reserved for spices.) Set aside $1^1/_2$ teaspoons of the spice mixture for the charmoula (see recipe).

TO MAKE THE STEW:

In a Dutch oven, heat the oil over medium heat. Add the onions and sweet potatoes and sweat for 10 minutes, or until the onions are tender. Stir in the garlic and the spice mixture and cook for 5 minutes. Deglaze the Dutch oven with 4 cups water, then add the parsnips, carrots, celery root, tomato paste, salt, pepper to taste, and lemon juice. Bring to a simmer, cover, and cook for about 20 minutes, or until the sweet potatoes have broken down and all the vegetables are tender.

Ladle into bowls. Drizzle the charmoula on top and serve hot.

---

charmoula

makes about 5 tablespoons

$^1/_3$ cup finely chopped fresh cilantro
$1^1/_2$ teaspoons reserved spice mixture (from the vegetable stew)
$^1/_2$ teaspoon tomato paste
$^1/_4$ teaspoon salt
$1^1/_2$ tablespoons fresh lemon juice
  3 tablespoons extra-virgin olive oil

In a small bowl, combine everything but the oil. Whisk in the oil. Let stand for a few minutes before serving.

cook's notes

℥ Be sure that the heat is very low when toasting the spices — otherwise they may scorch.

℥ Cut the sweet potatoes into the smallest dice you can manage if you really want them to break down and thicken the stew.

℥ If you don't have a spice grinder, use a mortar and pestle, working diligently to grind all the spices into a fine powder — no one wants to bite down on a big hunk of clove.

℥ Peel the celery root by cutting it square across the bottom and top, then use a paring knife to trim off the rugged outer layer edges.

serve with

Couscous with toasted almonds and golden raisins
Nadine's Onion and Black Pepper Rolls (page 229)
New Year's Honey Cake (page 264)

℥

to drink

A dry rosé
or a Blanc de Noir sparkling wine

SOURCE: *Comfort Me with Apples* by Ruth Reichl
COOK: Ruth Reichl after Danny Kaye

danny's lemon pasta

NOT TOO MANY PEOPLE KNOW that the irrepressible Danny Kaye was a spectacular born cook. Virtually anything he set his hand to in the kitchen was transformed. In her well-chronicled youth, Ruth Reichl, the editor of *Gourmet,* had the good fortune to enjoy a few meals with him. This lemon pasta was a particular favorite of hers, and she set about to re-create it. This is a truly divine pasta, rich with cream, butter, and Parmesan, with the cutting zing of lemon zest and lots of lemon juice. When you bring it to the table, there's a stunning fragrance of lemon.

serves 4

4 tablespoons (½ stick) unsalted butter
1 cup heavy cream
3 tablespoons fresh lemon juice
1 pound fresh egg fettuccine
   Salt

2 teaspoons finely grated fresh lemon zest
   Freshly ground black pepper
   Freshly grated Parmesan cheese, for serving

In a large heavy skillet, melt the butter. Stir in the cream and lemon juice and cook until warm. Remove from the heat, cover, and keep warm.

Cook the pasta in a large pot of salted boiling water until al dente, 2 to 3 minutes. Reserve ½ cup of the pasta cooking liquid and drain the pasta. Add the pasta to the skillet with the lemon zest and 2 tablespoons of the pasta cooking liquid; toss well. (Add more pasta cooking liquid, 1 tablespoon at a time, to thin the sauce, if necessary.) Season the pasta with salt and pepper to taste. Serve immediately with Parmesan cheese.

serve with
Antipasto of thin, crisp bread sticks,
sliced melon, and serrano ham, with drinks
Salad of sharp greens
Butter-Toffee Crunch Shortbread (page 250) and sliced fruit
℃

to drink
Chardonnay

main dishes

pasta with born-again zucchini and pesto

ESSENCE-OF-SUMMER PASTAS so often turn out to be about tomatoes, but this one is much subtler. It takes a wallflower vegetable, zucchini, which we all love to malign for being tasteless and watery, and makes it interesting. John Thorne treats zucchini as though it were eggplant, a technique you sometimes see in Middle Eastern recipes. The salted zucchini lolls around in a bowl for a while, then releases its considerable water. Finally, it gets twisted dry in a towel.

You may never have realized how bloated zucchini is, but once it's slimmed down, it has a whole new chewy texture and some actual flavor — and is indeed born again.

This is a great, nothing-fancy summer supper for two.

serves 2

2 medium zucchini
1 tablespoon coarse salt
2 tablespoons olive oil
1 garlic clove, minced
¼ teaspoon powdered red chile (see note)
¼ teaspoon salt

½ pound regular or thin spaghetti
½ cup homemade or good-quality store-bought pesto
Parmesan cheese, for serving
Freshly ground black pepper, for serving

Cut the zucchini in half crosswise. Slice each half into slivers about the size of a kitchen match. In a medium bowl, toss the zucchini with the coarse salt and let stand for 30 minutes, turning over occasionally. Meanwhile, put a big pot of salted water on to boil.

When the water is about to boil, in a large skillet, combine the oil, garlic, powdered chile, and salt over medium heat and cook until the garlic turns translucent (see note). Drain the liquid from the zucchini, spread an old but clean kitchen towel in the sink, and turn out the zucchini onto it. Wrap the zucchini up in the cloth and twist as tightly as you can, extracting every possible bit of moisture.

Cook the pasta according to package directions until al dente. Meanwhile, add the wrung-out zucchini to the skillet and cook, stirring frequently but gently, until the pasta is almost ready. Scoop out $1/4$ cup of the pasta cooking water and add to the zucchini, then stir in the pesto.

Remove the skillet from the heat. Drain the pasta and divide it between two plates, doling the sauce out on top. Serve with freshly grated Parmesan and lots of freshly ground black pepper.

cook's notes

- ℰ John Thorne suggests a rich-flavored, earthy, not-too-hot New Mexican chile powder from chimayo chile peppers. A good-quality paprika would also work quite well. Cayenne may be a little on the hot side.

- ℰ In our experience, garlic goes from white to scorched in seconds, so you may look in vain for it to turn translucent. As soon as it's fragrant, it's ready.

- ℰ The zucchini will not be overly salty after the salt treatment, and you definitely do not want to rinse it. Most of the salt gets wrung out with the liquid.

tip

Tom Colicchio, the superstar chef/owner at Craft in New York, shared a terrific pesto tip in the *New York Times*. Colicchio first blanches the basil leaves in boiling water for 15 seconds, then quickly plunges them into ice water to cool. He also blanches the garlic to soften its bite. After squeezing the basil dry, he proceeds with the pesto recipe, grinding the basil and garlic together in a food processor with the usual extra-virgin olive oil and Parmesan cheese. This is an amazing trick: the pesto tastes more, not less intense, and acquires a subtle complexity and super-creamy texture in the bargain. It also stays beautifully bright green.

serve with

"Squash and Smash" Tomato-Olive Salad (page 65)
made with parsley (not basil) and arugula
Crusty bread
Bowls of vanilla ice cream and sliced peaches
sprinkled with Spiced Almond Powder (page 294)

ℰ

to drink

Washington State Semillon (for white) or Pinot Noir (for red)

main dishes

SOURCE: *New York Times*
COOK: Arthur Schwartz

spaghetti with fried eggs and roasted red peppers

THIS STRIKES US AS A truly great recipe — tasty, comforting, economical, flavorful without being too heavy or oily, and made in half an hour from pantry staples. It's also fun to make, since you have to break the fried eggs into the pasta and then toss it. In case you're wondering, no, it doesn't taste the least bit eggy.

The recipe comes from Naples, where they know a thing or two about pasta. The basic idea (and a really smart one) is to use softly fried eggs, oil and some of the pasta cooking water to make a pasta sauce. We're sure the Neapolitans play around with this recipe, as we're tempted to do, with whatever's in season or hanging around in the kitchen: prosciutto, anchovies, cooked greens, or asparagus.

serves 4

2 red bell peppers

1/4 cup finely chopped fresh flat-leaf parsley

1 tablespoon salted capers, thoroughly rinsed, coarsely chopped if large

1 large garlic clove, minced
Sea salt and freshly ground black pepper

3 heaping tablespoons coarse bread crumbs

5 tablespoons extra-virgin olive oil

12 ounces spaghetti

2 large eggs
Freshly grated Parmigiano-Reggiano and Pecorino cheese, for serving

Roast the peppers under the broiler or on a gas burner with the flame on low. Turn them regularly so that they char all over. When they are fully blistered, place them in a paper or plastic bag. Let cool, then peel the peppers. When you cut them open, catch any pepper liquid in a small bowl. Trim off the stem ends, scrape out the seeds, and cut out the ribs, then slice lengthwise into 1/4-inch-wide strips.

In a small baking dish, combine the peppers and any captured juices, parsley, capers, and garlic. Season with salt and pepper to taste. Sprinkle the bread crumbs on top and set aside.

Preheat the oven to 350 degrees. Bring a large pot of salted water to a boil. Just before it boils, sprinkle 2 tablespoons of the oil over the red-pepper mixture and bake for 10 minutes. Add the pasta to the boiling water and cook according to package directions until al dente. After a few minutes, scoop out 1 cup of water and set aside.

Meanwhile, in a medium skillet, heat the remaining 3 tablespoons oil over medium heat. When it shimmers, crack in the eggs and fry, sunny side up, until the whites are set and the yolks are still runny. Remove from the heat.

Drain the pasta and pour it into a large warmed serving bowl. Using 2 forks, toss in the pepper mixture and fried eggs, adding some of the egg-cooking oil. As you toss, break the whites into pieces and let the yolks act as a sauce; they'll spread over the pasta and cook further from the heat. Add a little of the reserved pasta water if the sauce gets too thick. Season with salt and pepper to taste. Serve, passing the cheese on the side.

cook's notes

- You can also used brined capers, of course; just be sure to rinse them carefully.
- You can speed things up by using jarred piquillo peppers from Spain or a good brand of jarred roasted red peppers.

serve with

Mesclun salad

Olive bread

Almond Crisps (page 253) or amaretti cookies and clementines

to drink

Valpolicella
or young Chianti

SOURCE: *Boston Globe*
COOK: Barbara Lynch

rigatoni with sausage and cannellini beans

WE'RE GREAT FANS OF BARBARA LYNCH, the chef/owner of Boston's No. 9 Park. Like the name of her restaurant (simply the street number), her cooking is direct, honest, and puts on no airs. This hearty, earthy dish was inspired by her love of pasta e fagioli, the classic soup of pasta, beans, and sausage. The cannellini beans add creaminess and richness to the dish, and the little bit of butter stirred in at the end brings it all together and prevents it from feeling too sticky or starchy in your mouth.

What we love about this dish — besides how delicious it is — is that it relies mostly on pantry staples (a can of tomatoes, a can of beans, some red wine, a box of dried pasta, and a hunk of good Parmesan) and delivers big flavor. All you need to buy fresh is the Italian sausage.

Using both hot sausage and crushed red pepper flakes makes it nicely piquant — but not overly spicy. If you're a spicephobe, you could certainly use less crushed red pepper.

serves 6

2 tablespoons extra-virgin olive oil
4 garlic cloves, minced
1 large onion, coarsely chopped
1 pound hot Italian sausage, casings removed
1 cup dry red wine
1 28-ounce can peeled Italian tomatoes, drained and coarsely chopped, liquid reserved
½ teaspoon crushed red pepper flakes

Salt and freshly ground black pepper
1 pound rigatoni
1 19-ounce can cannellini beans, rinsed and drained
½ cup freshly grated Parmesan cheese, plus more for serving
2 tablespoons chopped fresh basil, plus basil leaves for garnish
2 tablespoons unsalted butter, cut into small pieces

In a large deep skillet, heat the oil over medium heat. Add the garlic and cook, stirring, until golden, about 1 minute. Add the onion and sausage and cook, breaking up the sausage with a wooden spoon, just until it loses its pink color, about 7 minutes. Add the wine, increase the heat to high, and cook until reduced by half, about 10 minutes. Stir in the tomatoes and their liquid, the red pepper flakes, and salt and pepper to taste. Reduce the heat to medium and cook until slightly thickened, about 30 minutes.

Meanwhile, in a large pot of boiling salted water, cook the rigatoni according to package directions until al dente. Drain, reserving 1 cup of the pasta cooking water.

Add the rigatoni to the sauce and gently stir in the beans, 1/2 cup Parmesan, the chopped basil, and butter. Reduce the heat to low and cook, stirring gently, until heated through, about 3 minutes. Add some of the reserved pasta cooking water if the pasta looks dry. Transfer to warmed bowls, garnish with the basil leaves, and serve. Pass additional Parmesan at the table.

cook's notes

- Use a decent red wine — perhaps the one you plan to serve with the pasta — like a Chianti or bigger Italian red.
- Sometimes it's impossible to find 19-ounce cans of beans (Progresso is a brand that comes in that size) and all you can find are 15-ounce cans. That's fine; it won't make a big difference in this dish. We've even made this dish without the beans and loved it just the same.
- For top-shelf canned tomatoes, look for San Marzano or Muir Glen brands.

tip

According to the *New York Times*, British diva cook Nigella Lawson cheerfully admits to draining the leftover wine from her guests' glasses and storing it in plastic bags in the freezer for cooking. Surprisingly, freezing wine doesn't completely ruin it; this is a good idea for small leftover amounts.

serve with

Olive Shortbread [variation of Curried Almond Shortbread] (page 12), with drinks
Big green salad
Warm garlic bread
Anarchy Cake (page 268)

to drink

An earthy Barbera
or Châteauneuf-du-Pape

SOURCE: *Macaroni and Cheese* by Joan Schwartz
COOK: Nora Pouillon

greek macaroni and cheese

FACED WITH AN ENTIRE BOOK OF MAC AND CHEESE recipes, we gulped and did a little bake-off. Our favorite was a surprise even to us; the idea of using a lot of feta cheese wasn't obvious, but it turned out to be terrific. Feta is lighter than the usual sharp Cheddar, and its piquant charms are highlighted by baby spinach and sweet little cherry tomatoes. This distinctive macaroni and cheese reminds you of Greek salad, pasta salad, even pastitsio. In the end, we couldn't stop eating it.

Nora Pouillon is a Washington, D.C., chef who uses only organic ingredients, but this dish also tastes great made with ordinary supermarket offerings.

This is one of those bizarre loaves-and-fishes recipes. It supposedly serves 4 to 6, but we served 10 people, with seconds.

serves 4 to 6 generously

Kosher salt
1 pound macaroni
1/2 pound baby spinach, washed and stemmed
1 1/2 pounds feta cheese, crumbled (about 6 cups)
2 1/3 cups whole milk
2/3 cup olive oil
2 tablespoons fresh lemon juice
2 teaspoons freshly ground pepper
1/2 pound cherry tomatoes, halved

1/2 cup coarsely chopped pitted black olives (optional)
1 tablespoon minced garlic
2 teaspoons minced fresh thyme
3/4 teaspoon minced fresh rosemary
1/2 teaspoon crushed red pepper flakes, or to taste
1/2 cup freshly grated Parmesan cheese
1/4 cup mixed chopped fresh herbs, such as rosemary, thyme, and parsley

Preheat the oven to 350 degrees, with a rack in the middle. In a large pot, bring 6 quarts salted water to a boil. Add the pasta and cook according to package directions until al dente, 8 to 10 minutes. Drain and place in a large bowl. Set aside.

In a large saucepan, bring 4 quarts salted water to a simmer over medium-high heat. Have ready a large bowl of ice water and a slotted spoon. Add the spinach to the simmering water (in three or four batches) and submerge it. Cook for about 15 seconds, remove with the slotted spoon, and plunge into the ice water. Let the spinach cool completely, drain it, and squeeze out the excess water. If the leaves are large, chop them into bite-sized pieces. Set aside.

In a blender or food processor, puree the feta with the milk, oil, lemon juice, 1 teaspoon salt, and the pepper, in two batches if necessary. The mixture will not be completely smooth; there will be small chunks of cheese remaining. Stir the cheese mixture into the cooked pasta, then stir in the reserved spinach, cherry tomatoes, olives (if using), garlic, thyme, rosemary, and crushed red pepper flakes.

Pour the pasta mixture into a 9-x-13-inch baking dish and sprinkle with the Parmesan and mixed herbs. Bake until heated through and the top is slightly browned, 25 to 30 minutes. Serve hot.

cook's notes

- To minimize the number of pots you use, cook the spinach first in the water for the pasta. Scoop it out with a slotted spoon, then cook the pasta in the same water.
- This mac and cheese is perfectly delicious the next day, so you can make it ahead.
- Speed things up by using prewashed baby spinach.

serve with

Garlicky Sun-Dried Tomato Spread (page 19), with drinks
Cucumber salad
Orange-Almond Lace Cookies (page 246)

to drink

Viognier
or medium-bodied rosé

SOURCE: *Boston Globe*
COOK: **Clem Silva after Ursie Silva**

sea clam pie

IN PROVINCETOWN, ON THE VERY TIP of Cape Cod, there has been both an artists' community, drawn by the spectacular light, and a community of Portuguese fishermen, drawn by the amazingly rich waters just off Provincetown. There are still strong traces of the Portuguese culture, though the fishermen are now few, and the artists have mostly disappeared as well. Provincetown is now mainly a tourist destination, but the traditional Portuguese bakery and restaurants still thrive.

At the top of the list is Clem & Ursie's, where "Little Clem" and his sister Debby cook the Portuguese specialties of their parents, for whom the restaurant is named. Every year, Ursie Silva would make this sea clam pie for the community, and it's a great dish, full of flavor and spicy from the linguiça sausage. The bread cubes soak up the delicious juices and get crisp in the oven.

You can make the pie with the crust or without, in which case it's a casserole (see note).

serves 6

2 tablespoons olive oil
1 large onion, chopped
2 garlic cloves, chopped
½ pound linguiça (Portuguese sausage), removed from its casing and diced

4 cups chopped clams, thawed if frozen
1 cup bread cubes
2 tablespoons clam broth, if needed
1 prebaked 10-inch piecrust

Preheat the oven to 350 degrees. In a large skillet, heat the oil over medium-high heat. Cook the onion and garlic, stirring, for 5 minutes, or until the onion is soft. Add the linguiça and cook, stirring, for 5 minutes more.

Transfer the mixture to a large bowl and stir in the clams and bread cubes. If the mixture seems dry, add enough clam broth to moisten it. (Too much makes the crust gummy.)

Spread the clam mixture in the piecrust. Bake for 30 minutes, or until the top is brown. Serve hot.

❧ If you make the pie without the crust, grease the pie pan, spread the clam mixture in it, and bake for 30 minutes.

❧ If you can't find linguiça, substitute chorizo or Italian sausage.

❧ Sea clams, which are large, are sometimes available in plastic containers, usually frozen, at supermarkets and fish markets.

serve with

A platter of sliced tomatoes with onions and basil
Garlic bread

❧

to drink

Chenin Blanc

SOURCE: *Good Housekeeping*
via Women.com Recipe Finder
COOK: Unknown

chile-dusted scallops with black bean salsa

WE HAVE A SECRET FONDNESS for tasty fifties-style recipes that require you to open a can of this and a can of that and throw them together. The cans in this case contain corn and beans. Add some scallops, fresh lime juice, cilantro, and a few other lively ingredients, and you have an almost instant dinner.

This dish begs for some avocado, so either start with guacamole or serve a green salad with tomatoes and avocado.

serves 4

1 15-to-19-ounce can black beans, rinsed and drained
1 15.25-to-16 ounce can whole-kernel corn, drained
¼ cup finely chopped red onion
¼ cup loosely packed fresh cilantro leaves, chopped
½ teaspoon salt
2 tablespoons fresh lime juice

1 pound sea scallops
1 tablespoon chili powder
1 teaspoon sugar
2 teaspoons vegetable oil

Fresh cilantro leaves and sliced hot red chiles, for garnish
Lime wedges (optional)

In a large bowl, mix the beans, corn, onion, chopped cilantro, ¼ teaspoon of the salt, and the lime juice. Set salsa aside.

Rinse the scallops under cold running water to remove any sand from their crevices; pat dry with paper towels. In a medium bowl, mix the chili powder, sugar, and the remaining ¼ teaspoon salt. Add the scallops and toss to coat.

In a large nonstick skillet, heat the vegetable oil over medium-high heat until very hot. Add the scallops and cook for 3 to 5 minutes, turning once, or until the scallops are lightly browned on the outside and opaque throughout.

Arrange the salsa and scallops on 4 dinner plates and garnish with the cilantro leaves and red chiles. Serve with lime wedges, if you like.

cook's note

℀ Much as we love the idea of cooking from cans, we actually prefer using frozen shoepeg corn kernels, thawed, in this recipe. Choose corn without sauce; you'll need two 9-ounce packages for this recipe.

serve with

Guacamole with Lemon and Roasted Corn (page 24), with drinks
Butter lettuce with croutons and a creamy dressing
Capirotada (Mexican Bread Pudding) (page 274)

℀

to drink

Sauvignon Blanc
or a simple white Bordeaux

SOURCE: Thyme package,
Dahn Brothers Fresh Herbs
COOK: Unknown

scallops with lemon-thyme cream

A GOOD RECIPE FOUND ON THE BACK of a box is rare indeed, so we get excited when we find one. This intriguing one appeared on an innocent-looking package of fresh thyme. A closer look revealed that we were supposed to use the entire package of thyme in this delicate dish — couldn't be, we thought, but in fact, the beauty of this recipe is the way the thyme is generously used but doesn't overpower the other flavors at all. You end up with buttery scallops, fragrant thyme, and sharp lemon to balance it all out — quite delicious.

Although the procedure is simple, you'll need to use two skillets to make this dish, but we think that's a small price to pay for something so fast and yet so elegant. It's ideal for a weeknight after-work dinner party.

serves 4 to 6

2 tablespoons butter
Juice of 2 lemons
3/4 ounce fresh thyme leaves, plus 4
   sprigs saved for garnish

1/2 cup whipping cream
2 pounds large sea scallops
   Salt and freshly ground black
   pepper

In a small skillet, melt 1 tablespoon of the butter over medium heat. Add the lemon juice and thyme leaves and cook until the liquid is almost gone, about 3 minutes. Reduce the heat to low and add the cream slowly, stirring constantly. After all the cream has been added, reduce the heat to a simmer.

Meanwhile, season the scallops with salt and pepper. In a large skillet, heat the remaining 1 tablespoon butter over high heat. When the foaming subsides, add the scallops and cook for about 3 minutes per side, or until the scallops are no longer translucent (do not overcook or the scallops will be tough). Transfer the scallops and any remaining pan juices to a serving platter and cover with the lemon-thyme cream. Garnish with the thyme sprigs and serve hot.

cook's notes

🎵 Look for good dry sea scallops and remove the little muscles from their sides.

🎵 Balance is key here; you don't need more than 3 tablespoons thyme leaves or $\frac{1}{3}$ cup lemon juice.

🎵 To strip the leaves from the thyme, hold the stem by the root end and strip down the stem, using your thumb and forefinger to pluck off the leaves.

🎵 Heavy cream may be used in place of whipping cream.

serve with

Steamed asparagus

White rice

French Butter Cookies (page 244) and fresh fruit

🎵

to drink

Chardonnay
or white Burgundy

SOURCE: *New York Times Magazine*
COOK: Jason Epstein

jason's best crab cakes ever

"BEST EVER" USUALLY SENDS US RUNNING in the other direction, but these crab cakes sounded so good that we had to give them a try. And it's true — these are the best crab cakes we've ever tasted. Jason Epstein has forgotten whose recipe this originally was, but there's no forgetting these.

The crab cakes are extravagant in every way, starting with the high price of crab, and they're incredibly rich with butter and cream. The piquant jalapeño and delicate scallions are terrific together, even better because they're gently sautéed in (what else?) butter. But the truly brilliant thing here is using the bread crumbs on the outside of the crab cakes, but none on the inside to muffle the flavors and gum up the crab. Dipped in egg and fried in butter, the crumb-coated cakes are delectably crisp on the outside, a perfect foil for the succulent crab.

serves 6

12 tablespoons (1½ sticks) unsalted butter, plus 1–2 tablespoons for sautéing crab cakes
1 cup finely chopped scallions (including some of the firm greens)
½ cup finely chopped jalapeño peppers
¾ cup heavy cream

2 teaspoons dry mustard
Pinch of cayenne pepper
2 pounds jumbo lump crabmeat, drained well, patted dry, and picked over for shell fragments
2 large eggs
2 cups fresh white bread crumbs
1–2 tablespoons vegetable oil

In a large skillet, melt the 1½ sticks butter over medium-high heat. Sauté the scallions and jalapeños for about 2 minutes, or until bright green. Add the cream and bring to a boil. Reduce the heat to medium and cook, stirring, for 3 to 4 minutes, or until thickened. Remove from the heat and stir in the mustard and cayenne. Let cool for 5 minutes.

In a large bowl, gently stir together the crabmeat and scallion mixture. Form uniform cakes by placing spoonfuls of the crab mixture on a baking sheet. Immediately place in the refrigerator to firm up, about 2 hours.

When ready to serve, beat the eggs in a shallow bowl and place the bread crumbs in a separate shallow bowl. In a large skillet, heat the remaining 1 to 2 tablespoons butter and 1 to 2 tablespoons oil over medium heat. Working with half the crab cakes at a time (keep the rest in the refrigerator), dip each cake into the beaten eggs and then coat with the bread crumbs. Sauté the crab cakes until browned, 2 to 3 minutes per side, turning only once or they will break. Repeat with the remaining crab cakes. Drain on paper towels and serve immediately.

cook's notes

- A bit of salt may brighten the flavors: cook a bit of the crab mixture to see if it needs salt.
- Your guests may want some lemon wedges to squeeze over the crab cakes, but taste them all by themselves first.
- Miniature crab cakes are great cocktail-party fare. The cooking time is just slightly less for little crab cakes.

serve with

Simple green salad with lemon vinaigrette
Cherry Tomato Gratin (page 212)
Parker House rolls
Lemon Pound Cake (page 260) with raspberries

to drink

Champagne

SOURCE: *Italian Holiday Cooking*
by Michele Scicolone
COOK: Michele Scicolone

shrimp with garlic and toasted bread crumbs

THESE SHRIMP ARE A TRADITIONAL Christmas Eve treat, and as Michele Scicolone notes, they disappear faster than you can say Buon Natale! They're good with cocktails or as a first course, but we like them best as a light meal, served with salad and good bread.

This is a very easy way to serve hot shrimp. You can have the shrimp all prepped in their pan, ready to bake. They'll hold for an hour, and they cook quickly, in just 10 minutes or so.

Don't stint on the lemon wedges: That last squeeze of fresh lemon really brings out the best in these shrimp.

serves 4

1 cup fresh bread crumbs, made from Italian or French bread

1/3 cup minced fresh flat-leaf parsley

1 large garlic clove, finely chopped
Salt and freshly ground black pepper

About 1/4 cup olive oil

1 1/2 pounds large shrimp, peeled and deveined

Lemon wedges, for serving

Preheat the oven to 450 degrees. Lightly oil a large baking sheet. In a medium bowl, combine the bread crumbs, parsley, garlic, and salt and pepper to taste. Add 3 tablespoons oil, or enough to moisten the crumbs.

Arrange the shrimp in a single layer on the baking sheet, curling each one into a circle. Spoon a little of the crumb mixture onto each shrimp and drizzle with a little more oil. Bake for 10 to 15 minutes, depending on the size of the shrimp, or until the shrimp turn pink and the crumbs are lightly browned. Serve with lemon wedges.

serve with

Sugar Snap Pea and
Prosciutto Salad
(page 61), as a starter
Rice or orzo
Lemon and Goat Cheese Cheesecake (page 272)

℘

to drink

A dry Chenin Blanc

SOURCE: *Williams-Sonoma Taste*
COOK: Barbara Kafka

asian sole

BARBARA KAFKA DUSTS delicate fillets of sole with powdered shiitake mushrooms and then rolls them into little spirals (paupiettes) and bakes them with ginger, sesame oil, and cilantro — Asian flavors that uplift the mild taste of the sole. The mixture seasons the fish as it bakes, and afterward you thicken it into a quick and tasty, salty-sweet-hot sauce (using the Asian technique of adding a little cornstarch) to serve on top.

serves 6 to 8

1½ tablespoons toasted sesame oil
½ ounce dried shiitake mushrooms
8 4-ounce sole fillets
⅓ cup rice vinegar
3 tablespoons tamari
⅓ cup thinly sliced scallions (white parts only)

1 tablespoon finely diced fresh ginger
½ cup chopped fresh cilantro
1 teaspoon sugar
2 tablespoons cornstarch mixed with 1 tablespoon cold water

Preheat the oven to 350 degrees with a rack in the bottom third. Wipe a glass pie dish or other baking dish with some of the sesame oil. Discard the shiitake stems and break the caps into pieces. Grind in a blender until reduced to a fine powder (you should have about ⅓ cup). Sift the mushroom powder onto a large sheet of aluminum foil.

Pull the sole fillets apart along the center membrane and remove any threads from the membranes. Coat the fillets lightly in the mushroom powder. Starting at the thick end, roll each fillet into a paupiette and place in the prepared baking dish, spiral side up. Add the vinegar, tamari, and remaining sesame oil to the baking dish. Sprinkle the fillets with the scallions, ginger, and the remaining shiitake powder.

Bake the fish for 18 minutes, remove from the oven, and turn off the oven. Transfer the fish to an ovenproof serving dish and return to the oven with the door open.

Pour the liquid from the baking dish into a small saucepan (you should have about ³/₄ cup). Add the cilantro and bring to a boil. Add the sugar and cook for 2 minutes. Add the cornstarch mixture and stir the sauce until thickened, about 30 seconds. Remove the fish from the oven. Spoon the sauce over and serve.

cook's notes

- Be sure to get toasted sesame oil, not the hot chile sesame oil.
- You can use soy sauce in place of tamari.
- Sole is a nice delicate fish, but it's not always around. Flounder is often all you will find. If the fillets are very small, as flounder tends to be, you may want to leave them whole (not pulling them apart down the center). If you have lots of small fillets rather than a few large ones, you may need a slightly larger baking dish — any shallow gratin or baking dish will do.
- When rolling the fillets into paupiettes, roll with the membrane side in (this is the side where the skin was and tends to retract when cooked).
- You may want to baste the fillets once about halfway through baking.
- Sprigs of fresh cilantro make a nice garnish.

tip

On Arthur Schwartz's New York radio show, we heard a great tip from David Pasternack, the master fish chef at Esca. When you're frying or sautéing anything fishy and you want just a light crisp coating on the fish — such as sole — use Wondra, the granulated flour, instead of regular flour. You can season the flour first with a little paprika or cayenne, pepper, even a little salt. This way, you get a veil of crisp coating, nothing pasty or too thick.

serve with

Spicy Maple Walnuts (page 1), with drinks
Jasmine rice
Stir-fried watercress or pea tendrils
Coconut-Basil Macaroons (page 252)

to drink

An off-dry Alsatian Riesling
or Bonny Doon's Pacific Rim

SOURCE: *How to Read a French Fry*
by Russ Parsons
COOK: **Russ Parsons after Paula Wolfert**

oven-steamed salmon with cucumber salad

THIS SUCCULENT WAY OF COOKING salmon is basically French. The combination of low oven temperature and a pan of water in the oven to moisten the fish with steam produces a silken, brightly colored salmon that's extremely delicate and not at all fishy.

Russ Parsons, the food editor of the *Los Angeles Times,* takes the technique and plays with the seasonings, sending the classic cucumber salad accompaniment off in an Asian direction, using cilantro, sesame seeds, and sesame oil. The salad and salmon are perfect partners, and they're put together with a minimum of fuss. This is clean, elegant food that's great for a summer dinner party.

serves 6 to 8

CUCUMBER SALAD

5 cucumbers
  Salt
2 tablespoons snipped fresh chives
1 teaspoon sesame seeds, toasted
1 tablespoon rice vinegar
½ teaspoon toasted sesame oil
2 tablespoons chopped fresh
   cilantro

1 salmon fillet (about 3 pounds)
  Salt and freshly ground black
  pepper

TO MAKE THE SALAD:

Peel the cucumbers, cut them lengthwise in half, and scoop out the seedy centers with the tip of a teaspoon. Cut each half into three strips lengthwise, then into 2-inch sections. Salt the cucumbers and drain in a colander for 20 minutes.

When the cucumbers have drained, rinse them under cold running water and drain again. Transfer them to a bowl and add the chives, sesame seeds, vinegar, and sesame oil and mix well. Taste and adjust the seasonings — the flavor of the sesame oil should be almost undetectable, the cucumbers should be slightly tart from the vinegar, and the herbs should be in balance. Just before serving, add the cilantro and mix well.

TO MAKE THE SALMON:

Preheat the oven to 300 degrees. Remove the skin and any pin bones from the salmon fillet. Trim the sides to form a roughly rectangular shape that is fairly consistent in thickness. Place the salmon on a baking sheet and season liberally with salt and pepper.

Place a roasting pan in the bottom of the oven and fill it with boiling water. Place the baking sheet on the middle rack of the oven and cook until you see the white fat begin to emerge on top of the salmon, about 20 minutes. Carefully slide the salmon onto a serving platter, surround it with the cucumber salad, and serve immediately.

cook's notes

- We like the salmon rubbed with a little of the toasted sesame oil before it goes into the oven.
- The tastiest cucumbers, in our opinion, are Kirbys, usually found at farmers' markets and often at supermarkets as well. These are old-fashioned pickling cucumbers, and they have a deeper flavor.
- Be sure to pat the cucumbers dry before mixing them with the remaining ingredients.

serve with

Edamame with Szechwan Pepper-Salt (page 2), with drinks
Almond Crisps (page 253) and Roasted Apricots with Cardamom (page 286)

to drink

Pinot Noir (for red)
or Washington State Riesling (for white)

source: *Weber's Big Book of Grilling*
by Jamie Purviance and Sandra S. McRae
COOK: Jamie Purviance and Sandra S. McRae

simple salmon

SIMPLE IS RIGHT. A quick marinade of ingredients found in most pantries makes this an easy and tasty way to gussy up regular salmon fillets. The marinade is lightly sweet with a slight bite from the horseradish and Dijon mustard. The indirect grilling method means no fussing around, and you don't even flip the fish as it cooks. The salmon comes off the grill moist and slightly smoke-kissed. You might miss the grill marks across the top of the fillets, but we love the neat trick of sliding the fish off its skin when it's done, leaving the skin behind on the grill rack and the fillet intact. This trick solves the problem with grilling delicate fish; no more sticking to the grill.

If you don't have a covered grill, try this marinade on the Oven-Steamed Salmon on page 130 and cook it in the oven.

serves 6

¼ cup extra-virgin olive oil

¼ cup soy sauce

1 teaspoon rice vinegar

¼ cup Dijon mustard

3 tablespoons prepared horseradish

2 tablespoons light brown sugar

6 salmon fillets with skin (about 6 ounces each and 1 inch thick)

In a medium bowl, whisk together the oil, soy sauce, vinegar, mustard, horseradish and brown sugar. Place the salmon fillets in a large zip-top plastic bag and pour in all but ⅓ cup of the marinade; reserve the remaining marinade. Press the air out of the bag and seal tightly. Turn the bag to distribute the marinade, place in a large bowl, and refrigerate for 15 to 30 minutes.

Set up a charcoal or gas grill for indirect grilling and preheat it to high (see note). When the grill is hot, remove the fillets from the bag and discard the marinade. Place the fillets, skin side down, on the center of the grill away from the heat. Cover and grill indirectly over high heat until the salmon is opaque throughout, 10 to 12 minutes. During the last 2 minutes of grilling time, brush the fillets with the remaining ⅓ cup marinade. Slide a spatula between the skin and flesh and transfer the fillets to serving plates. Serve warm.

℘ Cooking with indirect high heat on a grill is similar to roasting in an oven. Ideally, you want to place the fish on the grill in an area not directly over the coals. For a charcoal grill, this means piling all the hot coals to the sides of the grill, and for gas, it means lighting only half of the burners. With the grill cover down, the grill acts more like an oven, cooking the fillets from all sides.

tip

How do you deal with a barbecue brush that's sticky with sauce and oil? Wash the brush in liquid dish soap and very hot water, rinse well, and shake dry. Place the brush in a cup with the bristles pointing down, cover the bristles with coarse salt, and keep the brush in the cup until the next time you grill. The salt draws moisture out of the bristles and keeps them fresh and dry between uses. From "The Clever Cook," *Kansas City Star* (tip originally appeared in *365 Quick Tips,* by the editors of *Cook's Illustrated,* published by Harvard Common Press).

serve with

Wasabi peas, with drinks
Scallion Noodles (page 213)
Coconut-Ginger Blondies (page 250)

℘

to drink

Lightly chilled Tavel rosé
or Fumé Blanc

SOURCE: Eric Ripert, after *Gourmet*
COOK: Eric Ripert

smoked salmon croque monsieur with baby watercress salad

CROQUE MONSIEUR SOUNDS SO MUCH more glamorous than grilled ham and cheese sandwich, and somehow it always seems more elegant, too. But how about grilled smoked salmon and Gruyère cheese? With some caviar (see note below) and snipped chives to up the ante? This terrific sandwich is the brainchild of French chef Eric Ripert of Le Bernardin, Manhattan's upscale fish restaurant. Ripert has perfect pitch when it comes to balancing flavors, and this extremely simple but celestial sandwich is a good example. (We first spotted a different version in *Gourmet*. Eric Ripert was then kind enough to share his preferred version, which is served at Le Bernardin.)

This dressed-up croque monsieur can be a light supper, a lunch, a snack, a substantial bite with cocktails. We think it even works for breakfast.

serves 6

CROQUE MONSIEUR
- 12 slices sandwich bread, 1/2-inch thick
- 4 ounces Gruyère cheese, very thinly sliced
- 12 ounces sliced smoked salmon
- 1 tablespoon finely grated lemon zest or preserved lemon (see note)
- 1 tablespoon thinly sliced chives
- 6 ounces osetra caviar
- 6 tablespoons unsalted butter, softened

SALAD
- 1/4 teaspoon Dijon mustard
- 1 tablespoon lemon juice
  Salt
- 1/4 cup olive oil
- 3 cups baby watercress salad
  Fine sea salt and freshly ground pepper to taste

Place the twelve bread slices on a table. On six slices, place the Gruyère cheese and on the other six slices, place the smoked salmon. Sprinkle the salmon slices with lemon zest, the Gruyère slices with chives. Place one ounce of caviar on the salmon and close the sandwiches. Slice the crusts off the edges of the sandwiches and discard. Spread the butter over the outside of each sandwich. (The recipe may be made in advance to this point. Tightly wrap each sandwich in plastic and refrigerate until ready to serve.)

Make the vinaigrette by whisking together the mustard, lemon juice, and a pinch of salt. Whisking constantly, drizzle in the olive oil. Set aside.

Preheat two large nonstick sauté pans over medium high heat. Add three sandwiches to each pan with the Gruyère side down and sauté for two minutes, or until nicely golden. Turn them over and sauté for one minute on the salmon side.

To serve, cut the sandwiches, using a serrated knife, on the diagonal, then on the diagonal again (to make four triangles). Toss the watercress with enough vinaigrette to coat, and season to taste with salt and pepper. Place four triangles on each plate and divide the salad evenly among the plates and place next to the croque monsieurs. Serve immediately.

cook's notes

- Although the caviar is wonderful in this over-the-top sandwich and it would be perfect for an intimate New Year's Eve celebration, the sandwich is still great without it.
- If you have a large griddle, you can cook all the sandwiches at once.

tip

Preserved lemons can be found in markets that specialize in Middle Eastern food. If you want to make your own, we like this recipe, which appeared in *Gourmet* this year. Unlike the traditional version, these lemons can spoil in just a few weeks, so you might want to make just half the recipe.

12–14 lemons (3½–4 pounds)
⅔ cup kosher salt
¼ cup olive oil

Have ready a clean 6-cup screw-top glass jar. In a large saucepan of boiling water, boil 6 of the lemons for 5 minutes. They'll bob and spin around; you don't need to do anything to them. Drain them and let cool.

Cut the cooled lemons into 8 wedges each, for a total of 48 pieces. In a medium bowl, toss them with the salt, then pack into the jar. Juice the remaining lemons to measure 1¼ cups. Add enough juice to cover the lemons and seal the jar. Let stand at room temperature, shaking gently once a day, for 5 days. Add the oil, replace the lid, and store in the refrigerator for up to 1 month.

SOURCE: *Cooking Light*
COOK: Leslie Revsin

chicken thighs with garlic and lime

MORE AND MORE COOKS are discovering the joys of chicken thighs, which are arguably the tastiest meat on the chicken and go very well with any number of flavor combinations. This unusual Texas recipe has Southwest flavors: lime, cumin, oregano, and cilantro. It starts on top of the stove, then goes into the oven, and finally the pan drippings are turned into a lovely sauce for the chicken.

The only problem is that the recipe serves just two. If you're cooking for more people, you can make this dish in a roasting pan and let it cover two burners on the stovetop.

serves 2

1 tablespoon minced garlic
1½ teaspoons ground cumin
½ teaspoon dried oregano
¼ teaspoon salt
⅛ teaspoon freshly ground black pepper
2 tablespoons fresh lime juice

4 6-ounce chicken thighs, skinned
3 tablespoons fat-free low-sodium chicken stock
1 tablespoon white wine vinegar
2 teaspoons chopped fresh cilantro
2 lime wedges

Preheat the oven to 350 degrees. In a small bowl, combine the garlic, cumin, oregano, salt, pepper, and 1 tablespoon of the lime juice. Rub the garlic mixture over the chicken and place the chicken in a medium ovenproof skillet.

In a small bowl, combine the remaining 1 tablespoon lime juice, the stock, and the vinegar and pour over the chicken. Bring to a boil over medium-high heat. Remove from the heat. Wrap the handle of the skillet with foil. Cover and bake for 30 minutes, or until a meat thermometer registers 180 degrees.

Remove the chicken from the skillet and keep warm. Place the skillet over medium-high heat and bring the liquid to a boil. Cook until reduced to ¼ cup, about 3 minutes. Spoon the sauce over the chicken, sprinkle with the cilantro, and serve with the lime wedges.

serve with

Watercress salad with avocado, grapefruit sections, and a light citrusy vinaigrette
White rice
Pecan Brittle with Black Pepper (page 254)

℘

to drink

Bell Mountain Vineyards Chardonnay

SOURCE: *Fine Cooking*
COOK: Bill Devin

chicken thighs baked with lemon, sage, rosemary, and thyme

BILL DEVIN WORKS FOR A SPANISH food exporter and lives in Tarragona, Spain. This recipe is his take on the excellent Catalan rotisserie chicken, which is stuffed with lemon wedges and herbs and turned on a spit. The trick he's come up with is to roast chicken thighs on lemon slices and herbs, so that the meat gets infused with lemon-herb flavor. Allioli — the classic Spanish garlicky mayonnaise — rubbed under the skin before cooking does two things: it separates the skin from the meat so the skin gets super-crisp (the high oven temperature helps, too) and adds a lot of flavor.

serves 6

ALLIOLI
- 2 large garlic cloves
  Kosher or sea salt
- 3–4 tablespoons extra-virgin olive oil

- 12 chicken thighs, trimmed of fat, rinsed and patted dry
- 2 large lemons, each cut into six 1/4-inch rounds

- 1 bunch fresh rosemary, snipped into twelve 2-inch pieces
- 1 bunch fresh thyme, snipped into twelve 2-inch pieces
- 12 fresh sage leaves
  Salt and freshly ground black pepper

TO MAKE THE ALLIOLI:

Using a mortar and pestle, mash the garlic with a large pinch of salt to create a coarse paste (or use a small mixing bowl and the back of a spoon, or mince the garlic very finely on a cutting board). Add the oil very slowly in drops while pounding and grinding the paste until the allioli is thick, creamy, and emulsified.

Put the chicken in a large bowl. Rub the allioli all over the chicken, including under the skin. Cover and refrigerate for at least 2 hours or overnight.

Preheat the oven to 425 degrees with a rack in the middle. Arrange the lemon slices in a single layer in a large shallow roasting pan or a 9-x-13-inch baking dish. Top each slice with a piece of rosemary, a piece of thyme, and a sage leaf. Place the chicken thighs, skin side up, on top; sprinkle them generously with salt and pepper. Bake until the skin is golden and the juices run clear, 45 minutes to 60 minutes.

Sometimes the lemons and chicken produce a lot of juices, in which case you can make a delicious pan sauce. Transfer the chicken (keeping the herbs and lemon slices underneath) to a plate and cover loosely with aluminum foil. Tilt the pan to pool the juices in one corner. Spoon off the fat that rises to the top. Set the pan over medium heat (if the pan isn't flameproof, pour the juices into a small skillet) and scrape up any stuck-on bits. Let the juices boil and reduce so they thicken to a saucy consistency. Drizzle the sauce around, not on, the chicken to maintain the crisp skin. Serve the chicken pieces sitting on their beds of lemon and herbs.

cook's notes

- Be sure to really smash the garlic to a paste when making the allioli, otherwise it won't emulsify. A mortar and pestle is definitely the best.
- It may look as if you don't have enough allioli, but trust us, it's potent and goes a long way.

serve with

Bacon-Wrapped Dates with Almonds (page 5), assorted olives, and sliced Manchego cheese, with drinks
Sautéed spinach with roasted red peppers and toasted pine nuts
Crusty bread
New Year's Honey Cake (page 264)

to drink

A rich Rioja Gran Reserve

SOURCE: *How to Cook* by Delia Smith
COOK: Delia Smith

stir-fried chicken with lime and coconut

THE CHEERY BRITISH COOK DELIA SMITH has become a TV house-hold presence in America, where fans of her reliably delicious food are legion. Her new book is full of wonders such as toad in the hole and bubble and squeak, but we passed those by in favor of this startlingly uncomplicated work-night supper dish that we return to again and again. Smith manages to capture the haunting flavors of Southeast Asian cuisine in a format so simple it amazes us every time.

Though the quantities are calibrated for two diners, you can easily double the recipe — just use two pans.

serves 2

2 boneless skinless chicken breast halves (preferably free-range)

Grated zest and juice of 1 large lime

2 teaspoons olive oil

1 hot green chile pepper, seeded and finely chopped

2/3 cup canned unsweetened coconut milk

2 teaspoons Thai fish sauce (nam pla)

4 scallions, cut into 1-inch shreds (including the greens)

6 tablespoons chopped fresh cilantro

Cooked jasmine rice, for serving

Cut the chicken into bite-sized pieces. In a medium bowl, combine the chicken and lime zest and juice. Stir well and let marinate for 1 hour.

In a wok or large skillet, heat the oil over high heat. Add the chicken and stir-fry for 3 to 4 minutes, or until golden. Add the chile and stir-fry for 1 minute more. Add the coconut milk, fish sauce, half the scallions, and 3 tablespoons of the cilantro. Cook for 1 to 2 minutes more. Serve with jasmine rice and sprinkle the remaining scallions and cilantro over the top.

serve with

Curried Almond Shortbread (page 12)
Zesty Coleslaw with Peanuts (page 53)
Almond Crisps (page 253) and fruit sorbet

℮

to drink

Chenin Blanc

SOURCE: *Indian Regional Classics* by Julie Sahni
COOK: Julie Sahni

butter chicken

IT NEVER OCCURRED TO US to make butter chicken at home, though it's one of our favorite dishes at Indian restaurants. But one look at this recipe and we had to try it. This delectably rich concoction is actually just leftover chicken, brilliantly cooked in a savory sauce. In this version, the richness is tempered by the occasional surprising bite of fresh ginger as well as the zing of cilantro.

One of the best parts of this dish is how incredibly convenient it is. You can pick up a rotisserie chicken on the way home (or use leftover chicken) and have this main dish ready in less time than it takes to cook the rice. Butter chicken itself makes a great leftover; it's just as good two days later.

serves 4

4 tablespoons (½ stick) unsalted butter

2 small roasted chickens, cut into serving pieces and skinned

2 teaspoons ground cumin

SAUCE

2 cups canned tomato puree

1 cup heavy cream

¼ cup julienned fresh ginger

½ cup finely chopped fresh cilantro leaves and tender stems

Coarse salt and freshly ground black pepper

1–4 green chile peppers, stemmed and chopped with seeds (optional)

In a large nonstick skillet, melt 2 tablespoons of the butter over medium-high heat. Add the chicken pieces, sprinkle with cumin, and sauté, turning, for 3 minutes.

Add the sauce ingredients (including the chile, if using) and simmer until the chicken absorbs some of the sauce and becomes meltingly tender, about 15 minutes. Stir in the remaining 2 tablespoons butter. (The dish may be made ahead and refrigerated for up to 2 days. Reheat and check the seasonings, adding more pepper and chopped cilantro if necessary.) Transfer to a warmed serving dish and serve.

𝕮 We think the chicken is easier to eat and absorbs the sauce better if it's taken off the bone and cut into chunks before it goes into the sauce.

𝕮 If you can find it, use San Marzano canned tomato puree.

serve with

Spicy Maple Walnuts (page 1) with drinks
Basmati rice
Watercress salad with avocado
Coconut-Basil Macaroons (page 252)

𝕮

to drink

A lush, floral Rhône Valley Viognier

SOURCE: *New York Times*
COOK: **Amanda Hesser**

lemon chicken

FOR AN ARTICLE ON THE JOYS of crème fraîche, Amanda Hesser devised this terrific recipe, which has since become one of our favorites. It's very pure, with only the flavors of lemon, salt and pepper, and crème fraîche. But the effect of those minimal ingredients on the chicken (dark meat, the tastiest) is remarkable. The dish is deeply flavored with what seems to be the essence of chicken, with a wonderfully complex-tasting sauce. There's a sprinkle of lemon zest on top to enliven it further. The chicken is crisp, because most of the fat roasts out in the oven and is poured off before the sauce is made.

Although it could hardly be less complicated, this is a dish fit for company because it's also elegant. And adding crème fraîche makes it taste, well, French. We like to make it just with chicken thighs instead of whole legs with thighs attached, which will be easier for your guests to eat as well.

serves 4

1½ tablespoons butter
1½ tablespoons olive oil
4 whole chicken legs (with thighs attached)
Coarse sea salt or kosher salt

Freshly ground black pepper or ground multicolored peppercorns
Grated zest and juice of 1 lemon
½ cup crème fraîche

Preheat the oven to 375 degrees. Heat a large ovenproof skillet over medium-high heat. After 3 minutes, add the butter and oil. Season the chicken generously with salt and very generously with pepper. Place the chicken, skin side down, in the skillet and brown well on both sides, turning once.

Transfer the skillet to the oven. Bake for 15 minutes, or until the juices run clear when the chicken is pierced with a knife.

Return the skillet to the stovetop. Transfer the chicken to a platter and keep warm. Remove all but about 1 tablespoon of fat from the skillet. Place over medium heat, add the lemon juice, and stir to scrape up any pan drippings. Simmer for l minute, then add the crème fraîche and stir until melted and bubbling. If the sauce is too thick, add a few tablespoons of water. Pour the sauce over the chicken and sprinkle with lemon zest and additional pepper. Serve hot.

cook's note

℘ Because the ingredients are so few, it's important to buy the tastiest chicken you can find, which will probably be free-range. Thighs will fit in the pan better than legs and will also be easier to deal with on the plate.

serve with

Nutty Roasted Cremini (page 193)
Simple green salad
An assortment of artisan cheeses, slices of dense walnut bread, and ripe pears
French Butter Cookies (page 244) and espresso

℘

to drink

Red Burgundy
or Oregon Pinot Noir

SOURCE: *Atlanta Journal-Constitution*
COOK: **Reagan Walker**

chicken fricassee
with lemon, saffron, and green olives

THIS GEM SURFACED AS ONE OF THE *Atlanta Journal-Constitution*'s top 10 recipes from 2001. Reagan Walker went to France to take some cooking classes at Julia Child's old cottage in Provence, and out of the dozens of recipes she returned with, this affordable dish is her hands-down favorite, especially for a casual dinner party. Delectable aromas from the kitchen will greet your guests at the door — always a good way to start an evening.

The combination of lemon, saffron, tomatoes, and green olives creates a wonderful sunny, tangy flavor — especially welcome in the dark winter months. Although heavy cream is added to finish the sauce, it doesn't have the heaviness associated with many cream sauces — in fact, this sauce is actually rather thin, so you'll want to serve bread to sop it up or even consider serving the fricassee in shallow bowls if you want more sauce.

serves 4

1 3½-pound chicken, cut into 8 pieces
Coarse salt and freshly ground black pepper
¼ cup olive oil
2 medium carrots, peeled and diced
1 large onion, diced
1 celery rib, diced
3 garlic cloves, chopped
¼ cup dry white wine
½ cup chicken stock
2 large tomatoes, peeled, seeded, and chopped

2 ounces (about ¼ cup) cracked and pitted green olives
1 tablespoon freshly crushed coriander seeds
1–2 large pinches saffron
Juice of 1 lemon
¾ cup heavy cream
1 preserved lemon, cut into quarters, then sliced (see note)
1 bunch fresh cilantro, thick stems discarded and leaves chopped

Season the chicken pieces with salt and pepper. In a large sauté pan, heat the oil over medium-high heat. Add the chicken and brown on all sides, turning with tongs, for about 10 minutes. Add the carrots, onion, celery, and garlic and sauté until the vegetables are limp but not browned. Add the wine and bring to a boil.

Add the chicken stock, tomatoes, olives, coriander seeds, and saffron and return to a boil. Cover the pan with parchment paper and then with a lid, reduce the heat to medium-low and simmer for about 45 minutes, or until the chicken is tender.

Transfer the chicken to a serving platter and keep warm. Increase the heat to medium-high, add the lemon juice, and scrape the bottom of the pan to loosen the browned vegetables. Add the cream and preserved lemon slices and boil until the liquid is reduced by half or until slightly thickened. Strain if desired (though the bits taste great) and season with salt and pepper to taste. Pour the sauce over the chicken and scatter the cilantro over the top. Serve immediately.

cook's notes

- To double this recipe and serve 8, you'll need two large sauté pans.
- Preserved lemons can be found in markets that specialize in Middle Eastern foods or in gourmet specialty stores, or make your own (see page 135). Alternatively, you can substitute 1 small lemon (peel on), very thinly sliced.
- The nice part of cutting up a whole chicken is that you get a mix of white and dark meat. If you'd rather not cut up a chicken, use chicken pieces, preferably a mix of breast and thighs. You'll need about 2½ pounds of chicken pieces.

serve with

Fiesolana (Italian Cabbage Salad with Ham and Fontina) (page 68), as a starter
Red potatoes roasted with olive oil and herbes de Provence
Baguette for sopping up the sauce
Roasted Apricots with Cardamom (page 286) and softly whipped cream

to drink

Côtes de Provence red
or dry rosé

SOURCE: *The San Francisco Chronicle Cookbook,*
Volume II, edited by Michael Bauer
and Fran Irwin
COOK: Nancy Oakes

boulevard's staff turkey breast

WE OFTEN SEE THOSE SINGLETON TURKEY BREASTS in the freezer case at the supermarket and think, but what would I do with that? All too often, they're dry and tasteless, with a depressing texture — so we usually pass them by.

But here's what they do with this convenient cut of poultry at San Francisco's Boulevard Restaurant, where it's a staff favorite. The secret is a honey brine, flavored with mustard, hot pepper, and a bit of rosemary. You end up with a beautifully sweet-spicy, lightly salty turkey roast that also makes great sandwiches, salads, and leftovers. And once you've made the most of this partial bird, the carcass makes very good soup.

Note that this recipe is for a partial breast, not the whole gigantic thing.

serves 6

HONEY BRINE

2 quarts water or apple cider (see note)

³/₄ cup honey (or less if using cider — see note)

¹/₂ cup kosher salt

2 tablespoons Dijon mustard

1¹/₂ teaspoons crushed red pepper flakes

1 4-inch rosemary sprig

1 3–3¹/₂-pound bone-in turkey breast half

1 tablespoon olive oil

TO MAKE THE BRINE:

In a large pot, bring the water or cider to a boil over high heat. Pour the water or cider into a container just large enough to hold the turkey breast; let cool for 5 minutes. Add the honey, salt, mustard, and pepper flakes and whisk until the honey dissolves. Add the rosemary. Let cool to room temperature, then refrigerate until well chilled.

Place the turkey breast in the chilled brine. Weight with a plate if necessary to keep it completely submerged. Refrigerate for 1 to 2 days.

Remove the turkey breast from the brine, place it in a roasting pan, and bring to room temperature. Preheat the oven to 350 degrees.

Roast the turkey for 30 minutes, then brush with the oil. Continue roasting, basting occasionally with the drippings, for about 30 minutes more, or until an instant-read thermometer inserted in the thickest part of the meat, away from the bones, registers 150 degrees. Remove from the oven and let rest for 30 minutes before carving and serving.

cook's notes

- Chef Nancy Oakes recommends using cider or apple juice instead of water for the brine — pricey but very delicious. If you do that, cut the amount of honey in half.
- Often this cut of turkey comes frozen, in which case you can thaw it in the refrigerator right in the brine to get more flavor. Brine for 2 days.

serve with

Pan-Roasted Carrots (page 192)
Mashed Potatoes
Ported Rhubarb (page 285), as relish
Matzo Buttercrunch (page 256)

to drink

Zinfandel

SOURCE: *Food & Wine*
COOK: Tom Douglas

spice-rubbed turkey with sage gravy and wild mushroom stuffing

SEATTLE CHEF TOM DOUGLAS cooks all the time at home for his family, so we were especially interested to see what he makes for Thanksgiving. And it was such an interesting meal that we made it for our Thanksgiving, too — and had guests clamoring for the recipes.

There are several unusual elements here: first of all, Douglas makes, hands down, the best turkey gravy you'll ever taste. The secret is his rich turkey stock, made with a whopping seven pounds of turkey parts well ahead of time. You end up with about three quarts of delicious stock, which flavors the stuffing as well.

The turkey itself is rubbed with sage butter and left naked in the fridge overnight so it will have a particularly crisp skin. The stuffing, which is cooked separately, is full of woodsy flavor, with its wild mushrooms, hazelnuts, dried cranberries, and an echo of sage.

A number of these elements can be made ahead — the stock, the sage butter, and the dressing — which makes it possible to have a relatively stress-free Thanksgiving and still produce a stunning feast. You must start the turkey the day before roasting and serving.

serves 12

TURKEY AND GRAVY

10 tablespoons (1¼ sticks) unsalted butter: 6 at room temperature, 4 melted

¼ cup plus 2 tablespoons minced fresh sage

Kosher salt and freshly ground black pepper

1½ teaspoons coriander seeds

1 15-pound turkey, cavity fat removed, neck and wing tips reserved for stock, gizzard reserved for the gravy

2 large shallots, halved

½ orange, quartered

¾ cup plus 1 tablespoon all-purpose flour

2 quarts Turkey Stock (see recipe page 153)

Wild Mushroom Stuffing

In a small bowl, mash the 6 tablespoons room-temperature butter with ¼ cup of the sage and season with salt and pepper to taste.

In a small skillet, toast the coriander seeds over medium heat until fragrant, about 1 minute. Let cool, then transfer to a spice grinder and grind to a powder. In a small bowl, mix the ground coriander with $1^1/_2$ tablespoons salt and $1^1/_2$ teaspoons pepper.

Starting from the cavity end of the turkey and using your fingers, carefully separate the skin from the breast meat. Gently rub the sage butter under the skin, evenly coating the breast. Sprinkle the turkey inside and out with the seasoned salt. Refrigerate the turkey, uncovered, overnight. Bring the turkey to room temperature before roasting (allow 3 hours).

Preheat the oven to 350 degrees. Put the shallots and orange half in the cavity of the turkey and tie the legs together. Set the turkey and gizzard on a rack in a roasting pan. Brush the 4 tablespoons melted butter over the turkey and roast for about $2^1/_2$ hours, basting every 30 minutes. Halfway through roasting, rotate the turkey for even cooking. Cover the breast loosely with aluminum foil during the last hour of roasting. The bird is done when an instant-read thermometer inserted in the inner thigh registers 165 degrees. Transfer the turkey to a carving board and let rest for at least 30 minutes.

Cut the gizzard into $^1/_4$-inch dice. Pour the pan juices into a measuring cup. Spoon off $^1/_2$ cup plus 3 tablespoons of the fat, add it to the roasting pan, and set the pan on 2 burners over medium heat. Stir the flour into the fat until blended, then gradually whisk in the turkey stock, scraping up the browned bits on the bottom of the pan. Reduce the heat to low and simmer until no floury taste remains, about 20 minutes. Add the reserved pan juices, gizzard, and the remaining 2 tablespoons sage. Season with salt and pepper to taste.

Carve the turkey, arrange it on a platter, and serve with the gravy and Wild Mushroom Stuffing.

cook's notes

- If you have no spice grinder, you can use ground coriander instead of grinding your own.
- Decorate the turkey platter with sprigs of sage and fresh cranberries.

We found an eyebrow-raising tip in *Gourmet:* You can get some butchers to remove the turkey bones for you, so that you just cut straight down through the meat, stuffing and all. There's usually a minimal charge for the service, and you may have to give advance notice. And you won't have a high-rise bird; yours will be more the shape of a very large meat loaf. If you don't have an expert carver in residence, this tip could save you a huge amount of grief.

wild mushroom stuffing

The stuffing can be made a day ahead and refrigerated overnight.

serves 12

1 2-pound loaf peasant bread, crusts trimmed, bread cut into 1½-inch cubes

⅓ cup extra-virgin olive oil

Salt and freshly ground black pepper

½ cup dried porcini mushrooms (about 1 ounce)

1 cup boiling water

1½ cups hazelnuts (about 6 ounces)

1 cup (2 sticks) unsalted butter

1 medium onion, chopped

2 celery ribs, finely chopped

2 large shallots, minced

2 pounds mixed wild mushrooms, tough stems trimmed and the rest finely chopped

3 cups Turkey Stock (recipe follows)

1 cup dried cranberries (about 4 ounces)

¼ cup chopped fresh parsley

1 tablespoon chopped fresh thyme

2 teaspoons chopped fresh sage

Preheat the oven to 375 degrees. Butter 2 large baking dishes. On 2 large rimmed baking sheets, toss the bread cubes with the oil and season with salt and pepper to taste. Bake for about 20 minutes, or until golden. Set aside to cool. Reduce the oven temperature to 350 degrees.

In a small heatproof bowl, soak the dried porcini in the boiling water until softened, about 20 minutes. Rub the porcini to remove any grit, then remove them from the liquid and coarsely chop. Slowly pour the soaking liquid into a small saucepan, leaving behind any grit. Boil the liquid over high heat until reduced to ¼ cup, about 5 minutes. Remove from the heat and set aside.

Spread the hazelnuts on a rimmed baking sheet and toast for 12 minutes or until richly browned. Transfer to a kitchen towel and let cool completely. Rub the hazelnuts in the towel to remove their skins. Coarsely chop the hazelnuts. Set aside.

In a large skillet, melt 4 tablespoons of the butter over medium-low heat. Add the onion and celery and cook until softened, about 10 minutes. Scrape the onion-celery mixture into a very large bowl. In the same skillet, melt the remaining 12 tablespoons butter over medium-high heat. Add the shallots and cook, stirring, until softened, about 3 minutes. Add the fresh mushrooms, dried porcini and their reduced soaking liquid, and salt and pepper to taste. Cook over high heat until the liquid evaporates, about 15 minutes. Add the mushrooms to the onion mixture, along with the toasted bread cubes, turkey stock, hazelnuts, dried cranberries, parsley, thyme, and sage. Toss well and season with salt and pepper to taste.

Spread the stuffing in the prepared baking dishes and cover with aluminum foil. Bake for about 30 minutes, or until heated through. Uncover and bake until crusty, about 25 minutes more. If the stuffing is made a day ahead and chilled, it will take slightly longer to bake.

turkey stock

You can make the stock ahead and freeze it for up to 1 month or refrigerate it for up to 3 days.

makes about 3 quarts

7 pounds turkey parts, such as wings, thighs, and drumsticks

14 cups water

Reserved turkey neck and wing tips (optional)

1 large onion, thickly sliced

1 large carrot, thickly sliced

1 large celery rib, thickly sliced

2 garlic cloves, sliced

1 teaspoon kosher salt

Freshly ground black pepper

Preheat the oven to 400 degrees. In a large roasting pan, roast the turkey parts for about 1 hour, turning occasionally, until well browned. Transfer to a large pot.

Set the roasting pan over 2 burners. Add 3 cups of the water and bring to a boil, scraping up the browned bits from the bottom of the pan. Transfer the liquid to the pot. Add the neck and wing tips (if using) to the pot, along with the onion, carrot, celery, garlic, salt, several pinches of pepper, and the remaining 11 cups water. Bring to a boil. Reduce the heat to medium-low, partially cover, and simmer for about 2¹/₂ hours. Strain the stock and skim off the fat before using.

**We tend to go a little nuts
when the house is full at Thanksgiving.
Serve with some or all of these:**

Spicy Maple Walnuts (page 1)

Party Cheese Crackers (page 10)

Pureed Sweet Potato Soup (page 28)

Pan-Roasted Carrots (page 192)

Roasted Winter Squash (page 194)

Party Potatoes (page 200)

Creamed Scallions (page 207)

Sweet Potato Spoon Bread (page 224)

Grape Salsa (page 226)

Cranberry and Dried Cherry Relish (page 227)

Corn Bread with Fennel Seeds, Dried Cranberries,
and Golden Raisins (page 238)

Pecan Whiskey Cake (page 266)

Cranberry Puff-Up (page 281)

℘

to drink

American Pinot Noir
or Zinfandel

SOURCE: *Chile Pepper*
COOK: **Kenneth Smith**
after Jason Clevenger and Tom Cowman

upperline roast duck with ginger-peach sauce

THE UPPERLINE IS EVERYTHING a true New Orleans restaurant should be: lively, charming, personal, intimate, with great subtle Southern food that has a definite Crescent City accent. It's in an old — nearly 125 years old — house in the Garden District, and the minute you walk in, you feel at home. The most popular item on the menu is this terrific duck, which actually has two sauces; the other one is made with port and garlic cloves, and diners choose the one they want with their crisp, succulent, never-greasy duck.

This dish is flexible; you can skip the sauce altogether if you'd rather, and you can make the duck ahead and stop at several points along the way, right up to the moment the duck is boned.

The serving portions are very generous; the duck could easily serve four, with several side dishes.

serves 2

1 5-pound duckling
2 tablespoons Dijon mustard
1 tablespoon soy sauce
1 medium onion, chopped
1 medium carrot, peeled and chopped
1 tablespoon chopped garlic
2 tablespoons dried thyme
Salt
1 teaspoon freshly ground black pepper

SAUCE

2 ripe peaches, peeled, or 1 pound unsweetened frozen peaches, thawed
$1/4$ cup frozen orange juice concentrate
$1/4$ cup mango chutney
1 teaspoon peeled and grated fresh ginger
1 tablespoon Cointreau or Grand Marnier

In a large pot, bring 1 gallon of water to a boil. Meanwhile, cut shallow slits in the duck skin. Remove the liver (reserve it for another use) and cut off the wing tips. When the water is boiling, carefully lower the duck into it and parboil the duck for about 15 minutes.

Transfer the duck to a platter and let cool. Meanwhile, preheat the oven to 450 degrees. Rub the duck with the mustard and soy sauce. Stuff the inside of the duck with the onion, carrot, garlic, thyme, 1 tablespoon salt, and pepper.

Place the duck, breast side up, on a rack in a roasting pan. Roast for 1 hour and 15 minutes, then reduce the oven temperature to 350 degrees. Roast for 30 to 40 minutes more, or until the juices in the leg run clear when it's pricked. Let the duck stand for at least 15 minutes before carving.

Meanwhile, pit and slice the peaches, if using fresh. In a medium saucepan, combine the peaches, orange juice concentrate, chutney, ginger, and Cointreau or Grand Marnier over medium-low heat. Simmer for about 15 minutes. Add salt to taste.

When ready to serve, preheat the oven to 500 degrees. Split the roasted duck lengthwise with a heavy knife. Remove the breast bones and rib cage. Place the duck halves on a broiler pan and roast until the skin sizzles, about 8 minutes.

To serve, spoon the sauce onto 2 plates and place the duck on top.

cook's notes

- You'll need a tall pot to parboil the duck; a stockpot or a large pasta pot will work.
- If you're using a frozen duck, as you most likely will be, make sure it's completely thawed before you start this recipe.

serve with

Whipped Root Vegetables (page 205) or white rice
Steamed green beans
Pan-Roasted Carrots (page 192)

to drink

Australian Shiraz

SOURCE: *Williams-Sonoma*
New American Cooking: The Heartland
COOK: **Beth Dooley**

blue plate meat loaf

WE'VE BEEN ON THE LOOKOUT for a couple of years now for a really great classic meat loaf. And finally we've found one; this Midwestern "moist and honestly seasoned" meat loaf really delivers the goods. No sun-dried tomatoes here. What makes it different? The buttermilk-soaked bread crumbs add moisture and a slight flavor edge. The meat mixture is optimum: beef (chuck if possible); turkey (or veal, which we prefer); and — surprise — good country sausage meat. Bacon strips on top are not only attractive but also baste the meat loaf while it cooks.

Instead of being cooked in the usual loaf pan, this meat loaf stands on its own on a rimmed baking sheet, so that the sides brown and the fat drains off during the cooking.

Like all really good meat loaves, this one is excellent cold and makes first-rate sandwiches.

serves 4 to 6

½ cup fresh bread crumbs
½ cup buttermilk
1 pound ground beef
½ pound bulk pork sausage meat (see note)
½ pound ground turkey or veal
1 small yellow onion, minced

¼ cup minced fresh flat-leaf parsley
1 large egg, lightly beaten
½ teaspoon freshly ground black pepper
¼ teaspoon salt
3 slices hickory-smoked bacon (optional)

Preheat the oven to 350 degrees. In a small bowl, soak the bread crumbs in the buttermilk until it's absorbed, about 3 minutes.

In a large bowl, combine the soaked bread crumbs, beef, sausage, turkey or veal, onion, parsley, and egg. Gently mix together with your hands. Add the pepper and salt and mix again.

Turn the mixture onto a rimmed baking sheet and shape it into a loaf about 9 x 3 inches. If using the bacon, lay the strips across the loaf lengthwise.

Bake, basting occasionally with the pan juices, until the meat loaf is lightly browned and firm and an instant-read thermometer inserted into its center registers 160 degrees, 45 to 55 minutes. Let the meat loaf sit for about 10 minutes to reabsorb the juices. Using a serrated knife, cut the loaf into 1½-inch-thick slices. Transfer to individual plates and serve.

cook's notes

- Bulk sausage is most likely to be found in the freezer case, but if you can't find it, you can use Italian sausage links and remove the casings.
- If it seems as if there isn't enough salt in the recipe, remember that there's sausage meat, so in the end it's perfectly seasoned.
- Much depends on shaping the loaf properly. Don't make it too high in the middle or it will take too long to cook through. Try to shape it so it's flat on top without manhandling the meat too much.

serve with

Cumin Apple Chips (page 225) and Maytag Blue and Wisconsin Colby cheeses, with drinks
Buttered noodles or mashed potatoes
Peas or green beans
Green Onion Buttermilk Biscuits (page 233)
Cranberry Puff-Up (page 281)

to drink

Pinot Noir
or Shiraz

SOURCE: Ellen Ryan, *Washington Post*
COOK: Patrick Kennedy

new york spiedies

UNTIL THIS YEAR, we'd never even heard of a spiedie (pronounced speedy), but suddenly, references to these delectable kabob sandwiches popped up all over the place. Spiedies are a specialty of the area around Binghamton, New York, in the Southern Tier (and nowhere else in the entire country), and they're so enormously popular that there's a Spiedie Fest cook-off every year in Endicott, New York. This year's winner was Patrick Kennedy, and here's his recipe.

The best thing about a spiedie, which may have originated with an immigrant from the Abruzzi area of Italy, is that the meat is left to develop its rustic flavors in a savory marinade for up to three days. Then it's grilled and tucked into good squishy Italian bread. The buttered bread soaks up all the juices, and the whole is transformed into much more than the sum of its parts. You may balk at buying onion powder and garlic powder if they're not in your cupboard already, but trust us, these are great.

serves 10

2 cups vegetable oil
1 cup vinegar
8 garlic cloves, chopped
1 tablespoon dried thyme
1 tablespoon dried oregano
1 tablespoon garlic powder
1 tablespoon onion powder

Zest of 1 lemon
5 pounds top round roast, cut into 1½-inch pieces
1 loaf soft Italian bread, thickly sliced
Butter for the bread (optional)

At least 1 day ahead, in a large bowl, combine the oil, vinegar, ½ cup water, garlic, thyme, oregano, garlic powder, onion powder, and lemon zest. Reserve ½ cup marinade, cover, and refrigerate. Add the meat to the remaining marinade and toss to coat. Cover and refrigerate, turning occasionally, for at least 24 hours and up to 3 days.

Preheat a grill to high. Transfer the meat to skewers and discard the marinade. Grill the skewers, turning occasionally and basting with the reserved marinade, until the meat is cooked through, 8 to 10 minutes. Serve immediately with the bread, buttered if desired, on the side. To eat, fold the bread over the contents of a skewer and pull the skewer out, leaving the meat sandwiched within the bread.

cook's notes

℮ You don't have to grill the spiedies; you can also broil them quite successfully.

℮ You may want to add some salt to the meat just before or after you grill it, since there's none in the marinade.

℮ The recipe cuts in half perfectly for a smaller group.

serve with

Radish Salad (page 52)
Salad of inner leaves of escarole with a sharp-creamy dressing
Lemon Pound Cake (page 260)

℮

to drink

Watermelon Punch (page 299) and cold beer

SOURCE: *The Southwest* by Kathi Long
COOK: Kathi Long

chicken-fried steak with chipotle gravy

EUROPEANS — AND EVEN SOME YANKEES — think chicken-fried steak is a myth, but it's alive and well in the Heartland and the South because it's so good. In this version, Midwestern cream gravy meets Southwestern chile and spices, a great idea. This isn't fancy steak, it's good old full-of-flavor chuck, which needs pounding to make it super-tender.

Cream and milk make the creamy gravy very rich, but once you spring for fried steak, why worry about a little gravy? The gravy tends to be a bit thick — pastier than what you might normally be used to unless you're a Midwesterner — but it seems right for chicken-fried steak. If you want it thinner, just add a bit more milk — or use less cream and more milk.

serves 6

STEAKS

1 1/2 pounds 1/2-inch-thick chuck steak, divided into 6 equal pieces

1 1/2 cups all-purpose flour

2 tablespoons ground ancho chile

1 tablespoon coarse salt

2 teaspoons freshly ground black pepper

2 teaspoons dried oregano, preferably Mexican

2 teaspoons cumin seeds, toasted and ground (see note)

Oil (preferably peanut), for frying

CHIPOTLE GRAVY

3 tablespoons all-purpose flour

1 cup milk

1 cup heavy cream

1 tablespoon sauce from chipotle chiles in adobo sauce, or to taste

2 teaspoons fresh thyme leaves

1 teaspoon coriander seeds, toasted and ground (see note)

1/2 teaspoon freshly ground white pepper

Coarse salt

TO MAKE THE STEAKS:

One at a time, place the pieces of meat between sheets of plastic wrap and, using a meat pounder, pound the steaks to an even 1/4-inch thickness. In a medium bowl, stir together the flour, ground chile, salt, pepper, oregano, and cumin. Coat each steak with the seasoned flour, shaking off any excess.

In a large cast-iron skillet, heat 1/4 inch oil over medium heat. Add the steaks and fry, turning once, until golden, 4 to 5 minutes per side. Transfer to paper

main dishes

towels to drain. Keep warm. Discard all but 3 tablespoons of the oil from the skillet.

TO MAKE THE GRAVY:

Return the skillet to medium heat and stir in the flour. Cook, stirring, for 3 minutes; do not brown. Gradually whisk in the milk and cream and simmer until thickened, about 3 minutes. Stir in the adobo sauce, thyme, coriander, white pepper, and salt to taste.

Place the steaks on warmed individual plates and ladle 4 to 6 tablespoons of gravy over each one. Serve at once.

cook's notes

- If you don't have ancho chile powder, you can use another ground chile, but do avoid the chili powder that is a mix of spices meant for seasoning chili stew.
- Once you open a can of chipotles in adobo, transfer it to a glass jar and keep covered in the refrigerator. It will last for weeks, if not months.
- To get the full flavor of spices, such as coriander and cumin, buy them whole and toast and grind them yourself. To toast, in a heavy dry skillet, heat the spice over medium heat, shaking often, until it just begins to change color and becomes fragrant. Pour onto a plate to cool and then grind in a spice grinder or with a mortar and pestle. You can substitute preground spices, but the flavor will be somewhat paler.

tips

- In *The Valentino Cookbook,* chef Piero Selvaggio suggests using a plastic storage bag instead of plastic wrap for pounding meats. It's much sturdier and easier to work with.
- We found some great steak tips from David Rosengarten in the *Rosengarten Report,* his food lovers' newsletter. Choose a thick steak, preferably prime or choice, and ideally dry-aged for at least 4 weeks (an expensive detail that contributes a lot to the flavor). You want darkish pink to lightish red meat, with white fat (yellow fat is from old animals). The fat should be running through the meat in "a wispy swarm of streaks," not long lines, for best flavor. Take another tip from Peter Luger, the Brooklyn steakhouse: about 1 minute before the steak is done, pour clarified butter over both sides or brush the steak with room-temperature butter. Let it stand for at least 5 minutes to reabsorb the juices.

Spicy Margarita Raisins (page 4) mixed with roasted salted peanuts, with drinks
Mashed potatoes or soft flour tortillas
Cybill's Greens (page 206)
Leafy green salad with mango, avocado, and cilantro
Capirotada (Mexican Bread Pudding) (page 274)

℘

to drink

Cold lager
or Gewürztraminer

main dishes

SOURCE: **Macy's De Gustibus Cooking School**
COOK: **Eileen Weinberg**

barbecued brisket

FEW DISHES WILL BE SO GRATEFULLY received as a good barbecued brisket. This is a Texas-style brisket, with just a little heat and quite a few vegetables to round out the flavors. The key ingredient here is a homemade sweet-sour barbecue sauce, which takes only 10 minutes to cook. You can make a double batch and freeze half to use later on chicken, ribs, or even grilled burgers.

You need to start the brisket a day ahead, so the basic cooking will be done and the meat can absorb some of its very tasty juices. The next day, you chop up the brisket and some vegetables and bacon and add the barbecue sauce. A couple of hours in the oven and it's ready to serve a mob. You can also reheat the brisket very successfully, you can smoke it if you'd like, and you can freeze it (but not in aluminum foil).

serves 12

1 8-to-10-pound beef brisket
2 tablespoons paprika
2 tablespoons salt
1 tablespoon coarsely ground black pepper
1½ cups roughly chopped celery
1½ cups roughly chopped onion
1½ cups roughly chopped carrots
  Olive oil

½ pound bacon
2 cups diced red bell pepper
2 cups diced onion
1 whole unseeded jalapeño pepper
3–4 cups diced fresh tomatoes
2 tablespoons minced garlic
4 cups Barbecue Sauce (recipe follows)
  Cooked rice or sandwich buns, for serving

The day before you plan to serve the brisket, preheat the oven to 350 degrees. Rub the brisket with a mixture of the paprika, salt, and pepper. Place most of the celery, onion, and carrots in the bottom of a roasting pan. Place the seasoned brisket on top and scatter the remaining celery, onion, and carrots over it. Pour 2 cups of water around the brisket. Seal the roasting pan well with aluminum foil and bake for 3 to 4 hours, or until fork-tender. Cool overnight in the pan in the refrigerator.

The next day, preheat the oven to 400 degrees. Dice the brisket into 1-inch chunks, discarding any excess fat.

In a Dutch oven, heat a thin film of oil over medium heat. Sauté the bacon, red pepper, onion, and jalapeño until tender. Add the tomatoes and garlic and cook for 10 minutes. Add the brisket and the barbecue sauce. Cook, covered, for 2 hours, or until tender, removing the cover for the last 15 minutes of cooking.

Serve the brisket hot over rice or on buns.

cook's notes

- You can use organic canned diced tomatoes instead of fresh, if tomatoes aren't in season.
- You can use a high-quality commercial barbecue sauce instead of making your own, but it won't be quite as good.

barbecue sauce

4 cups ketchup

2 cups cider vinegar

1 cup corn oil

3/4 cup Worcestershire sauce

2 cups packed dark brown sugar

1/2 cup yellow mustard

2 tablespoons chopped garlic

3 tablespoons fresh lemon juice

In a large saucepan, mix together all the ingredients over medium heat. Cook for 10 minutes; do not boil. The sauce can be frozen for several months.

SOURCE: *Second Helpings from Union Square Café* by Danny Meyer and Michael Romano
COOK: Michael Romano

italian beef stew

LET'S SAY YOU'RE IN THE MOOD for a good stew, but the very thought of flouring and browning little bits of beef in endless batches is more work than you can even contemplate. This unusual stew is the perfect solution. You just dump the meat, unfloured, into hot fat and let the liquid emerge from it into the pot. As it continues to cook, the liquid concentrates and the meat browns in its own juices. It's a deeply flavored, tender stew that leaves the cook blessedly free for an entire hour before dinner.

You take it the rest of the way in the oven in two stages; first it cooks with wine, then with tomato sauce. You end up with a delicious stew that has a definite Italian accent — in fact, leftovers are great as a pasta sauce.

serves 4

2 tablespoons vegetable oil
3 pounds trimmed beef chuck, cut into 1-to-1½-inch cubes
1 cup chopped onion
1 tablespoon minced garlic
1 bay leaf
2 teaspoons coarse sea salt
¼ teaspoon freshly ground black pepper

1 tablespoon tomato paste
1 cup red wine
2 cups tomato sauce (store-bought is fine)
1 tablespoon sliced fresh sage leaves
2 tablespoons chopped fresh parsley

Preheat the oven to 350 degrees. In a straight-sided ovenproof skillet (with a tight-fitting lid) large enough to hold the meat in one layer, heat the oil over high heat until smoking. Add the meat and cook, stirring occasionally, until all the juices have evaporated and the meat is browned, 20 to 25 minutes. (Turn the heat down if necessary to keep the meat from burning.)

Reduce the heat to medium. Stir in the onion, garlic, bay leaf, salt, and pepper and cook until the onion is soft but not brown, about 3 minutes. Stir in the tomato paste, cook for 1 minute. Add the wine, bring to a boil, cover tightly, and bake in the oven until almost all the liquid has evaporated and the meat is tender, about 1 hour.

Stir in the tomato sauce and sage, return the skillet to the oven, and continue baking until the meat is soft enough to cut with a spoon, about 1 hour more. Transfer the stew to a warmed deep platter, sprinkle with parsley, and serve piping hot.

serve with

Salad of sliced orange, fennel, and black olives
Whipped Root Vegetables (page 205)
Pistachio Gelato (page 292) and biscotti

℘

to drink

Barolo
or Cabernet Sauvignon

SOURCE: *The Elements of Taste*
by **Gray Kunz and Peter Kaminsky**
COOKS: **Gray Kunz and Todd Humphries**

braised short ribs of beef

THIS SENSATIONAL RECIPE is just one part of an elaborate dish devised at New York's Lespinasse when Gray Kunz was the chef there and worked with Todd Humphries to perfect it. It was the most popular dish on the menu, and it's easy to see why. The spice mix that dusts the short ribs and reappears in the braising liquid is intensely aromatic and heady, and it gives the ribs a flavor that's almost intoxicating.

At Lespinasse, the dish was served with pureed parsnips or mashed potatoes, a sauce that included papaya pickle, and a topping of crisp potatoes, fresh horseradish, and a few other elements. For the home cook, though, the ribs and some mashed potatoes will do just fine.

Because the spice mix is so strong, it needs to be carefully balanced, so taste it and correct it if necessary. The cooks are very insistent that the spices be freshly ground, and of course, they're best that way. But we've also tried it with preground spices, and it's still plenty delicious.

serves 8

SPICE MIX
1/4 cup coriander seeds
1 tablespoon allspice berries
1 tablespoon cumin seeds
1 tablespoon Szechwan peppercorns
1 teaspoon whole cloves
1 bay leaf
1 tablespoon black peppercorns
1 tablespoon ground cinnamon
  Kosher salt

BRAISING LIQUID
2 28-ounce cans diced tomatoes
1 cup tamarind paste (available in Indian markets)
1 cup chopped peeled fresh ginger

1/3–1/2 cup dark brown sugar, to taste (depending on the tanginess of the other ingredients)
3 tablespoons tomato paste
3 tablespoons Spice Mix
2 garlic cloves
5 tablespoons Worcestershire sauce
3 tablespoons mango pickles (available at Indian markets; optional)

8 pounds beef short ribs, trimmed of excess fat
  Kosher salt
  Spice Mix
3 tablespoons corn oil

TO MAKE THE SPICE MIX:

In a medium dry skillet, toast the coriander, allspice, cumin, Szechwan peppercorns, cloves, and bay leaf over low heat. Add the black peppercorns and grind in a spice grinder or with a mortar and pestle until the mixture is medium fine. Put the spice mix on a plate and stir in the cinnamon and a pinch of salt. Reserve 3 tablespoons for use in the braising liquid; set the remainder aside.

TO MAKE THE BRAISING LIQUID:

In a food processor, combine all the ingredients, including mango pickles (if using), and 4 cups water and pulse to a smooth paste.

Preheat the oven to 350 degrees. Season the short ribs liberally with salt and dust liberally with the spice mix. In a large Dutch oven or braising pan, heat the oil over medium-high heat. Add the ribs and brown on all sides, 6 to 8 minutes, in batches if necessary.

In a large saucepan, bring the braising liquid to a boil. Pour it over the ribs, cover the pan, and braise in the oven until the ribs are very tender, about 3 hours. Transfer the ribs to a platter and cover with aluminum foil. Degrease the braising liquid and bring it to a simmer. It is very important to balance the flavors and to season particularly strongly. The recipe will be overly tangy if you don't, so season as needed with additional salt, brown sugar, Worcestershire sauce, and the remaining spice mix. Any leftover spice mix can be stored in a sealed container for future use. Spoon the sauce over the ribs and serve hot.

serve with

Whipped Root Vegetables (page 205) or mashed potatoes
Sharp green salad
Ginger Puddings with Bittersweet Chocolate Sauce
and Ginger Caramel Crunch (page 276)

℘

to drink

A big, spicy Zinfandel
or Amarone

main dishes

SOURCE: *Fine Cooking*
COOK: Ris Lacoste

individual beef wellingtons with mushroom, spinach, and blue cheese filling

WARNING: THIS RECIPE IS A LOT OF WORK, but sometimes you want a dish that screams impressive, and this updated classic is a knockout. Fortunately, you can do all this work ahead so when it's time for the big soiree, you just pop these babies directly from the freezer into the oven, and about an hour later, voilà, you've got a spectacularly elegant main course. The various elements — beef tenderloin, creamy Maytag Blue cheese, caramelized onions with sherry, herb-marinated portobellos, and a bit of sautéed spinach — are all hiding beneath the burnished pastry crust.

This recipe solves several Wellington problems. First, by baking the pastry packages when they're frozen solid, you avoid the twin problems of the pastry being soggy and the meat overcooking. This way, the frozen beef doesn't even start to cook until the pastry is well on its way to becoming browned and baked through. When you cut into your pastry package, the beef is perfectly pink and the pastry is baked just right. Using puff pastry (rather than the traditional brioche) gives you a lighter and flakier pastry crust. The initial high heat of the oven helps the pastry to "puff" a little and come out crisp and flaky.

The best way to make these is to spread out the work over two days (and that all takes place up to a week before the party). Prepare all the components of the Wellingtons the day before or the morning of the day you intend to assemble them. Then, when everything is well chilled and ready, make a little assembly line and turn these out. Once assembled, the Wellingtons must freeze for at least six to eight hours (ideally overnight) and up to a week. Make sure you have plenty of room in your freezer before starting. If they're not frozen solid, they won't cook right.

serves 6

PASTRY
  All-purpose flour, for rolling
3 1-pound packages frozen puff pastry (6 sheets total),
    such as Pepperidge Farm

MUSHROOMS

2 large portobello mushrooms, stems removed

6 tablespoons olive oil, plus more for cooking

2 garlic cloves, minced

1/2 teaspoon lightly chopped fresh thyme leaves

1/2 teaspoon very roughly chopped fresh rosemary

Coarse salt and freshly ground black pepper

CARAMELIZED ONIONS

4 tablespoons (1/2 stick) unsalted butter

3 medium onions (about 6 ounces each), thinly sliced

1/2 cup medium-dry sherry, such as amontillado

Coarse salt and freshly ground black pepper

SPINACH AND CHEESE

12 cups tightly packed spinach (about 14 ounces)

2 tablespoons unsalted butter

Coarse salt

Pinch of freshly ground white pepper (optional)

6 ounces Maytag Blue cheese or another good-quality blue, such as Roquefort

STEAKS AND ASSEMBLY

6 5-to-6-ounce beef tenderloin steaks (choose equal-sized center-cut portions)

Coarse salt and freshly ground black pepper

About 3/4 cup olive oil

4 large eggs

Flour

TO ROLL AND CUT THE PASTRY:

On a floured work surface, roll out each of the 6 pastry sheets to just over 1/8 inch thick and, using a sharp knife, cut out a 10-inch round from each one. From the scraps, cut out 12 leaves or other shapes to use as decoration. Layer the pastry rounds and decorations between pieces of waxed or parchment paper, wrap the bundle well in plastic wrap, and freeze again.

TO COOK THE MUSHROOMS:

In a medium shallow bowl, toss the portobellos with the oil, garlic, thyme, and rosemary. Cover and marinate in the refrigerator for 2 hours. Remove the portobellos from the marinade (they will have soaked up most of it) and season them with salt and pepper to taste. In a medium heavy skillet, heat a thin film of oil over medium-high heat. Sear the portobellos until softened and browned, about 5 minutes per side. Transfer to paper towels and flip them once to drain both sides. When cool, cut each mushroom cap in half crosswise and cut the halves into strips about $1/2$ inch thick.

TO CARAMELIZE THE ONIONS:

In a large heavy skillet, melt the butter over medium heat. Add the onions, reduce the heat to medium-low, and cook slowly, stirring occasionally, until well browned, soft, and sweet, 30 to 40 minutes. Add the sherry and cook until the skillet is dry. Season with salt and pepper to taste. Set aside to cool. Place the cooled onions in a colander set in a bowl, cover, and refrigerate.

TO MAKE THE SPINACH AND CHEESE:

Wash the spinach well and remove any stems. Have ready a bowl of ice water. In a large skillet, combine 6 cups of the spinach, a touch of water, 1 tablespoon of the butter, a pinch of salt, and a little white pepper (if using) over medium-high heat. Toss just until wilted and immediately transfer to the ice water to shock the color and stop the cooking. Scoop the spinach from the ice water and put it in a colander to drain. Squeeze as much water out of the spinach as you can, a small handful at a time. Set aside on paper towels to continue draining. Repeat with the remaining spinach, butter, salt, and white pepper (if using). Cover with plastic wrap and refrigerate. Divide the blue cheese into six 1-ounce portions. Try slicing the whole piece into 6 slices; if it crumbles, just evenly divide it. Cover and refrigerate.

TO SEAR THE STEAKS:

Season each steak very generously on both sides with salt and pepper. Rub the seasoning into the meat to keep it in place. In a large skillet, heat $1/8$ inch oil over high heat until just smoking. Sear the steaks for 2 minutes per side, or until brown and crisp on the outside. Be sure that your skillet is very hot so you just sear the beef and don't overcook it, and don't crowd the pan or it will steam rather than sear. (Check the sides to be sure the steaks are still red in the middle.) Work in batches if necessary. Refrigerate the beef until chilled or until ready to use, up to 24 hours.

Arrange the mushrooms, caramelized onions, spinach, cheese, and steaks on your counter. Divide the portobello strips into 6 portions. Make sure the caramelized onions are well drained (they tend to collect liquid as they sit) and divide them into 6 portions. Squeeze the spinach again, divide it into 6 portions, and leave it on paper towels for further draining. Cover a large rimmed baking sheet (that fits in your freezer) with parchment paper. Have ready a ruler, a small sharp knife, and a pastry brush. In a small bowl, whisk 2 of the eggs with 1 teaspoon water for an egg wash.

Lightly flour one area of your counter (the cooler the area, the better). Take 1 pastry round and 2 decorative pieces from the freezer and set them on the floured surface. Work quickly to maintain the integrity of the pastry. Lightly score a 4-x-3-inch rectangle in the center of the round; don't cut through the pastry. Extend the lines of the rectangle and cut out the corners of the round created by the line extensions, leaving a cross of pastry with the 4-x-3-inch scored center. Give a spinach portion one last squeeze and spread half of it over the rectangle center of the pastry, being careful to keep within the score marks. Follow with a portion of cheese, a portion of onions, a steak, a portion of portobellos in a single layer, and the rest of the spinach portion. Spread each layer as evenly as possible. Brush a light coating of the egg wash on each of the four panels of pastry.

Check to be sure that the pastry is now pliable enough to fold without breaking (wait a minute or two for it to soften if it is too cold and stiff). Fold each side panel onto the top, stretching the dough a bit if necessary to make the ends meet or slightly overlap. Follow suit with the top and bottom panels. Seal the panels together by pressing in the top panel where it meets the bottom panel and by pinching each of the four sides together where the panels meet. Don't worry if the package doesn't look gorgeous; it's more important that it's well sealed so the juices don't leak out.

Hold the package upright in your hands, securing all the seals and smoothing the rough spots to make the package into a neat, rounded block. Set it seam side down and gently press the top and sides to make them as even all the way around as possible. Brush the top and sides with the egg wash. Put the decorations on top and brush with the egg wash. (You'll be cutting the package in half to serve, so separate the decorations.) Set the Wellington on the parchment-lined baking sheet. Put the sheet in the freezer to set and chill the pastry. Repeat with the remaining 5 Wellingtons, adding each to the sheet in the freezer as you go. After they chill for an hour, wrap them well in plastic individually and return them to the freezer.

TO COOK THE WELLINGTONS:

Preheat the oven to 400 degrees. In a small bowl, make another egg wash with the remaining 2 eggs and 1 teaspoon water. Remove the Wellingtons from the freezer (do not thaw) and brush them with a fresh coat of egg wash. Put them on a lightly greased heavy rimmed baking sheet and cook for 20 minutes. Reduce the oven temperature to 350 degrees and cook until a meat thermometer registers 110 degrees (be sure the tip of the thermometer is inserted in the center of a package), 35 to 40 minutes more. Set them aside to rest for no longer than 10 minutes. The tightly enclosed beef will continue to cook out of the oven, so if you have to wait for more than 10 minutes, trim the sides of the pastry to let out some of the hot steam and reduce the internal temperature. Cut each Wellington in half, arrange on warm plates, and serve immediately.

cook's notes

- Be sure to get the right size tenderloin steaks. If they are too small or too large, they won't cook in the time directed. Look for center-cut tenderloin steaks, which are the thickest and most evenly shaped.
- Pay attention when searing the beef that the skillet is very hot before you add the beef. Season each steak generously and be certain not to overcook them — the center should still appear very rare. They will come up to medium-rare in the oven.
- Do not try to bake these before they have frozen solid — it won't work.

tip

In an issue of *Fine Cooking* that came out after this recipe appeared, a reader wrote in to suggest a way to streamline the assembly of the Wellingtons: Make a template for cutting the pastry. Trace a circle the same size as the pastry circles (10 inches) on a piece of waxed paper and fold it into quarters to find the center. Then mark the 4-x-3-inch rectangle and cut out the corners, creating a cross-shaped template. It's easier than having to measure each time.

serve with

Caviar and toast, with champagne
Christmas Salad (page 47), for a starter
Valentino's Chocolate Truffle Cake (page 262)

ℰ

to drink

A big, elegant California Cabernet Sauvignon
or Crozes-Hermitage

main dishes

SOURCE: *Louisville Courier-Journal*
COOK: Sarah Fritschner

pork chops adobado

TODAY'S LEAN PORK CHOPS present a problem for the home cook: instead of being succulent, they're often dry and chewy. The way around the problem is to brine them, but that takes time and forethought. Here's another way to transform skinny pork chops into something wonderful, using a hot oil treatment. The adobado method is Portuguese, and it delivers a lot of flavor for a minimal amount of effort.

Into the hot oil go some terrific seasonings: garlic, cumin, paprika, and oregano — all delicious with pork. If you have only half an hour to spare, a hot oil bath will work wonders. If you can remember to do it a day ahead, the overnight oil soak, similar to the treatment New York Spiedies (page 159) get, will make a huge difference.

serves 4

2 tablespoons olive oil
3–5 large garlic cloves, minced
1 teaspoon dried oregano
1 tablespoon paprika
1 teaspoon ground cumin

1 teaspoon salt, or to taste
1/2 teaspoon freshly ground black pepper, or to taste
4 boneless pork chops (about 1 inch thick)

In a small skillet, combine the oil, garlic, and oregano over low heat. Cook for 2 minutes, or until aromatic. Stir in the paprika, cumin, salt, and pepper. Remove from the heat.

Place the pork chops in a shallow dish and pour the seasoned oil over them. Rub the oil mixture into the pork and let stand for at least 30 minutes at room temperature, or refrigerate all day or overnight.

Broil or grill for about 5 minutes per side, or until the pork is done to your taste. Serve hot.

cook's notes

❧ Let the seasoned oil cool a little before rubbing it onto the pork — otherwise, it will start to cook the outside of the meat, not a good thing.

❧ If you're broiling the chops, don't put them too close to the heat source. About 4 to 5 inches away is good. If the surface starts to burn, lower the heat or the rack.

❧ Adjust the cooking time to suit the thickness of the chops. Or use an instant-read thermometer and take the chops off when they reach 155 degrees.

serve with

Rice pilaf

Romaine leaves with oranges, toasted almonds, and slices of sweet onion

Cinnamon-Caramel Hot Chocolate (page 295), for dessert

❧

to drink

Grenache
or Syrah

SOURCE: *The Glorious Foods of Greece*
by Diane Kochilas
COOK: Diane Kochilas

pork stew with leeks, orange, and mint

THIS CLASSIC GREEK DISH is called tigania (which means "of the frying pan"). It's a basic stew that's been given an extra dimension with a dry marinade of paprika, crushed red pepper flakes, orange zest, and mint, not to mention the unusual choice of red wine for cooking pork. After gently simmering in the wine, the pork comes out fork-tender and looking and tasting more like beef.

The stew has all the considerable satisfaction of Old World cooking, yet the combination of flavors feels up to date and appealing.

serves 4

1½ pounds boneless pork shoulder, trimmed of fat and cut into 1½-inch cubes

1 tablespoon grated fresh orange zest

1 teaspoon sweet paprika

½ teaspoon crushed red pepper flakes, or more to taste

½ teaspoon dried mint

Salt and freshly ground black pepper

⅓ cup extra-virgin olive oil

1 large red onion, chopped

1 large leek (white part only), well washed and chopped

1 cup dry red wine, plus more if needed

In a medium bowl, toss the pork with the orange zest, paprika, crushed red pepper flakes, mint, and salt and pepper to taste. Cover and refrigerate for at least 1 hour.

In a large heavy skillet, heat the oil over medium-high heat. Add the pork and cook, stirring, until browned on all sides. Transfer to a plate with a slotted spoon. Reduce the heat to medium, add the onion and leek, and cook, stirring, until translucent, 7 to 8 minutes. Return the pork to the skillet and add the wine. Cover, reduce the heat to low, and simmer until the pork is tender, 1 to 1½ hours. Add water or more wine to the skillet if necessary to keep the stew moist. Taste and adjust the seasonings. Serve warm.

cook's notes

- You can extend the marinating time for up to several hours — it will only add to the flavor of the stew.
- For evenly sized cubes of pork, buy a 1½-pound hunk of pork shoulder and cut it up yourself.
- Like any good stew, this keeps well and tastes even better when reheated the following day.

serve with

Layered Salad of Bulgur, Fennel, Pine Nuts, Dill, and Mint (page 48)
Parsleyed new potatoes
Toasted pita bread
Lemon and Goat Cheese Cheesecake (page 272)

to drink

Mourvèdres
or Tempranillo

SOURCE: *Secrets of Saffron* by Pat Willard
COOK: Pat Willard

portuguese pork sausage and clams with saffron

THIS INTRIGUING DISH IS MADE with Italian sausage and clams, peppered with jalapeño and given complexity with saffron-infused white wine. Just before serving, it gets a little shower of cilantro. This is a dish for a chilly night, served over rice so that the lovely sauce gets its due.

Although its flavors are complex, this recipe is extremely simple, starting off with an oven browning and finishing with a quick sauté and simmer on the stovetop. You can use a small pork roast instead of the sausage, but it will need to cook longer, of course.

If there are any leftovers, this dish tastes just as good the next day. Remove the clams from their shells before you refrigerate it.

serves 6

1/2 cup white wine
Pinch of saffron (about 40 threads)
1 1/2 pounds Italian sausage (hot, sweet, or a mixture)
3 tablespoons olive oil
1 jalapeño pepper, sliced

1 large garlic clove, minced
1/2 cup chicken stock
Juice of 1 lemon
3 dozen littleneck clams, scrubbed clean
Handful of fresh cilantro leaves, chopped

Preheat the oven to 400 degrees. In a small bowl, combine the wine and saffron and set aside to steep. Place the sausage in a shallow roasting pan and pour 1 tablespoon of the oil over it. Roast for 30 to 40 minutes. Remove the sausage from the pan and cut into serving pieces. Set aside.

In the same pan on top of the stove, heat the remaining 2 tablespoons oil over medium heat. Sauté the jalapeño and garlic until the garlic turns golden and the jalapeño skin begins to blister. Reduce the heat to medium-low and add the saffron-infused wine (be careful — the oil may splatter). Stir, scraping up any browned bits that are stuck to the pan. Add the stock, lemon juice, reserved sausages, and clams. Increase the heat to medium-high, cover, and simmer until the clams are open; discard any unopened clams. Just before serving, stir in the cilantro. Stir hot.

cook's note

℮ You may want to remove the seeds from the jalapeño if you'd like less heat. They'll be even hotter the next day, if you have leftovers.

tip

In her book *Secrets of Saffron,* Pat Willard explains that saffron threads need to be steeped in a liquid to bring out their flavor and color. The maximum time is 20 minutes, and the steeping liquid will determine to some degree the flavor of the saffron. Steeping it in a cold liquid, such as vinegar or alcohol, brings out an element of hotness. If you add the saffron during the middle of the cooking process, the flavor will be more subtle than if you add it at the end. Baking seems to mellow saffron, making it almost sweet.

If you forget to steep the saffron, just add it to the liquid in the recipe and microwave it for a minute or two — 1 cup liquid will take 1½ minutes.

serve with

Rice
Rustic peasant bread
Crème Fraîche Panna Cotta with Berry Puree (page 279)
℮

to drink

Off-dry Riesling
or Chenin Blanc

main dishes

SOURCE: *Born to Grill*
by Cheryl Alters Jamison and Bill Jamison
COOKS: Cheryl Alters Jamison and Bill Jamison

honey-bourbon ham steak

WHAT TO DO WITH A HAM STEAK? The Jamisons have a truly great idea, and it works on the grill as well as under the broiler. The glaze seems born for ham, with its honey sweetness, garlic, dry mustard, and the big taste that pulls it all together: bourbon. The flavor is delicate and unusual enough that you can serve this ham to company. We've even tripled the amounts and made a glaze for a whole ham from the same recipe — and it was equally delicious.

Start to finish, it's probably 15 minutes to produce this very tasty ham. That makes it an option for breakfast or brunch as well, for hearty eaters. Since the glaze produces a delectable caramelized surface on the ham steak, you could just cut it in strips and serve it on a platter alongside eggs.

serves 4

HONEY-BOURBON GLAZE

3 tablespoons honey

2 tablespoons bourbon

1 tablespoon soy sauce

2 garlic cloves, roasted and mashed (see note)

1/2 teaspoon dry mustard

2 1-pound fully cooked bone-in ham steaks (about 1/2 inch thick)

TO MAKE THE GLAZE:

In a food processor, combine all the ingredients and process until smooth.

Preheat the grill or broiler to high.

Grill uncovered or broil the ham steaks for 7 to 9 minutes, turning once midway and brushing with the glaze, and glazing again in the last 2 minutes of cooking. If grilling covered, cook for 6 to 8 minutes, glazing and turning in a similar manner. If you wish, pour any remaining glaze over the ham steaks after removing them from the grill. Serve hot.

The only problem is remembering to have some roasted garlic on hand. If all else fails, bake some potatoes to serve with the ham and tuck a head of garlic inside some foil, then drizzle with olive oil before you twist the foil closed. When the potatoes are almost done, the garlic's done.

serve with

Sweet Potato Spoon Bread (page 224)
Cybill's Greens (page 206) or buttered lima beans
Apple-Chile Cobbler (page 290)

to drink

Lightly chilled Beaujolais-Villages (for red)
or Sylvaner (white)

SOURCE: *Zarela's Veracruz*
by Zarela Martínez with Anne Mendelson
COOK: Zarela Martínez after Lupita Guzmán

chile-braised spareribs

WE CAN'T REMEMBER ever seeing a dish of stovetop ribs before, but as Zarela Martínez points out, it's a terrific technique that's much beloved in Mexico and ought to be better known here. The meat is started in a small amount of liquid, then browned in its own rendered fat after the liquid evaporates. As Martínez says, it's a sort of braising in reverse, and it concentrates the flavor of the meat more than any other technique except roasting.

A few other little tricks from the Mexican kitchen contribute even more flavor: both the chiles and the garlic are griddle-roasted to bring out their flavors. Then the chiles are soaked not in water but in good homemade stock.

The succulent ribs are deeply flavored with just the chiles, garlic, and cloves. These ribs are a great choice for a rainy summer day when you'd hoped to be able to cook ribs on the grill. Everyone will feel lucky when these are served up.

serves 4

2 pounds meaty pork spareribs, chopped into 2-inch lengths

1½–2 teaspoons salt, or to taste

1 cup boiling water

4 ancho chiles, stemmed and seeded

4 cups pork or chicken stock, heated

5 garlic cloves

5 whole cloves

Season the spareribs with 1½ teaspoons of the salt. Pour the boiling water into a heavy medium Dutch oven or large heavy saucepan over medium-high heat. Add the ribs, reduce the heat to medium, and cook stirring occasionally, for about 30 minutes. During the last 5 to 10 minutes, start checking carefully as the water boils off. At this stage, the meat will be starting to render some of its fat. Keep cooking, stirring frequently to prevent scorching, until it is literally frying in its fat, 5 to 10 minutes more. It should be deep golden but not over-browned.

As soon as you've started the meat, begin the chile sauce. Rinse and griddle-dry the chiles following the directions below. Place in a medium bowl and cover with the hot stock; let sit for 20 minutes. Griddle-roast and peel the garlic according to the directions below; set aside. In a small heavy skillet, toast the whole cloves over medium-high heat until fragrant, about 1 minute. Grind the cloves using a mortar and pestle. In a blender, combine the chiles and their soaking liquid, garlic, and cloves. Puree very thoroughly.

Pour the chile sauce over the browning spareribs. Cover and cook over medium-low heat for 20 minutes more, or until the ribs are very tender. Taste for salt, add a little if desired, and serve.

cook's notes

ℰ To griddle-dry the chiles: Rinse them lightly under cold running water and shake off the excess. Heat a griddle or cast-iron skillet over medium-high heat until a drop of water evaporates instantly. Place the chiles on the griddle, being careful not to crowd them. Heat them for about 30 seconds, turning occasionally, just until their moisture evaporates and you smell their toasted fragrance. Do not let them scorch, or they will ruin the dish. Transfer them out to a bowl as they are done, cover generously with boiling water, and let stand for 15 to 20 minutes. Drain thoroughly before proceeding.

ℰ To griddle-roast the garlic: Heat a heavy skillet over medium-low heat until a drop of water sizzles the minute it hits the pan. Add the garlic cloves, without crowding, and roast them gently, turning frequently, for about 8 minutes, or until the skins are blackened and the interiors are soft.

serve with

Guacamole with Lemon and Roasted Corn (page 34)
Beans and rice
Flour tortillas

ℰ

to drink

Watermelon Punch (page 299)
or margaritas

SOURCE: *O, The Oprah Magazine*
COOK: Quincy Jones

oven-baked ribs

LISTEN UP: NOT ONLY ARE THESE AMAZING RIBS Oprah's favorite ribs of all time, but Ray Charles feels exactly the same way. We agree; these are tender, not greasy or sweet or gloppy, and they have lots of different flavors in each bite.

There are a few secrets here: one is the dry marinade in which the ribs luxuriate for two whole days, and the other is their leisurely time in the oven, six to eight hours, depending on your patience. So this is no last-minute impulse; you have to start thinking about these ribs days ahead of time, and then you have to devote the day to cooking them. But there's nothing difficult here — and it does seem right that the world's best ribs should take some time.

The first two ingredients — Spike seasoning and Ac'cent — may come as a big surprise. We'd never even heard of Spike but had the wit to look for it in a natural food store. It's a mix of 39 seasonings, heavy on the salt, and there are actually three kinds of Spike. You want the Original.

Just do what Quincy Jones says. The recipe makes a lot of ribs, but you'll be happy to have leftovers. Or you can easily cut the recipe in half.

serves 8

2 teaspoons Spike seasoning (see above)
1 teaspoon Ac'cent seasoning
1/2 teaspoon freshly ground black pepper
5 racks baby back ribs (about 5 pounds total)
6 garlic cloves, minced
2 large jalapeño peppers, minced

2 green bell peppers, seeded and thinly sliced
2 red bell peppers, seeded and thinly sliced
2 yellow bell peppers, seeded and thinly sliced
2 large onions, halved and thinly sliced

In a cup, combine the Spike and Ac'cent seasonings and the pepper. Sprinkle 1/4 teaspoon of this seasoning mixture on each side of each of the rib racks. In a small bowl, combine the garlic, jalapeños, and remaining seasoning mixture. Rub the garlic mixture on the top and bottom of the ribs.

Line a large roasting pan (17-x-11 inches) with enough heavy-duty foil to wrap all the ribs or use a foil roasting bag (see note). Spread a layer of bell peppers and onions on top of the foil. Place 2 rib racks side by side on top of the vegetables. Continue to layer the peppers and onions and ribs. Tightly wrap the ribs in the foil and refrigerate for 2 days.

Remove the pan from the refrigerator and let stand at room temperature for 30 minutes. Preheat the oven to 400 degrees. Before placing the ribs in the oven, reduce the oven temperature to 300 degrees. Bake the foil-wrapped ribs for 6 to 8 hours. Remove the ribs. If there are any pan juices, spoon off and discard the fat, reserving the juices. Cut each rack into 3 sections and serve with the vegetables and any pan juices.

cook's note

At low temperatures, many ovens have trouble holding an even temperature, and you may find — as we did twice — that the ribs have gotten too dry. To avoid this problem, use an oven roasting bag (the kind intended for turkeys) instead of foil. This is an especially good idea if you're making a half recipe, which will dry out much more quickly.

serve with

Steamed rice
Tomato and cucumber salad
Green Onion Buttermilk Biscuits (page 233)
Double-Crust Jumble Berry Pie (page 282)

to drink

Cold beer
or dry rosé

SOURCE: Lamb roast label, Sam's Club
COOK: Unknown

lemony leg of lamb, greek style

WE FOUND THIS RECIPE ON A boneless leg of lamb from New Zealand. It's now our recipe of first resort when we buy one of these exceptionally lean roasts, because it's so simple and satisfyingly seasoned with delectable Greek flavors. It makes a lamb roast that's as good cold as it is hot from the oven. Best of all, there are no tricky leg bones to maneuver around when carving at the table; you can just slice it like a loaf of bread.

New Zealand is the only other place in the world besides Ireland where there are no predators; if Adam and Eve had met there, no snake would have come along to get everyone in trouble. It also has a wonderful climate and lots of grassland, so New Zealand sheep are happy and range-fed, which means their meat is much leaner and they haven't been subjected to hormone-laden feed. So keep an eye out for this tasty lamb.

serves 6

1/3 cup all-purpose flour
1 tablespoon grated fresh lemon zest
1 tablespoon dried oregano
1 tablespoon dried rosemary, coarsely crumbled

3 garlic cloves, minced
6 tablespoons fresh lemon juice
Salt and freshly ground black pepper
1 boneless leg of lamb (about 4 pounds for New Zealand lamb)

Preheat the oven to 425 degrees. In a small bowl, combine the flour, lemon zest, oregano, rosemary, and garlic. Stir in the lemon juice to form a paste. Season with salt and pepper to taste. Make 1/2-inch-deep incisions all over the lamb. Rub the lemon paste over the lamb, making sure it gets inside the incisions. Pour 3/4 cup water into a roasting pan and place the lamb on a rack in the pan.

Roast the lamb for 30 minutes. Reduce the oven temperature to 350 degrees and roast until an instant-read thermometer registers 155 degrees for medium (some roasts have a pop-up thermometer that will spring at this point). If you prefer medium-well, roast for 10 minutes more.

Let the roast stand, covered, for 10 minutes before carving. Skim any fat from the pan, spoon the pan juices over the sliced lamb, and serve.

If the lamb is not from New Zealand or Australia, a leg will be larger and fattier (unless it's range-fed) — adjust the roasting time accordingly.

serve with

Spiced Spinach with Yogurt (page 208), as a starter
Fresh Zucchini, Almonds, Curry, and Mint (page 209)
Evelyne's Gratinéed Potatoes (page 199)
Butter-Toffee Crunch Shortbread (page 250) with fruit salad

to drink

A robust Bordeaux-style red

side dishes

SOURCE: *New York Times*
COOK: Tom Colicchio

pan-roasted carrots

PAN-ROASTING BRINGS OUT THE NATURAL sweetness of carrots, and that's underscored here by the touch of honey at the end of the cooking time. The carrots get a bit caramelized, and they're perfumed with sprigs of fresh rosemary. When you bring these carrots to the table, expect a chorus of oohs and aahs as the rosemary fragrance wafts up and people get their first glimpse of this beautiful dish.

The recipe comes from Tom Colicchio, the chef at Manhattan's Craft restaurant, known for its exquisite comfort food that's as straightforward as possible — high-class home cooking.

serves 4

2 tablespoons extra-virgin olive oil
16 long, thin carrots, trimmed and
    peeled
Fleur de sel and freshly ground
    black pepper

4 sprigs fresh rosemary
4 teaspoons honey
1 tablespoon butter

In a large sauté pan, heat the oil over low heat. Add the carrots and fleur de sel and pepper to taste. Cook, turning the carrots occasionally, until golden brown on all sides, 15 to 20 minutes.

Add the rosemary during the last 5 minutes of cooking. Just before serving, add the honey and butter and mix well. Serve hot.

cook's notes

❧ High rollers can spring for the very expensive fleur de sel, which is indeed delicious. Sea salt will do fine.

❧ You want skinny, in-season carrots for this dish. You can use big old carrots, but first cut them crosswise into quarters and then cut each quarter in half lengthwise. They will also need to cook quite a bit longer to become tender. Because they're less sweet, they may not brown much until you add the honey and butter. If so, just turn the heat up a bit at that point and you can get a nice caramelization.

❧ The carrots should cook in a single layer. They'll shrink as they cook, so don't worry if they're a little tight in the pan at first.

SOURCE: *Vegetables from Amaranth to Zucchini*
by Elizabeth Schneider
COOK: Elizabeth Schneider

nutty roasted cremini

WE PRESENTED THESE MUSHROOMS to a mushroom-loathing member of our immediate family, and to our astonishment he pronounced them wonderful. Mushroom lovers will be even more entranced by this brilliant side dish. The mushrooms stay juicy and a little chewy but take on a wonderful roasty aroma from the spices, sherry, and hazelnuts.

Elizabeth Schneider suggests cooking the mushrooms in the hot oven after a roast has come out and is standing, waiting to be carved. That's a great idea, for everything from chicken to roast beef.

serves 4 to 6

1 tablespoon sherry
1 teaspoon Chinese five-spice powder or ground fennel seeds or aniseeds
About ½ teaspoon kosher salt

1½ pounds small cremini mushrooms, wiped clean and stems discarded
2 tablespoons hazelnut oil
⅓ cup coarsely chopped roasted husked hazelnuts
Freshly ground black pepper

Preheat the oven to 450 degrees with a rack in the top third. In a large bowl, combine the sherry, five-spice powder or fennel seeds or aniseeds, and the salt, mixing well. Add the mushrooms and oil, tossing to coat as evenly as possible. Place the mushrooms in a single layer in a roasting pan.

Roast until cooked through and browned, 10 to 15 minutes. Toss the mushrooms with the hazelnuts, and pepper to taste. Serve hot.

tip

To roast the hazelnuts, which can be done earlier: Preheat the oven to 450 degrees. Arrange the nuts on a baking sheet and mist with water. Roast for 10 to 15 minutes, or until fragrant and beginning to color. Let cool slightly. Schneider husks the nuts by chopping them in a food processor, using the plastic blade. After removing the husks, she returns the nuts to the processor and chops them with the metal blade. Any stubborn husks can be ignored.

side dishes

SOURCE: *Wine Country Living*
COOK: **Michael Chiarello**

roasted winter squash

CARAMELIZED, TENDER, SWEET, and delicious. A combination of earthy molasses, a little sweet balsamic vinegar, and a dash of sugar coats cubes of butternut squash. Michael Chiarello is the very famous entrepreneurial Napa Valley chef who's always pushing the envelope of classic dishes by giving them a Napa twist. While Chiarello roasts this squash in the fireplace, you can get the same fire-roasted flavor in a hot oven. Our guests simply devoured these tender sweet chunks of buttery squash. The squash is just as good warm as it is hot out of the oven, which gives the cook a lot of flexibility. Of course, if you have a fireplace you can cook in, your oven is freed for other things.

You can make this dish with other winter squash, such as acorn. Rosemary or thyme would work in place of sage, although sage is especially nice on the holiday table, and this is the year we can't seem to get enough of sage.

serves 6 to 8

3 pounds butternut squash
Salt and freshly ground black
   pepper
8 tablespoons (1 stick) unsalted
   butter

2 tablespoons finely chopped fresh
   sage
2 tablespoons sugar
1/4 cup dark unsulfured molasses
1/4 cup balsamic vinegar

Preheat the oven to 400 degrees. Line a heavy rimmed baking sheet with heavy-duty aluminum foil.

Peel the squash with a vegetable peeler or sharp paring knife. Halve lengthwise, discard the seeds, then cut into 1-inch cubes. Place in a large bowl and season with salt and pepper to taste.

In a medium skillet, melt the butter over medium-high heat. When the butter stops foaming and turns a light brown, remove from the heat and immediately add the sage, sugar, molasses, and vinegar. (Stand back so as not to get splattered.) Mix well and return to medium-low heat to simmer for 1 to 2 minutes.

Pour the vinegar-butter mixture over the squash and toss well. Spread the squash in a single layer on the baking sheet. Roast, tossing at least once, until the squash is very tender and caramelized, about 1 hour. Serve warm.

cook's notes

- To cook the squash in the fireplace: Instead of placing the squash on a baking sheet, wrap it in two or three double-thickness packages of aluminum foil. Place just in front of the hot coals in the fireplace. Turn from time to time and cook for about 1 hour, or until the squash is tender.

- You might want to put a splatter screen over the skillet when you add the seasonings to the hot butter, because it really does splatter and can burn you if you're too close.

- The squash is very rich and buttery. If you like, you could reduce the butter to 4 tablespoons (½ stick).

- Be sure to have a baking sheet large enough to hold the squash in a single layer — otherwise, the cubes will steam rather than roast.

SOURCE: *How to Grill* by Steven Raichlen
COOK: Steven Raichlen

barbecued stuffed cabbage

HERE'S ONE OF THOSE amaze-your-friends recipes, a bit like the Beer Can Chicken popularized by the same cook, Steven Raichlen (which appeared in our 2000 edition of *The Best American Recipes*). In both cases, these ingenious American dishes had long been popular on the barbecue circuit, and no one knows who first had such a bright idea. But this cabbage is pure genius: delicious, the work of moments, and stunning to look at.

The buttery cabbage develops a sweet-smoky taste and picks up the bacon flavor from the bacon-and-onion stuffing. You can use regular old green cabbage or sweeter and milder savoy, which Raichlen prefers. Barbecued cabbage is a perfect accompaniment for smoked turkey or pork.

The only problem with this terrific cabbage is knowing when it's done. The best way is to buy exactly the size of cabbage specified; then you can't go wrong with the timing.

serves 6 to 8

4 tablespoons (½ stick) butter

4 slices bacon (¼ pound, preferably artisanal), cut crosswise into ¼-inch slivers

1 small onion, finely chopped

1 medium savoy or green cabbage (about 2 pounds)

¼ cup good store-bought barbecue sauce

Coarse salt and freshly ground black pepper

In a medium bowl, soak 2 cups wood chips in cold water to cover for 1 hour. Drain and set aside.

In a medium skillet, melt 1 tablespoon of the butter over medium heat. Add the bacon and onion and cook until just beginning to brown, 3 to 5 minutes. Drain the bacon and onion in a strainer set over a bowl and reserve the drippings. Transfer the drained bacon and onion to a small bowl. Crumple a piece of aluminum foil and shape it into a ring about 3 inches in diameter.

Cut the core out of the cabbage by angling your knife down about 3 inches and cutting out a cone — the cutting circle should be about 3 inches in diameter. Discard the core. Cut the remaining 3 tablespoons butter into dice. Stir the barbecue sauce into the bacon-and-onion mixture. Prop the cabbage upright on the aluminum-foil ring, cavity up. Place the bacon-and-onion mixture in the cavity and top with as many pieces of butter as will fit. Using a basting brush, paint the outside of the cabbage with the reserved bacon drippings (save any remaining drippings for basting pork chops or making baked beans). Season the cabbage lightly with salt and generously with pepper.

Set up the grill for indirect grilling and preheat to medium. If using a gas grill, place all the wood chips in the smoker box or in a smoker pouch and preheat on high until you see smoke, then reduce the heat to medium. If using a charcoal grill, toss all the wood chips onto the coals.

Place the cabbage on its foil ring in the center of the hot grill rack away from the heat. Cover and grill the cabbage until very tender and easy to pierce with a skewer, 1 to 1^1/$_2$ hours. If using a charcoal grill, you'll need to add 12 fresh coals per side after 1 hour if the cabbage is not done.

To serve, peel off any dried-out or charred outside leaves and discard. Cut the cabbage into wedges and serve.

cook's notes

- We like to fold the outer leaves down when serving the cabbage, which gives it a nice rustic look.
- Bacon isn't the only flavor option; you can also use kielbasa or chorizo and just cook the sausage with the onions.
- If you'd rather, you can smoke the cabbage at 225 degrees for 2^1/$_2$ to 3 hours.

SOURCE: *New York Times Magazine*
COOK: Julia Reed

puree of cauliflower with curry

CAULIFLOWER SEEMS FINALLY to have emerged from rehab, where it's gotten over its harsh cabbagy reputation and become a subtle, sweet, delectable vegetable. Here it's steamed, pureed, and perked up with a hint of curry. People are intrigued by this lovely dish, and then they can't stop eating it. You can add cream or not, as you like. You can make the puree rough or smooth. On its own, it's a very light accompaniment; with a little cream added, it takes on more gravity.

One of the great virtues of this dish, aside from its taste, is that you can make it ahead and settle it into a gratin dish to be reheated when you're ready to serve.

serves 6

1 2-pound cauliflower head
Heavy cream (optional)
2 tablespoons unsalted butter, at room temperature, plus more to taste

2 teaspoons hot curry powder, such as Madras
1/2 teaspoon salt
1/2 teaspoon freshly ground white pepper

Trim off the leaves and cut out the central core of the cauliflower; break it into florets. Peel the core and slice. Halve the florets lengthwise.

In a medium saucepan, bring 1/2 cup water to a boil over medium heat. Add the cauliflower core and florets, cover, and cook until tender, about 5 minutes.

Drain the cauliflower, reserving the cooking water, and place in a food processor. Add 1/4 cup of the cooking water, heavy cream, if using, the 2 tablespoons butter, the curry powder, salt, and pepper and process to the desired consistency, adding more cooking liquid or butter, if desired. Taste and adjust the seasonings. Serve immediately, or transfer the puree to a gratin dish and reheat in a 250-degree oven when ready to serve.

cook's note

℮ To bring out the flavor of the curry powder, warm it with the butter in a small skillet before adding it to the cauliflower in the food processor.

SOURCE: **Kathleen Brennan**, *Saveur*
COOK: **Evelyne Geoffray**

evelyne's gratinéed potatoes

COOKS IN FRANCE AND ANYWHERE else French cooking is admired argue about how to make the perfect gratin dauphinois (that's scalloped potatoes to us). Is it wall-to-wall cream and butter, is there any milk, is there stock, nutmeg or not, topped with cheese or not? We've almost never met a gratin dauphinois we didn't like, but we've also never tasted one as wonderful as this one.

This version was served for lunch to a group of French harvest grape-pickers at Chateau Thivin, who rose up afterward to sing, "This is the life, the life, the life . . ." Indeed, it is. This gratin has both milk and heavy cream, and it also has a magical ingredient, the star of so many dishes this year: crème fraîche. That gives it a subtle tang and a whole new dimension of elegance. It's also superb comfort food.

serves 8

2 cups milk
2 cups heavy cream
4 tablespoons (½ stick) butter
1 garlic clove, minced
6 large russet potatoes, peeled

Salt and freshly ground black pepper
Freshly grated nutmeg
1 cup crème fraîche

Preheat the oven to 400 degrees. In a large saucepan, bring the milk and cream just to a boil over medium-high heat. Meanwhile, grease a large baking dish with 1 tablespoon of the butter and scatter the garlic over the bottom.

Slice the potatoes thinly and arrange in slightly overlapping layers in the baking dish, seasoning each layer with salt, pepper, and nutmeg to taste.

Spread the crème fraîche over the potatoes, then pour the hot milk-cream mixture over them and dot with the remaining 3 tablespoons butter. Bake until brown and bubbling, about 1 hour. Serve warm.

SOURCE: *One Potato, Two Potato*
by Roy Finamore with Molly Stevens
COOKS: Roy Finamore and Molly Stevens

party potatoes

PROBABLY THE MOST FRUSTRATING part of preparing Thanksgiving dinner is the last-minute potato-mashing and gravy-making. If you have this recipe in your arsenal, you can knock off the mashed potatoes two days ahead and have them sitting pretty in the refrigerator, ready for a last-minute heating. But that's not the only time you need these potatoes; they're also great for a buffet or for any crowd.

These luxurious mashed potatoes have a couple of other virtues, too. They're light and fluffy because they're whipped with an electric mixer, and they're incredibly luscious because they have sour cream and butter plus cream cheese to give them a little edge.

serves 10 to 12

3 pounds russet potatoes, peeled and cut into chunks

Coarse salt

8 tablespoons (1 stick) unsalted butter, cut into ½-inch pieces

8 ounces cream cheese, at room temperature

½ cup sour cream, at room temperature

⅔ cup milk, warmed

Freshly ground black pepper

Paprika

In a large saucepan, cover the potatoes with cold water by at least an inch, add a good pinch of salt, and bring to a boil. Reduce the heat to medium, partially cover, and cook until the potatoes are very tender. Drain and return them to the pan over medium heat. Cook for a minute or two, shaking and stirring so the potatoes don't stick, until they are floury and have made a film on the bottom of the pan.

Remove from the heat and break up the potatoes with a handheld electric mixer on low speed. Gradually drop in 6 tablespoons of the butter and beat until it is absorbed. Refrigerate the remaining 2 tablespoons butter. Gradually add the cream cheese and sour cream, beating well after each addition. Finally, beat in the milk, a little at a time. You want the potatoes to be fluffy and light; if they seem to be getting too wet, don't add all the milk. Season with salt and pepper to taste. (If you don't have an electric mixer, use a hand masher to start and then use a wooden spoon to beat in the butter, cream cheese, sour cream, and milk. Beat the milk into the potatoes one third at a time, beating vigorously after each addition.)

Butter a 9-x-13-inch baking dish and spoon the potatoes into it. Smooth the top and then, with a spatula or fork tines, swirl or score the surface of the potatoes to leave little peaks that will brown nicely during baking. Refrigerate, covered tightly with plastic wrap, for up to 2 days before baking.

Preheat the oven to 350 degrees. Dust the top of the potatoes with paprika. Cut the remaining 2 tablespoons butter into small pieces and scatter them over the top. Bake until the potatoes are heated through and the top is lightly golden, about 1 hour. (Expect it to take only half the time if the potatoes haven't been re-frigerated.) Serve hot.

cook's note

🌿 If you'd like to do a little lily-gilding, you could add ¼ cup chopped fresh chives to the potatoes.

SOURCE: *La Bella Cucina* by Viana La Place
COOK: Viana La Place

potato "focaccia"

WE WERE INTRIGUED WHEN we learned this Italian recipe was discovered at a Sagra della Patata (potato festival) — and what better way to celebrate potatoes? This isn't the familiar bready focaccia but, rather, a deep gratin of creamy pureed potatoes layered with a piquant saucelike mixture of tomatoes, capers, and olives. Serve this focaccia as a side dish or make it into a light supper. Very comforting, tasty, filling, and pretty. It's good warm or at room temperature, which makes it useful for a buffet or large gathering. If there are a lot of other side dishes around, this one will easily stretch to feed 8 to 10.

The ideal dish to use for this is the glazed terra-cotta gratin dish called a tiella — one of a range of southern Italian clay pots in many sizes, small to gigantic. French clay gratin dishes also work particularly well here — but any gratin dish will turn out a fine potato focaccia.

serves 6

2 pounds small Yukon Gold potatoes

1 cup grated Pecorino cheese

3 large eggs, lightly beaten
Sea salt and freshly ground black pepper

3 medium onions, finely diced

1/2 cup dry white wine

1 bay leaf, preferably fresh

2 tablespoons extra-virgin olive oil, plus more for the baking dish and drizzling

4 medium ripe tomatoes, peeled and cut into large chunks

1/2 cup pitted oil-cured black olives

2 tablespoons capers

1/2 cup bread crumbs

Preheat the oven to 400 degrees. Place the potatoes in a large pot of cold water, bring to a boil, and boil until tender. Peel the potatoes and, while still warm, put them through a ricer into a large bowl to make a smooth puree. Add the cheese and eggs to the potato mixture and season with salt and pepper to taste. Set aside.

In a large saucepan, combine the onions, wine, bay leaf, and 1/4 cup water over medium-high heat . Cook until the liquid has almost completely evaporated and the onions are tender; expect this to take some time. Add more water as needed until the onions are completely tender.

Add the 2 tablespoons oil, the tomatoes, and a pinch of salt to the onions. Reduce the heat to medium and simmer for 10 minutes, or until the tomatoes thicken to a sauce. Add the olives and capers and simmer for 3 minutes more. Set aside.

Oil a baking dish (preferably a glazed clay one) that measures about 8 inches in diameter or a 10-inch oval gratin dish. Sprinkle a few of the bread crumbs on the bottom.

Spread half of the potato mixture on the bottom of the baking dish. Spread the tomato sauce over the potatoes. Carefully spread the rest of the potato mixture over the top. Sprinkle with the remaining bread crumbs and drizzle with oil. Bake for 40 minutes, or until the top is golden brown. Let cool for at least 10 minutes. Serve warm or at room temperature, cut into squares or wedges.

cook's notes

- Because of the acid in the white wine, the onions will never get so tender that they fall apart. The acid imparts a definite tang to their flavor and keeps them intact — so just cook until they offer little resistance when you bite down on one and all of their raw onion flavor has mellowed.
- If you don't bother to peel the tomatoes here, we bet few people will notice.
- Hold the potatoes in a clean kitchen towel or oven mitt to peel them while still warm.
- La Place always uses spring water or purified water when she cooks — and indeed, it may make a difference.

SOURCE: *O, The Oprah Magazine*
COOK: Rori Trovato

roasted potatoes with asparagus, cherry tomatoes, and black olives

THIS GORGEOUS DISH OF SAVORY roasted vegetables is easy and so good it's almost impossible to stop eating. There's just about nothing to do, in fact, except turn on the oven. It's a three-stage roasting process. First the potatoes go in the oven, then the asparagus, and finally the rest of the tomatoes and olives, the really tender ones, at the end of the roasting. You serve all the vegetables together on a platter, passing sour cream on the side if you like.

We've listed this recipe among the side dishes, but it can also be a satisfying vegetarian main dish.

serves 6

2 pounds fingerling potatoes, scrubbed and halved lengthwise
3 tablespoons extra-virgin olive oil
Salt and freshly ground black pepper
1 pound asparagus (about 16 spears), thick ends trimmed

1 cup cherry tomatoes
¼ cup pitted Kalamata olives
2 teaspoons chopped fresh thyme, or 1 teaspoon dried
Sour cream, for serving (optional)

Preheat the oven to 400 degrees. In a large bowl, toss the potatoes with 1 tablespoon of the oil and season with salt and pepper to taste. Spread the potatoes in a single layer on a rimmed baking sheet and roast, without stirring, for 15 minutes.

In the same bowl, toss the asparagus with 1 tablespoon of the oil. Add to the partially roasted potatoes and roast for 15 minutes more.

In the same bowl, toss the tomatoes, olives, and thyme with the remaining 1 tablespoon oil. Add to the partially roasted potatoes and asparagus and roast until the tomatoes soften, about 5 minutes more. Season with salt and pepper to taste. Serve hot, with a dollop of sour cream, if desired.

cook's note

℘ Fingerlings are delicious little upscale potatoes that can be hard to find. You can substitute small red new potatoes or Yukon Golds, which will need to be quartered.

SOURCE: *Beard House* magazine
COOK: Don Diem

whipped root vegetables

AT THE JAMES BEARD HOUSE in Manhattan, which was actually the famous cook's home, chefs from all over the country visit regularly to cook dazzling meals for a highly appreciative group of diners. This year, one of the chefs was Don Diem, from the Atlanta restaurant Noche. This side dish, which looks just like an airy version of mashed potatoes, is very light and full of subtle flavors. The vegetables are whipped rather than mashed, which gives them a quite different texture. You don't taste the turnips, but they're a big lightening factor, and the parsnips contribute an earthy sweetness.

The puree is a perfect side dish for a big-deal meal, such as a groaning-board holiday spread. It's especially good with pork or beef.

serves 6

3 medium parsnips, peeled and cut into ½-inch dice (about 3 cups)

2–3 medium turnips, peeled and cut into ½-inch dice (about 2 cups)

1 large Idaho potato, peeled and cut into ½-inch dice (about 2 cups)

Coarse salt

8 tablespoons (1 stick) butter, at room temperature

¼ cup sour cream, at room temperature

Pinch of ground nutmeg

Freshly ground white pepper

In a large saucepan, combine the parsnips, turnips, and potato with salted water to cover. Bring to a boil and cook until the vegetables are very tender, 30 to 40 minutes. Drain well. Place the cooked vegetables in a stand mixer fitted with the whip attachment and whip until mashed. Slowly incorporate the butter, sour cream, nutmeg, and salt and white pepper to taste, then whip on high speed for about 1 minute to lighten the mixture. Transfer to a heated serving dish and serve hot.

cook's note

If you have no stand mixer, you can make the puree in a food processor, but it will be a bit denser.

SOURCE: *Ballots to Shallots*
COOK: Cybill Shepherd

cybill's greens

WE RAN ACROSS AN INTERESTING new cookbook from the League of Women Voters of Tennessee, featuring recipes from mayors, senators, congressional representatives, just plain folks . . . and Elvis. Among them, we found this excellent recipe from actress Cybill Shepherd, who comes from Memphis. Ms. Shepherd definitely knows her greens: She mixes a combination of turnip, collard, kale, and mustard greens and cooks them down slowly with olive oil, onion, garlic and, perhaps surprisingly, hot chiles. The peppers don't stay in the finished dish, however; they're plucked out right before the greens are served, but their essence lives on, subtly bringing out the flavors of the greens in the same way a jolt of hot sauce or vinegar does once they're cooked.

serves 4

4 bunches greens (turnip, collard, kale, or mustard, or a combination)

1 or 2 hot chile peppers

1/4 cup olive oil

1 cup chopped sweet onion

6 garlic cloves, minced

1–2 teaspoons salt, or to taste

1/2 teaspoon freshly ground black pepper, or to taste

Thoroughly wash the greens. Rinse, soak, and rinse again. Pick over and remove any undesirable leaves. Break the greens into pieces and discard the stems. Cut the chiles in half lengthwise and discard the seeds and stems.

In a large pot, heat the oil over medium heat. Add the onion and garlic and cook for 1 to 2 minutes. Add the chile peppers and cook, stirring, until the onion is golden but not brown.

Add the washed greens and 2 to 3 cups water, cover, and simmer for about 1 hour, or until the greens are cooked down and tender. Discard the chile peppers, add salt and pepper, and serve hot.

cook's note

Some, of course, like it hot, in which case you can chop the chile peppers and just leave them in the dish.

SOURCE: *Gourmet*
COOK: **Edna Lewis**

creamed scallions

EVER SINCE WE READ EDNA LEWIS'S first cookbook, *The Taste of Country Cooking,* we've been fans of not only the cook and her book but also her way with scallions, serving them as a side dish. Lewis tries to find scallions no bigger around than a pencil — which in our experience usually means the farmers' market. But the bigger ones taste good, too, she concedes, and that's what we used when we tried this dish.

Cooked scallions have a wonderful sweet freshness, nicely underscored here by a fair amount of cream and a little garlic. This extremely easy recipe makes a good extra side dish, especially at a holiday meal, so that everyone gets just a few bites of this rich treat.

serves 4 to 6

2/3 cup heavy cream
1/4 teaspoon minced garlic
5 bunches scallions (about 30), trimmed and cut into 1/2-inch-thick pieces

1 tablespoon chopped fresh parsley
Salt and freshly ground black pepper

In a medium skillet, bring the cream and garlic to a boil. Reduce the heat and simmer briskly until reduced by half, about 7 minutes. Remove from the heat.

Meanwhile, in a medium heavy saucepan, combine the scallions and 3 tablespoons cold water over medium-high heat. Cover and cook until tender, 5 to 7 minutes.

Add the cream mixture to the scallions. Stir in the parsley and salt and pepper to taste, reduce the heat to medium, and cook, stirring, until piping hot. Serve immediately.

SOURCE: *Mediterranean Vegetables*
by Clifford A. Wright
COOK: Clifford A. Wright

spiced spinach with yogurt

THIS SYRIAN VEGETABLE DISH is very special indeed, and not just because it tastes so extraordinary. According to Clifford A. Wright, it's a rarity these days to find this dish on anyone's table in Syria. It's one of a group of Persian-influenced dishes called burani, named after the wife of a ninth-century caliph, which were popular in 13th-century Damascus. This fragrant spinach dish, which seems so simple, actually includes six spices beyond salt and pepper. But they're used with a very subtle hand, and to mesmerizing effect.

This burani is usually served as a starter, with warm Middle Eastern flatbread for dipping. It also makes a fine side dish, especially for lamb.

serves 4

2 pounds flat-leaf spinach, washed and trimmed of heavy stems
1 cup high-quality whole-milk yogurt
2 large garlic cloves, mashed with ¹/₂ teaspoon salt
2 tablespoons extra-virgin olive oil
1 teaspoon freshly ground coriander seeds
¹/₈ teaspoon freshly ground allspice

¹/₈ teaspoon freshly grated nutmeg
¹/₈ teaspoon freshly ground cardamom seeds
¹/₈ teaspoon freshly ground cloves
¹/₈ teaspoon ground cinnamon
Salt and freshly ground black pepper
¹/₃ cup chopped walnuts

Middle Eastern flatbread (pita bread) for serving

In a large saucepan, place the spinach, with only the water adhering to it from its last rinsing, over medium-high heat. Cover, and cook until the spinach wilts, about 5 minutes. Drain in a colander, pushing out excess water with the back of a wooden spoon.

In a small bowl, stir together the yogurt and garlic-salt mixture. Set aside.

In a medium skillet, heat the olive oil over medium-high heat. Add the spinach, spices, and salt and pepper to taste. Cook, stirring occasionally, until heated through, about 5 minutes. Transfer the spinach to a serving platter, spoon several dollops of the yogurt mixture over it, and sprinkle with the walnuts. Serve immediately with the flatbread.

SOURCE: *The Paris Cookbook* by Patricia Wells
COOK: Joël Robuchon

fresh zucchini, almonds, curry, and mint

THIS IS A FAMOUS-FRENCH-CHEF RECIPE, and although it's unusual and delicious, it happens to be extremely simple as well. If you live in California, you may have access to fresh almonds; for the rest of us, blanched almonds work perfectly here. The zucchini and almonds, both rather bland on their own, are tossed with curry powder, salt, and white pepper and left to absorb the seasonings for 15 minutes. Then they're quickly seared in a little olive oil until they turn golden. A little slivered mint, and they're ready to serve.

This really isn't quite like anything you've ever tasted before. Use high-quality ingredients — young zucchini, good almonds, an excellent curry powder — since everything counts in this recipe. It's particularly delicious with lamb.

serves 6

1 pound young zucchini, scrubbed, trimmed but not peeled, and cut into pieces roughly the size of an almond

½ cup fresh shelled almonds or whole blanched almonds

2 teaspoons curry powder, or to taste

Fine sea salt and freshly ground white pepper

2 tablespoons extra-virgin olive oil

24 fresh mint leaves, cut into fine slivers

In a large bowl, combine the zucchini, almonds, curry powder, and salt and white pepper to taste. Toss together, cover with plastic wrap, and set aside for 15 minutes to absorb the seasonings.

In a large nonstick skillet, heat the oil over high heat until hot but not smoking. Add the zucchini mixture and cook, shaking the pan frequently, until golden, 3 to 4 minutes. The zucchini should remain crunchy. Add the mint and toss to blend evenly. Taste and adjust the seasonings. Mound the warm zucchini mixture in a serving bowl, and serve immediately.

SOURCE: *The Best Vegetarian Recipes*
COOK: Martha Rose Shulman
after Maria Kaneva-Johnson

cabbage gratin
with red pepper and tomato

COOKED CABBAGE IS RARELY on anyone's list of favorite dishes, and that's because it usually hasn't been cooked long enough. If you think you don't like cabbage, you really should try this sweet, succulent Eastern European dish. The cabbage is almost roasted until it's caramelized and its native sweetness emerges. Balancing the sweetness is the tartness of tomatoes, with earthy red bell pepper to round out the flavors.

The dish is done when the edges are beginning to brown, which means the vegetables have reached their maximum sweetness.

serves 4 to 6

2 tablespoons extra-virgin olive oil

1 small or medium onion, finely chopped

1 medium red bell pepper, seeded and diced

1 1½-pound green cabbage, cored and finely chopped (about 8 cups)

Salt

1 small tomato, or half a 14-ounce can diced tomatoes (about ½ heaping cup)

1 teaspoon paprika

Freshly ground black pepper

2–3 plum tomatoes, thinly sliced

Preheat the oven to 350 degrees with a rack in the top third. Oil a 2-quart baking dish or gratin dish. In a large nonstick skillet, heat 1 tablespoon of the oil over medium heat. Add the onion and bell pepper and cook, stirring, until they begin to soften, about 3 minutes. Add the cabbage and ½ teaspoon salt, stir together, cover (use a pizza pan if your skillet doesn't have a lid), and reduce the heat to low. Cook, stirring occasionally, for 10 to 15 minutes, or until the cabbage is tender and limp. Add 3 tablespoons water, cover, and cook for 15 minutes more, or until the cabbage is thoroughly tender and its bright green color has faded. Stir in the chopped tomato, paprika, and pepper to taste and remove from the heat. Taste and add salt, if needed.

Transfer the mixture to the prepared baking dish. Arrange the sliced tomatoes over the top, sprinkle them with salt and pepper to taste, and drizzle on the remaining 1 tablespoon oil. Bake for 40 to 50 minutes, or until some of the cabbage and tomato slices are charred around the edges and the tomato slices are shriveled. Serve hot or at room temperature.

❧ You can make the dish a day ahead of serving — just cover, chill overnight, and reheat for 15 to 20 minutes at 300 degrees — or simply bring it to room temperature.

SOURCE: *The All New Good Housekeeping Cookbook*

COOK: *Good Housekeeping* staff

cherry tomato gratin

IN THE DEAD OF WINTER, when you start to imagine that you may never taste a really ripe tomato again, cherry tomatoes come to the rescue. This is an incredibly cheering gratin, with its bright red mini tomatoes and green parsley flecks. Cherry tomatoes are at their best in the summer, however, and that's also a great time for this dish, since it's lighter than most gratins and goes well with grilled meat or fish.

serves 6

¼ cup plain dry bread crumbs

¼ cup freshly grated Parmesan cheese

1 garlic clove, crushed in a garlic press

¼ teaspoon coarsely ground black pepper

1 tablespoon olive oil

2 pints ripe cherry tomatoes

2 tablespoons chopped fresh parsley

Preheat the oven to 425 degrees. In a small bowl, mix together the bread crumbs, Parmesan, garlic, pepper, and oil.

Place the cherry tomatoes in a 1½-quart casserole dish or a deep 9-inch pie dish. Top with the bread-crumb mixture and sprinkle with the parsley.

Bake until the tomatoes are heated through and the crumb topping is browned, about 20 minutes. Serve warm.

cook's notes

- The gratin is especially gorgeous baked in a white dish.
- Any leftovers can become a very tasty pasta sauce. Just reheat, add olive oil to taste, then toss with the pasta.
- You may need a bit more olive oil to moisten the bread crumbs.

SOURCE: *Pleasures of the Vietnamese Table*
COOK: **Mai Pham**

scallion noodles

THIS SATISFYING SIDE DISH of fresh egg noodles tossed with scallion-and-shallot-infused hot oil originally came from China but has migrated all over Asia in various versions. We can see why it's so popular; for one thing, it's quick to make and requires only a few ingredients. It reminds us of a very clean-tasting lo mein.

Scallion noodles are delicious with chicken and pork — especially off the grill. If you're grilling, you can boil and rinse the noodles in advance, then just throw the dish together in the few minutes it takes for the grilled meat to rest before serving.

In the time it takes to prepare a package of store-bought ramen noodles, you can make these infinitely tastier scallion noodles for a quick lunch or late-night snack. Toss in leftover bits of cooked meat or tofu if you want to fortify it.

serves 4

1 bunch scallions
3 tablespoons vegetable oil
2 shallots, thinly sliced
2 tablespoons soy sauce, or to taste

1 pound fresh egg noodles, boiled for 2 to 3 minutes, rinsed, and drained
Pinch of salt

Cut the white parts of the scallions into thin rings. Cut the green parts into 2-inch lengths.

In a large nonstick skillet, heat the oil over medium heat. Add the shallots and the white and green parts of the scallions. Stir until fragrant, about 1 minute. Add the soy sauce, noodles, and salt. Stir gently, being careful not to break the noodles. Turn several times so the noodles are coated evenly with the oil and are heated through. Transfer to a serving plate and serve immediately.

cook's notes

❧ If you can't find fresh Vietnamese egg noodles, known as mi, you can use fresh chow mein–style noodles or fresh linguine.

❧ Rinse the noodles thoroughly so that they won't stick together in a solid lump. And give them several good shakes when draining so you don't add a lot of water to the skillet.

side dishes

SOURCE: **Bruce Feiler,** *Gourmet*
COOK: *Gourmet* staff

persian rice with dill and pistachios

ALTHOUGH WE'VE HEARD lots of tales about the legendary Persian rice, cooked in a deep pot with butter on the bottom so it has a crunchy crust, we'd never actually tasted it before we found this recipe. Now we can't stop making it, and this stunning dish is inevitably the hit of our dinner parties.

This Persian rice is stunning — subtle and elegant, with the surprise of pistachios and dill.

The rice is layered in the pot with the dill and pistachios, then slowly steamed. When it's done, the rice is scooped out into a serving bowl and the pot gets a quick dip in cold water to release the crust, the famous *tah-dig*. Magically, the crust comes off in one piece — more or less — and you can either break it up to perch on top of the rice or simply cover the serving platter with the whole crust, letting each diner break off a little piece along with the rice. Or serve it separately, as the recipe suggests.

serves 8 to 10

3 cups basmati rice (1¼ pounds)

3 tablespoons salt

6 tablespoons (¾ stick) unsalted butter

⅔ cup chopped fresh dill

1 cup coarsely chopped natural pistachios (5 ounces)

In a large bowl, rinse the rice in several changes of cold water until the water runs clear. Drain in a large strainer.

In a large heavy pot, bring 4 quarts of water and the salt to a boil. Add the rice and cook for 5 minutes. Drain in a large strainer.

Wash the pot and return it to the stovetop. In the pot, melt the butter over medium-low heat. Spoon the rice over the butter, alternating with layers of dill and pistachios and mounding loosely, ending with the rice.

Using the handle of a wooden spoon, make 5 or 6 holes in the rice mound going all the way down to the bottom of the pot. Cover the pot with a kitchen towel and a heavy lid. Tuck the edges of the towel over the top of the lid so it won't burn.

Cook, undisturbed, until the rice is tender and a crust has formed on the bottom of the pot, 30 to 35 minutes. Spoon the loose rice onto a platter. Dip the bottom of the pot into a bowl of cold water for 30 seconds to loosen the crust. Remove the crust with a large spoon and serve it in a separate bowl or over the loose rice.

cook's notes

- You may think an enameled cast-iron pan, such as Le Creuset, would be perfect for this job, but be warned: it may crack the enamel. Choose a heavy stainless-steel pot instead.
- *Gourmet*'s tasters found that the best pistachios come from Iran and Turkey.
- Leftover rice makes great rice cakes: just mix with beaten egg, add salt and pepper to taste, and fry the rice cakes in a little butter.

SOURCE: *Nigella Bites* (television program)
COOK: Nigella Lawson

green pea risotto

THIS RISOTTO IS A SURPRISE: creamy, rich, with a lovely true pea flavor. Nigella Lawson, aka the Domestic Goddess, has been wise and used frozen petite peas, so we can have real springtime pea flavor in the middle of winter. What makes this risotto special is her trick of pureeing half the cooked peas in the blender with butter and cheese, which then enriches the risotto just before you serve it.

Lawson serves this as a main course, in which case it serves two. But we think it also makes a terrific side dish, especially with lamb chops. Use any light stock here — Lawson uses ham stock, which most of us don't have in our pantries, but chicken, vegetable, or veal stock would all be fine — just not beef.

serves 2 as a main course, 4 as a side dish

4 tablespoons (½ stick) unsalted butter, cut into 4 equal pieces

1 cup frozen baby peas

4 cups stock (see note above), heated

2 tablespoons freshly grated Parmesan cheese, plus more for serving

Pinch of freshly grated nutmeg

Freshly ground black pepper

Drop of oil

2 shallots or 1 small onion, minced

1 cup Arborio or Carnaroli rice

½ cup dry white wine or vermouth

Salt

Chopped fresh parsley (optional)

In a medium saucepan, melt 1 tablespoon of the butter over medium heat. Add the peas and cook, stirring occasionally, for 2 minutes. Remove half the peas and set aside. Add a ladleful of the hot stock to the peas remaining in the pan, cover, and cook gently until soft, about 5 minutes. Transfer the fully cooked peas to a mini-processor or blender along with 1 tablespoon of the Parmesan and 1 tablespoon of the butter. Season with nutmeg and pepper to taste and puree until smooth. Set aside.

Return the saucepan to medium heat and melt 1 tablespoon of the butter along with the drop of oil. Add the shallots or onion and cook, stirring with a wooden spoon, for about 4 minutes. Add the rice and stir until every grain glistens with the oniony fat. Pour in the wine or vermouth and let it bubble away and absorb.

Then add a ladleful of the hot stock and stir until this, too, is absorbed. Continue in this vein, patiently, for 10 minutes more. Add the reserved whole peas and then start again, a ladleful of stock at a time. In another 8 minutes or so, the rice should be cooked and the risotto creamy. Taste to see if it needs more cooking. It's hard to be precise with risotto; sometimes you'll find that you have stock left over, while other times you'll need to add hot water from the kettle.

When the risotto is tender and creamy, stir in the pureed pea mixture. Season with salt and pepper to taste. Beat in the remaining 1 tablespoon Parmesan and 1 tablespoon butter. Sprinkle with chopped parsley, if you like, and serve with extra Parmesan at the table.

cook's notes

- Keep the stock hot in a saucepan on a neighboring burner on low. It's also a good idea to have the teakettle on low and on hand since sometimes the rice will absorb more stock than others and you may need to add some hot water from the kettle.
- If you think of it, take the peas out in advance and let them thaw. If you forget, don't worry. You can use them straight from the freezer with no problem.

SOURCE: *Lidia's Italian-American Kitchen*
by Lidia Bastianich
COOK: Lidia Bastianich

sardinian old bread and tomato casserole

THIS MARVELOUS DISH IS ONE OF those brilliant Italian inventions made out of almost nothing: some stale bread, a few tomatoes, an onion, fresh oregano, and cheese. Since thrifty cooking is something of a lost art in American kitchens, you'll probably need to buy a fresh loaf of bread and let it get stale overnight to make this cross between a bread pudding and lasagna. But do make it; this is soul food.

It's great with both meat and fish or on its own as a light meal with a salad. Lidia Bastianich points out that it makes a fine brunch dish, topped with an egg fried in olive oil. That's the way we like it best.

serves 6

1 28-ounce can Italian plum tomatoes, preferably San Marzano
1 teaspoon sea salt, plus additional salt for water
1 pound day-old dry, crusty Italian bread, cut into 3/4-inch-thick slices (about 16)

4 tablespoons extra-virgin olive oil
1 large yellow onion, sliced (about 2 cups)
1/4 cup chopped fresh oregano
2 cups freshly grated Pecorino Romano cheese

Chop the tomatoes in a food processor, using on-and-off pulses. Don't over-process them or you'll incorporate too much air and the tomatoes will turn pink. Stir in 1 teaspoon salt.

In a small saucepan, bring 2 cups salted water to a boil. Lower the bread slices one by one into the boiling water for a second or two, just long enough to wet them. Place them on a kitchen towel on the counter to drain. Press the moistened bread lightly to remove excess water.

In a large skillet, heat 3 tablespoons of the oil over medium heat. Add the onion and cook, stirring, until golden, about 8 minutes. Pour in the tomatoes and bring to a boil. Reduce the heat so the sauce is simmering and cook until slightly thickened, about 20 minutes. Stir in the oregano and cook for 5 minutes more.

Preheat the oven to 375 degrees. Oil an 11-inch oval baking dish (or an equivalent baking dish) with the remaining 1 tablespoon oil. Spoon in enough of the tomato sauce to coat the bottom and arrange half the bread slices over the sauce, tearing them and wedging them as necessary to make an even layer. Spoon half the remaining tomato sauce over the bread and sprinkle 1 cup of the Pecorino over the sauce. Make another layer of the remaining bread slices, tomato sauce, and Pecorino. Bake until the casserole is heated through and the cheese topping is browned, about 25 minutes. Serve hot.

SOURCE: *Fine Cooking* recipe contest
COOK: Jan Curry

bacon bread pudding

WE FOUND THIS RECIPE AMONG the 10 finalists in a recipe contest for *Fine Cooking* magazine. The bread pudding wasn't even a contender; it was just used to prop up some herb-grilled chicken breasts. While the chicken didn't win the contest, we discovered ourselves thinking wistfully about this great bread pudding. It's custardy and creamy with just the right amount of crisp bacon to give it a salty-savory flavor. Gruyère cheese adds just enough sharpness. These little puddings are a painless way to turn out a dinner-party-fancy side dish for anything from a big roast to, yes, grilled chicken. It's also a great brunch dish.

Although the recipe makes these puddings in individual servings, we're also happy doubling the recipe and baking it in a 1½-quart baking dish to serve eight, family style.

serves 4

3 slices bacon, chopped
1⅓ cups whole milk
2 large eggs
Salt and freshly ground black pepper

3 cups cubed sturdy bread (about three ½-inch-thick slices)
⅔ cup freshly grated Gruyère cheese

Preheat the oven to 350 degrees. Butter four 6-ounce custard cups or ramekins. In a small heavy skillet, cook the bacon until crisp. Drain the bacon on paper towels and set aside.

In a medium bowl, whisk together the milk, eggs, and salt and pepper to taste. Stir in the bread cubes, cheese, and bacon. Divide the mixture among the custard cups. Arrange the cups in a baking dish, and add hot water to the baking dish to reach halfway up the sides of the cups. Bake until the puddings are set, 35 to 40 minutes. Run a knife around the edges of the cups to loosen the puddings and serve warm.

cook's notes

❧ Cut the bread into cubes about ½ inch in size so that they fit nicely into the custard cups.

❧ If the water you add to the baking dish is not hot, expect the puddings to take up to 10 minutes more to cook. The puddings are baked when the centers are just set.

❧ Using a rustic bread with a bit of heft to it will give the pudding more texture. A softer bread will make them custardy-soft throughout. Whatever bread you use, don't bother removing the crust; it adds texture and color.

❧ Don't be shy with the pepper grinder. Black pepper and salty bacon are a good match.

SOURCE: *Martha Stewart Living*
(television program)
COOKS: Johanne Killeen and George Germon

double corn polenta

SUMMER IS WRITTEN ALL OVER this sensational polenta, with its tomatoes and herbs and fresh corn. We also like the idea of this hearty dish for winter, made with cherry tomatoes, which taste good all year long, and frozen corn niblets.

This polenta could be served at almost any meal and be almost any course of that meal. We'd be as delighted to see it for brunch as we would for a main course, an appetizer, or a side dish at dinnertime. It's very rich and creamy, which made us think appetizer. On the other hand, it could be a good vegetarian main dish (figure four servings). We've put it with the side dishes, however, because we think it is superb alongside juicy grilled steaks or lamb. The recipe serves six to eight as a side, but it's flexible — you can also cut it in half for an intimate two-person supper.

serves 6 to 8

2 ripe tomatoes
1/4 cup extra-virgin olive oil
Coarse salt
1 cup heavy cream
2 tablespoons unsalted butter
1 cup medium-grind cornmeal
1 1/2 cups cooked corn kernels

2/3 cup loosely packed fresh mixed herbs, such as parsley, thyme, chives, and basil, coarsely chopped
2/3 cup freshly grated Parmesan cheese
4 large fresh basil leaves, for garnish

Core and roughly chop the tomatoes. In a small bowl, toss them with the oil. Season with salt to taste and set aside.

In a medium heavy saucepan, combine 4 cups water and the cream over medium-high heat. Bring to a boil. Add the butter and salt to taste and stir to melt the butter. Whisking constantly, add the cornmeal in a slow, steady stream. Continue to whisk until all lumps have disappeared. Reduce the heat to low, and gently simmer, stirring constantly with a wooden spoon, until the polenta is thick and creamy, about 20 minutes.

Fold in the corn, herbs, and Parmesan. Spoon into a heated serving bowl and top with the tomatoes and any accumulated juices. Tear the basil leaves into small pieces, and sprinkle them over the tomatoes. Serve immediately.

cook's note

When serving this as a main course, divide the polenta between 4 heated bowls and serve immediately.

SOURCE: *Time Out New York*
COOK: Michael Sullivan

sweet potato spoon bread

WE LOVE SWEET POTATOES and we love spoon bread, but we never would have thought of putting the two together. At Manhattan's Le Zinc restaurant, however, they're way ahead of us. The sweet potatoes and cornmeal are great foils for each other, both sweet and earthy in different ways. Everyone loves it, kids and adults alike, so it's a great dish for holiday meals. It's especially good with ham, but it also works with turkey instead of the usual sticky-sweet sweet potatoes. It would be a fine addition to the brunch table.

The spoon bread reheats well, so it can travel to a potluck or even be made a day ahead, which is a huge advantage.

serves 6 to 8

3 large sweet potatoes
1 cup heavy cream
3/4 cup cornmeal
3/4 cup brown sugar
3 tablespoons butter
1 tablespoon ground cinnamon

Salt and freshly ground black pepper
1/2 cup all-purpose flour
Pinch of nutmeg
1/2 cup honey
4 large eggs

Preheat the oven to 350 degrees. Bake the sweet potatoes for 1 to 1 1/2 hours, or until tender. Let cool and peel.

In a small saucepan, combine the cream, 1 cup water, the cornmeal, brown sugar, butter, cinnamon, and salt and pepper to taste over low heat. Cook until it starts to thicken, 8 to 12 minutes.

In a food processor, puree the cornmeal mixture, sweet potatoes, flour, nutmeg, honey, and eggs. Transfer the mixture to a large buttered baking dish and cook for 45 to 60 minutes, or until set.

cook's note

℟ Unless you're a huge fan of cinnamon, start with 1 teaspoon and taste the puree just before you add it to the baking dish. If it needs more cinnamon, add it judiciously and check the seasonings.

SOURCE: *Gourmet*
COOK: Katy Massam

cumin apple chips

WE CAN'T SAY ENOUGH ABOUT THESE amazing apple chips. They're crispy-crunchy like a good potato chip, but also sweet and tart. They're easy to make and keep well (up to a week in an airtight container). They're a good accompaniment to a salad, especially a creamy or curried one. We love the idea of serving them with cheese — something blue and creamy or something aged such as sharp white Cheddar or Cheshire.

makes 20 chips

> 3 tablespoons powdered sugar
> 1 teaspoon ground cumin
> 1 medium Granny Smith apple

Preheat the oven to 200 degrees with a rack in the middle. Line a baking sheet with a nonstick baking-sheet liner or parchment paper.

Into a small bowl, sift together the powdered sugar and cumin twice to mix them evenly. Sift half of the cumin-sugar evenly onto the baking sheet.

Using a mandoline or a very sharp knife, cut the apple crosswise into very thin slices (about $1/16$ inch thick). Arrange 20 of the largest slices nearly touching each other on the cumin-sugar-dusted baking sheet, then evenly sift the remaining cumin-sugar over them. (Save the remaining apple slices for another use.)

Bake the apple slices until pale and beginning to crisp, about $1^1/2$ hours. Immediately peel the chips off the baking sheet and cool on a wire rack.

cook's notes

- There's no need to remove the peel, seeds, or core from the apple slices — in fact, the core and seeds leave a pretty star-shaped pattern in the center of each chip.
- If you don't have a nonstick baking-sheet liner, don't be surprised if the chips stick a bit to the parchment. If this happens, just return the baking sheet to the oven for 3 minutes to soften and then peel them off.
- The chips won't feel crisp when you first pull them from the oven. They turn crunchy as they cool.

side dishes

SOURCE: *San Francisco Chronicle*
COOK: Jacqueline Higuera McMahan

grape salsa

WE WERE SNAGGED RIGHT AWAY by the very idea of a grape salsa, and the next thing we knew, we were serving it for Thanksgiving dinner. In fact, this entirely fresh-tasting, zippy salsa goes well with turkey, chicken, pork, or lamb.

It has some subtle flavors — lemon, almonds, chives, rice vinegar — as well as some lively ones — cilantro, jalapeño, cayenne. There seem to be different tastes in every bite, which tends to mean you take a lot of bites. It's refreshing, stimulating, and light all at once.

You can use red or green seedless grapes or a mixture, but we think red is prettiest, and maybe even tastiest.

makes about 2¼ cups

- 2 cups seedless grapes, halved
- 1 tablespoon fresh lemon juice
- 1 tablespoon rice vinegar
- 1 teaspoon mild-flavored olive oil
- 1 garlic clove, minced
- 1 jalapeño pepper, seeded and minced
- 2 tablespoons snipped fresh chives
- 2 tablespoons minced fresh cilantro
- Generous pinch of salt
- ⅛ teaspoon cayenne pepper
- Freshly ground black pepper
- ¼ cup toasted almond slivers, crushed

In a medium bowl, combine all the ingredients. Serve slightly chilled or at room temperature.

cook's note

Sometimes red seedless grapes have what appear to be tiny seeds. You don't have to remove them; these are just genetic leftovers, seeds that never develop, and you don't even notice them when you bite into the grape.

SOURCE: *Bon Appétit*
COOK: Rozanne Gold

cranberry and dried cherry relish

EVERY YEAR WE SEE DOZENS of new versions of cranberry sauce, but this one from the queen of brilliant minimalist food, Rozanne Gold (author of the 1-2-3 cookbook series), really caught our attention. Dried tart cherries with tart cranberries and cardamom? We had to try it, and now we don't think we'll spend a holiday season without it. This relish has a wonderful flavor that seems to go with everything from turkey to cold roast lamb to ham. It's great on sandwiches or on little tidbits to go with cocktails (smoked trout comes to mind), and we've even seen some houseguests dipping chips into it.

One of the best things about it, though, is that it must be made ahead — and you don't cook it at all, so it takes just a few minutes to put it together.

makes 2 cups

1 12-ounce package fresh cranberries

1 cup dried tart cherries (about 5 ounces)

1 cup packed light brown sugar

1/2 teaspoon ground cardamom

In a large bowl, mix together all the ingredients. Transfer half the mixture to a food processor and pulse until coarsely chopped. Repeat with the remaining mixture. Store the relish tightly covered in the refrigerator for at least 1 day and up to 2 days, stirring occasionally. Bring to room temperature before serving.

cook's note

Dried cherries can have pits that the pitting machine has missed — unpleasant discoveries in both the food processor and the mouth. Give the cherries a feel before they go into the relish to pick up any strays.

breads

SOURCE: *River Run Cookbook* by
Jimmy and Maya Kennedy and Marialisa Calta
COOK: Jimmy Kennedy

nadine's onion and black pepper rolls

JIMMY KENNEDY IS A SOUTHERN cook who migrated to New York City and then on to the mountains of Vermont. In his New York days, he was a partner in Nadine's restaurant in Greenwich Village, where they still serve these rolls to customers as soon as they sit down at the table. They're big, soft, doughy rolls with great flavor. Sweet onions and black pepper make these rolls unusually good — so good, they've been written up in *Gourmet* and various other media.

These are dinner rolls, that vanishing breed, and they're chewy with a good crumb, even a bit dense. You pull them apart and drag a piece across your plate to sop up any lingering gravy. They're so big, you might think about making them somewhat smaller — but in our experience, every bite gets eaten.

makes 12 rolls

6 tablespoons vegetable oil	5 cups all-purpose flour
2½ cups chopped onions (about 2½ medium)	1 tablespoon coarsely ground black pepper
1 scant tablespoon (1 packet) active dry yeast	1½ teaspoons poppy seeds
	2 teaspoons salt

In a large skillet, heat 2 tablespoons of the oil over medium-high heat. Add the onions, reduce the heat to medium, and sauté until they are quite soft, 10 to 12 minutes.

Into a small bowl, pour 1½ cups warm water and sprinkle the yeast on top. Let stand for 5 to 10 minutes. The yeast should start to bubble.

In a large bowl, mix the flour, pepper, poppy seeds, and salt. Stir in the yeast mixture and the remaining 4 tablespoons oil. Add the cooked onions and stir vigorously — a stand mixer with a dough hook works well, too.

Turn the dough out onto a floured work surface and knead until smooth, at least 4 to 5 minutes. Clean out the mixing bowl, grease it with a bit of oil, and place the kneaded dough in it. Cover with a clean kitchen towel or plastic wrap and let

breads

rise in a warm place for 1 hour. The dough should be doubled in size, and when you press it with your fingers, it should stay indented. If it doesn't, let it rise some more.

Knead the dough on a floured work surface for a minute or two. Cut it into quarters, then cut each quarter into 3 pieces to make 1 dozen rolls. With your hands, form each piece into an oval.

Place the rolls on greased baking sheets, cover with a clean kitchen towel, and let rise in a warm spot for 30 minutes. Preheat the oven to 400 degrees. Bake the rolls for about 20 minutes, or until golden.

cook's note

℘ If the dough seems too sticky, add ⅓ to ½ cup more flour. It should be a supple, smooth dough.

tip

Most plastic wrap is pretty disappointing in terms of its ability to cling tightly or seal anything. It's also often a nightmare to use, since it sticks to everything else. But try this tip we heard about this year: keep the plastic wrap in the fridge, and it will seal much better and not get all tangled up. True.

SOURCE: *Prairie Home Breads*
by Judith M. Fertig
COOK: Judith M. Fertig

hoosier ham and cheese biscuits

SMOKED HAM, CHEESE, and dry mustard transform plain biscuits into something much more special and savory. They come from the Heartland, specifically St. Joseph County, Indiana, where people are passionate about their biscuits. They're comforting, salty, smoky, and tender — and, like any good biscuit, quick to make. The simple and surprising technique eliminates the need to cut in the butter — instead, you pour melted butter into the baking pan and drizzle more over the top before they bake. This gives the biscuit a lovely browned bottom, golden top, crunchy exterior, and tender interior. It may look like a lot of butter when you pour it into the pan, but the biscuits will absorb it and be the better for it.

These should be served warm and make excellent companions for soup or chili. Like all biscuits, they're best served the same day.

makes about 24 biscuits

2 cups self-rising flour (see note)
¾ cup finely chopped smoked ham
    or prosciutto
¾ cup finely grated Cheddar or
    Asiago cheese

1 teaspoon dry mustard
⅔ cup milk
8 tablespoons (1 stick) unsalted
    butter, melted

Preheat the oven to 450 degrees. In a large bowl, stir together the flour, ham or prosciutto, cheese, mustard, and milk with a wooden spoon until you have a soft dough. Pour half of the melted butter into the bottom of a 13-x-9-inch baking pan. Turn the dough out onto a floured work surface and roll out or pat into a 10-x-6-inch rectangle. Using a serrated knife or pizza wheel, cut the rectangle of dough lengthwise in half, then cut crosswise into 3-x-¾-inch strips (or use canapé or cookie cutters to cut out shapes of your choice).

Place the dough strips or shapes into the buttered pan. Drizzle the dough with the remaining butter. Bake until the biscuits have risen and browned, about 15 minutes. Serve warm.

℀ Self-rising flour is convenient because it already contains baking powder and salt. But it's not convenient if you have to run to the store to buy some; just make your own. For every 1 cup flour, remove 1 teaspoon flour and replace it with 1 teaspoon baking powder plus ½ teaspoon salt.

℀ If you happen to have an end piece of ham or prosciutto, this is a good way to use it.

℀ If you use a cookie cutter, the yield may vary depending on the size of the biscuits they make.

tip

Ken Haedrich (*Soup Makes the Meal,* Harvard Common Press) has two good biscuit tips. One is to add 1 table-spoon cornstarch for every 2 cups flour to make especially light, tender biscuits. And, if you have no biscuit cutter, re-move both ends of a tomato-paste can, wash it well, and use it to cut the biscuits.

green onion buttermilk biscuits

IF YOU LIVE ON THE WEST COAST, you call them green onions; on the East Coast, they're scallions. They're delicious in biscuits, as we've seen in several recipes this year. This one wins our vote; it's a little sweet, which is a nice foil for the onions, it's made with butter and buttermilk (more thumbs-up from us), and it has a lovely golden glaze on top.

These biscuits are very good for breakfast or dinner, even Thanksgiving dinner, which is how the Day family in Missouri serves them. You can make them up to six hours ahead and reheat them, you can play with herbs (try adding some fresh dill), or you can substitute chives for the green onions/scallions — they're very versatile and easy to make.

The recipe makes a Thanksgiving kind of amount but cuts in half perfectly to serve six.

makes about 28 biscuits

4 cups all-purpose flour

1/4 cup sugar

2 tablespoons baking powder

2 teaspoons salt

3/4 cup (1 1/2 sticks) cold unsalted butter, cut into small pieces

1 1/2 cups chilled buttermilk, plus more if needed

1/4 cup finely chopped green onions (scallions)

1 large egg, beaten for glazing

Preheat the oven to 425 degrees. In a large bowl, whisk together the flour, sugar, baking powder, and salt. Add the butter and rub in with your fingertips until the mixture resembles coarse meal. Add the 1 1/2 cups buttermilk and green onions and stir until moist clumps form, adding more buttermilk by tablespoonfuls if the dough is dry.

Gather the dough together; divide in half. Flatten each half on a floured work surface to a 3/4-inch thickness. Using a 2-inch cookie cutter, cut out biscuits. Gather the excess dough, pat it out again, and cut out more biscuits.

Place the biscuits on ungreased baking sheets and brush each with the beaten egg. Bake the biscuits until cooked through and golden brown on top, about 16 minutes. Serve hot. You can make the biscuits up to 6 hours ahead. Let them stand on the baking sheets at room temperature and reheat in a 325-degree oven for 5 minutes just before serving.

cook's notes

- We like to double the green onions in this recipe, so you can really taste the onion flavor.
- Try to handle the dough as lightly as possible for the airiest biscuits.

tip

For great buttermilk biscuits, *The Baker's Dozen Cookbook* recommends kneading the dough briefly, about 15 turns, which will give it strength to rise. And more: To save last-minute time, you can make the dough to the point of adding the buttermilk up to 12 hours ahead. Cover the bowl tightly and chill it in the refrigerator until you're ready to add the buttermilk and bake the biscuits. These will taste a lot fresher than reheated biscuits.

SOURCE: *Moosewood Restaurant New Classics*
by the Moosewood Collective
COOK: Kip Wilcox

lemon-thyme biscuits

THESE VERY FRAGRANT BISCUITS celebrate that great combination of lemon zest and fresh thyme that lights all faces at the table. The biscuits are homey and elegant at the same time, great with soups or stews or roast chicken.

You can mix them in the food processor, which saves lots of time. Even a nonbaking beginner will turn out great-looking biscuits with no problems. The dough is wonderfully forgiving and easy to work with; if you don't usually feel comfortable rolling things out, these biscuits will be a snap.

serves 6

4 tablespoons (1/2 stick) cold butter, cut into small pieces

1 tablespoon grated fresh lemon zest

2 cups unbleached all-purpose flour

1 tablespoon sugar

2 teaspoons baking powder

1/2 teaspoon baking soda

1/2 teaspoon salt

2–3 tablespoons chopped fresh thyme

3/4 cup plus 2 tablespoons buttermilk, plus more for brushing

Preheat the oven to 425 degrees. Lightly oil a baking sheet. In a medium bowl or food processor, place the butter pieces and lemon zest. Sift the flour, sugar, baking powder, baking soda, and salt over the butter and lemon zest. By hand or in the food processor, mix the butter with the flour mixture until evenly distributed. Add the thyme and mix well. Add the buttermilk and stir or pulse briefly. The dough will be soft and a little sticky.

On a lightly floured work surface, pat the dough into a 9-inch circle about 1/2 inch thick. Slice it into 6 wedges. Place the wedges on the prepared baking sheet and brush the tops with a little buttermilk. Bake for 20 minutes, or until firm and golden brown. Serve immediately.

cook's note

🌱 For lemon zest, the best tool is a Microplane zester. Use it upside down, as though you were playing the fruit like a violin, and the zest will collect neatly on the back. Zip, zip, you're done.

breads

SOURCE: *The Baker's Dozen Cookbook,*
edited by Rick Rodgers
COOK: Carol Field

orange-rum sweet bread

AS MUCH AS WE LOVE THE BIG, bold, killer flavors of so many recipes these days, there are definitely times when all we crave is something good and simple and delicious. Here it is: a lovely, golden brown, mildly sweet loaf with a tender texture. Soft and fragrant with the scent of rum and orange, this bread goes well with morning coffee or afternoon tea. Carol Field also suggests serving it with a glass of vin santo. We volunteer that it toasts up beautifully.

Using a starter adds an extra step to this recipe, but it's largely unattended time, and it solves a big problem with sweet breads. Typically, the sugar in the dough makes the yeast ferment too quickly, which compromises the taste and texture of most sweet breads. The starter deliberately slows down the yeast action and ensures a delicate, full-flavored loaf.

makes 1 large loaf

SPONGE

1/2 cup whole milk, heated to lukewarm (100–110 degrees), or more if needed for the dough

2 1/2 teaspoons active dry yeast

2/3 cup all-purpose flour

DOUGH

1/4 cup dark rum

3 1/4 cups all-purpose flour, or more if

needed

1 teaspoon fine sea salt

3 large eggs, at room temperature

1/3 cup sugar

2 oranges

1/4 cup olive oil (not extra-virgin; see note)

1 large egg white, beaten with 2 teaspoons water, for glazing

TO MAKE THE SPONGE:

Into the bowl of a stand mixer, pour the warm milk and sprinkle the yeast on top. Let stand until the yeast dissolves, about 5 minutes. Add the flour and stir vigorously with a wooden spoon to form a thick batter. Cover tightly with plastic wrap. Let stand at room temperature until the sponge is bubbly and doubles in volume, 30 to 45 minutes.

TO MAKE THE DOUGH:

Add the rum to the sponge in the bowl. Attach the bowl to the mixer and fit with the paddle attachment. Add 1 cup of the flour and the salt and mix on low speed until smooth. Add 2 of the eggs and 1 cup of the remaining flour and mix until smooth. Beat in the remaining egg, then the remaining 1¹/₄ cups flour and the sugar. Grate the zest of the 2 oranges right into the bowl, removing the bowl from the stand if necessary to do so. (Reserve the zested oranges for another use.) With the mixer on low speed, add the oil in a slow, steady stream, then mix for 3 minutes. Switch to the dough hook and knead on medium-low speed until the dough is firm, elastic, and velvety with a barely sticky surface, about 3 minutes. If the dough seems too firm, beat in an additional tablespoon or so of milk; if too wet, add flour 1 tablespoon at a time.

Detach the dough hook and remove the bowl from the stand. Cover the bowl tightly with plastic wrap. Let stand until the dough is doubled in volume, about 3 hours.

Lightly oil a 2-quart round soufflé dish or charlotte mold. Turn the dough onto a floured work surface and shape it into a round. Fit rounded side up into the prepared dish. Cover with a moistened kitchen towel. Let stand at room temperature until the dough has risen to the top of the dish, about 2 hours.

Preheat the oven to 400 degrees with a rack in the middle. Brush the top of the dough with some of the egg white glaze. Bake for 15 minutes. Reduce the oven temperature to 350 degrees and bake until the bread is golden and sounds hollow when the bottom is tapped, about 20 minutes more.

Transfer to a wire rack and cool for 30 minutes. Remove from the dish and cool completely on the rack.

cook's notes

- Assertively flavored olive oil will overpower the bread, so choose the olive oil carefully. Traditionally, this recipe would have been made with a neutral-tasting pure olive oil, but if you can't find one, look for a milder type of extra-virgin, such as the French ones.
- If you don't have a 2-quart soufflé dish, you can use a slightly larger one, just don't wait for the dough to rise all the way to the top of the dish.

SOURCE: *Gourmet*
COOK: Gina Marie Miraglia

corn bread with fennel seeds, dried cranberries, and golden raisins

THIS CORN BREAD IS DISTINCTIVE in a number of ways, not least that it can be made three days ahead. That's because it's actually corny bread, not corn bread; there's a lot less cornmeal than regular flour in it. It reminds us of one of our favorite breads, the semolina loaf from Amy's bakery in Manhattan, which also contains fennel seeds and golden raisins. But the dried cranberries are a brilliant addition that makes this especially appropriate for the holidays. And frankly, we couldn't stop eating it.

The original recipe recommends baking 10 miniature loaves, which in our case meant buying 10 pans. But you can also bake the corn bread in two regular metal loaf pans, which is what we've done here. You shouldn't let lack of the right equipment stop you from making this delicious bread.

serves 10

1 1/3 cups all-purpose flour
2/3 cup yellow cornmeal (not coarse)
1/3 cup sugar
1 1/2 teaspoons baking powder
3/4 teaspoon baking soda
3/4 teaspoon salt
1 1/2 cups well-shaken buttermilk
3/4 cup (1 1/2 sticks) unsalted butter, melted and cooled

2 large eggs
1/2 cup golden raisins, coarsely chopped
1/2 cup dried cranberries, coarsely chopped
1 1/2 tablespoons fennel seeds, coarsely crushed with a mortar and pestle or pulsed in an electric coffee/spice grinder

Preheat the oven to 375 degrees with a rack in the middle. Butter two 8-x-4-x-3-inch metal loaf pans and dust with flour, knocking out any excess. In a large bowl, stir together the flour, cornmeal, sugar, baking powder, baking soda, and salt. In a medium bowl, whisk together the buttermilk, melted butter, and eggs and add to the flour mixture, stirring until just combined. Stir in the raisins, cranberries, and fennel seeds.

Divide the batter between the pans, smoothing the tops, and let stand for 10 minutes. Bake until the tops are pale golden and a tester inserted in the center of a loaf comes out clean, about 35 minutes. Transfer to a wire rack and cool for 10 minutes. Remove the loaves from the pans and cool completely on the rack.

cook's notes

- To make the corn bread up to 3 days ahead, bake it, cool it, and wrap it tightly in plastic wrap. Keep at room temperature.

- To make individual loaves, use ten 3-x-2-x-1½-inch loaf pans and bake for 20 to 25 minutes.

desserts

SOURCE: *New York Times*
COOK: Bill Yosses

the best chocolate chip cookies

AMERICA'S FAVORITE COOKIE turns up in dozens of guises every year, all enjoyable but none particularly outstanding. This one is different. New York chef Bill Yosses trained under the chocolate master himself, Robert Linxe at La Maison du Chocolat in Paris, so when he turned his attention to the all-too-often bland and dry chocolate chip cookie, we took note. They're just as easy to make as any other chocolate chip cookies, but these have two secret ingredients that up the taste ante: a little hazelnut butter (or peanut butter) and the pulp of a vanilla bean are beaten into the creamed butter and sugar. The results: a cookie with a hint of nuttiness and a chewy, moist texture that lasts for a few days.

Chances are you won't be able to identify the flavor of the nut butter, but you'll enjoy the richness it provides. And finally, instead of ordinary chocolate chips, chop bars of top-shelf bittersweet chocolate into rough quarter-inch pieces. You'll get a bigger hit of chocolate, and the cookies look prettier, too.

makes about 48 cookies

8 tablespoons (1 stick) unsalted butter, at room temperature
1 cup sugar
1/2 cup light brown sugar
1/4 cup unsweetened hazelnut butter or peanut butter
2 large eggs
1 vanilla bean, split lengthwise, pulp scraped out

2 1/3 cups all-purpose flour
1 teaspoon baking soda
1 teaspoon salt
12 ounces bittersweet chocolate, chopped into 1/4-inch or larger pieces
1/2 cup chopped nuts (optional)

Preheat the oven to 375 degrees. Line 3 baking sheets with parchment paper. In a stand mixer fitted with the paddle attachment, cream the butter and sugars. Add the hazelnut butter or peanut butter, beating until smooth. Beat in the eggs and the vanilla bean pulp, scraping down the bowl as needed.

In a large bowl, sift together the flour, baking soda, and salt. Gradually add the dry ingredients to the butter mixture, and mix on low speed until the dough comes together. Mix in the chocolate pieces and the nuts, if using. Drop heaping tablespoons of the dough 2 inches apart onto the prepared baking sheets, flattening them slightly by hand.

Bake until lightly browned, 9 to 12 minutes. Cool the cookie sheets on a wire rack before removing the cookies.

cook's notes

- Unsweetened hazelnut butter, sometimes called hazelnut paste, can be found at some health food and specialty stores. We found it at Kalustyan's, 123 Lexington Avenue, New York, NY 10016; 212-685-3451; www.kalustyans.com. Creamy peanut butter makes a fine substitute.

- Bill Yosses recommends using a chocolate with at least 60 percent cocoa.

SOURCE: *New York Times*
COOK: **Dorie Greenspan after Lionel Poilâne**

french butter cookies

FOR SOME AFICIONADOS, nothing says Paris like the ethereal but rich butter cookies found at the legendary Poilâne bakery on the Rue du Cherche-Midi. These are not at all like American cookies; instead, they're delicate, subtle, tender, with a slight crunch and a pale golden ivory color. The flavor is pure butter, preferably the rich, complex, slightly tangy cultured French butter, which is hitting our shores in huge amounts as American gourmets develop a taste for it. We even have some homegrown cultured butter now.

If you want to make these cookies and can't find French butter, look for Vermont Butter & Cheese Company's cultured butter or Plugrá, a widely distributed extra-rich butter favored by chefs. There's not even a pinch of salt or a drop of vanilla here to bump up the flavor — so it's all about butter, and using the right one is crucial. The cookies will still be good if you make them with premium American butter, but they won't have the touch of acidity that renders the French version so divine.

makes about 70 cookies

10 tablespoons (1¼ sticks) unsalted French or premium American butter, at room temperature

½ cup sugar
1 large egg, at room temperature
2 cups all-purpose flour

In a stand mixer, beat the butter on low speed until smooth. Add the sugar and continue to beat until it's blended into the butter. Add the egg and beat on low speed until it is incorporated. Add the flour and mix only until it disappears; do not overmix.

Transfer the dough to a work surface and knead it 6 to 8 times, or until it just comes together. Divide the dough in half, shape each half into a 4-inch disk, wrap in plastic, and chill until firm, about 4 hours.

Preheat the oven to 350 degrees with racks in the top and bottom third. Line 2 baking sheets with parchment paper.

Working with one disk at a time, roll out the dough on a heavily floured work surface until it is ¹/₈ to ¹/₄ inch thick. Using a 1¹/₂-inch round cookie cutter, cut out as many cookies as you can. Place the cookies on the prepared baking sheets. Gather any scraps into a disk, chill them, then roll them out and cut.

Bake the cookies for 8 to 10 minutes, or until set; they should not take on much color. Cool on a wire rack.

cook's notes

- To knead the dough: use the heel of your hand to smush and slide the dough across the board, gather it up with a bench scraper, and fold it back onto itself. Repeat 6 to 8 times, or until the dough is homogeneous and smooth. This is the same technique the French use for pâte sablé.

- When you remove the disks from the refrigerator, they may be too hard to roll out, since high-fat butter firms up so much. Either let them sit a bit or slap the disks a few times with a rolling pin to begin to flatten and soften them. Don't worry if the dough tears as you roll. Simply patch it and continue.

tip

TV cooking star Ming Tsai makes lovely Asian butter cookies by adding ¹/₂ teaspoon almond extract and ¹/₂ teaspoon five-spice powder to a standard rich butter cookie recipe like this one. Delightful!

SOURCE: *Dallas Morning News*
COOK: Sue Dauzat

orange-almond lace cookies

THESE COOKIES WON FIRST PLACE in the "decadent" category of the *Dallas Morning News* holiday cookie contest. They are reminiscent of the classic florentine but much less demanding to make. In fact, they come together in no time at all. Stir everything in a saucepan, then drop onto a baking sheet. They bake up beautifully lacy and golden. The texture is delicate, chewy, and satisfying, and the flavor is sweet and nutty, with a good shot of orange.

Even though the drizzle of chocolate is optional, we can't imagine making these without it — especially since it does such a nice job of dressing up these elegant cookies.

makes about 36 cookies

¾ cup (1½ sticks) unsalted butter
1½ cups finely chopped almonds
¾ cup sugar
1 tablespoon all-purpose flour
2 teaspoons finely grated fresh
    orange zest
½ teaspoon salt
1 large egg, beaten
    Melted chocolate, for garnish
    (optional)

Preheat the oven to 325 degrees. Line a baking sheet with parchment paper. In a medium saucepan, melt the butter over medium heat. Remove from the heat and stir in the almonds, sugar, flour, orange zest, and salt. Mix to combine and then stir in the beaten egg.

Drop tablespoons of the dough 3 inches apart on the prepared baking sheet. Bake until golden brown and crispy-lacy, 10 to 12 minutes. Let cool completely. If desired, drizzle melted chocolate over the top. These are best eaten the same day.

cook's notes

Don't even try to make these without parchment paper. The cookies will stick to your baking sheets and make a horrible mess.

Be sure to drop the cookies at least 3 inches apart on the baking sheet since they spread quite a bit — after all, that's what makes them lace cookies.

If you live in a dry climate, you may find that these will keep for a day or two. It's the humidity that will make them weepy and soft.

Use a semisweet or dark chocolate for the drizzle to best offset the sweet orange flavor in the cookie.

tip

If you want to drizzle chocolate over the cookies but don't have a small pastry bag and don't want to fashion one out of parchment, here's a solution. Melissa Murphy Hagenbart, a contributor to *Fine Cooking,* recommends dipping the tines of a fork into melted chocolate and then using it to trail the chocolate across the cookies.

SOURCE: *The All-American Cookie Book*
by Nancy Baggett
COOK: Nancy Baggett

snickerdoodles

SNICKERDOODLES ARE OLD-FASHIONED, completely American cookies you may remember from your childhood, or your grandmother's cookie plate. They're large, mildly spiced (especially if you take the nutmeg option, which we urge you to do) sugar cookies with a crispy-chewy texture that's very satisfying. The little bit of corn syrup in the recipe helps keep the cookies chewy in the center but crisp around the edges.

Despite their catchy name, snickerdoodles don't sound very exciting, but you'll be surprised at how fast they disappear — people just love them. This recipe is an adaptation of one from a 1902 Estherville, Iowa, cookbook.

makes about 35 cookies

2²/₃ cups all-purpose flour
2 teaspoons cream of tartar
1 teaspoon baking soda
½ teaspoon salt
¼ teaspoon ground nutmeg (optional)
1 cup (2 sticks) unsalted butter, slightly softened

1³/₄ cups sugar
1½ tablespoons light corn syrup
2 large eggs
2½ teaspoons pure vanilla extract

¼ cup sugar, combined with 1½ teaspoons ground cinnamon, for topping

Preheat the oven to 375 degrees with a rack in the top third. Grease several baking sheets or coat with nonstick cooking spray.

In a large bowl, thoroughly stir together the flour, cream of tartar, baking soda, salt, and nutmeg, if using; set aside. In another large bowl, with an electric mixer on medium speed, beat together the butter, sugar, and corn syrup until well blended and fluffy, about 2 minutes. Add the eggs and vanilla and beat until well blended and smooth. Beat in half of the flour mixture until evenly incorporated. Stir in the remaining flour mixture until evenly incorporated. Let the dough stand for 5 to 10 minutes, or until firmed up slightly. Put the cinnamon-sugar in a shallow bowl.

Roll portions of the dough into generous 1½-inch balls with lightly greased hands (the dough will be soft). Roll each ball in the cinnamon-sugar. Place about

2³/4 inches apart on the baking sheets. Using your hand, slightly pat down the tops of the balls.

Bake the cookies, one sheet at a time, for 8 to 11 minutes, or until just light golden brown at the edges. Reverse the sheet from front to back halfway through baking to ensure even browning. Transfer the sheet to a wire rack and let stand until the cookies firm up slightly, 1 to 2 minutes. Using a spatula, transfer the cookies to wire racks. Let stand until completely cooled. Let the baking sheets cool between batches to prevent the cookies from spreading too much.

Store in an airtight container for up to 10 days or freeze for up to 2 months.

tips

- If you're using cooking spray on the baking sheets, how do you avoid getting oily film all over your countertops as well? CleverChef.com has a very clever solution: open the dishwasher and spray the sheet while it's resting on the dishwasher door. Any sprayed oil will get washed away with the next load of dishes.

- Although the recipe says to grease your hands to roll the cookies into balls, we admit that we did it with ungreased hands and had no trouble. Where things can get messy, however, is when you roll the cookies in the cinnamon sugar. The neatest way to do this is to first shape a whole baking sheet worth of cookies, and *then* roll them in the sugar so you're not reaching back into the cookie dough with sugary hands

SOURCE: *In the Sweet Kitchen* by Regan Daley
COOK: **Regan Daley**

butter–toffee crunch shortbread

WE FOUND THIS RECIPE in a prizewinning Canadian cookbook that captured the hearts and minds of the American culinary world this year. We love Regan Daley's basic brown sugar shortbread with the brilliant addition of butterscotch morsels and candy toffee bits (like Heath Bar crunch). It's buttery and crumbly and easy to make. These cookies are a huge hit with everyone from candy-loving kids to more discriminating grown-up palates.

The little bit of rice flour or cornstarch in the dough makes the shortbread even tenderer than most. The only tricky part is making sure you cut the shortbread into fingers before it has cooled completely and set up. The recipe makes a big batch, but since they keep so well (they even freeze well) and are perfect for gift giving, we're happy making a full batch. You can, however, easily cut the recipe in half if you're feeling less exuberant.

makes fifty 3-inch fingers

2$\frac{1}{2}$ cups all-purpose flour

$\frac{2}{3}$ cup rice flour (cornstarch may be substituted)

$\frac{1}{2}$ teaspoon salt

1$\frac{1}{2}$ cups (3 sticks) unsalted butter, at room temperature

6 tablespoons fruit sugar or superfine sugar (see note)

6 tablespoons firmly packed light brown sugar

$\frac{3}{4}$ cup miniature butterscotch chips

$\frac{3}{4}$ cup English toffee pieces for baking, such as Skor or Heath Bar bits

Preheat the oven to 325 degrees with a rack in the middle. Butter a 9-x-13-inch metal baking pan. Line the bottom and up the two long sides of the pan with a piece of parchment paper. Leave about a 1-inch overhang on the sides to make removing the cooled shortbread easier.

Into a large bowl, sift the flour, rice flour or cornstarch, and salt; set aside. In the bowl of a stand mixer fitted with the paddle attachment or in a large bowl with a wooden spoon, beat the butter until very smooth. Gradually add the sugars and cream the mixture until it is very light and fluffy. If using a mixer, transfer the butter-sugar mixture to a large bowl. Add the flour mixture, about $\frac{1}{2}$ cup at a time, fully incorporating each addition before adding the next. Use your fingers to knead the final portion of the flour mixture into the dough, keeping your palms off the dough as much as possible so the warmth doesn't turn the butter oily. When the last of the flour is fully blended, add the butterscotch chips and toffee bits and knead them into the dough until evenly distributed.

Press the dough firmly into the prepared pan and use the back of a metal spoon to smooth the surface. Prick the dough all over with a fork. Bake for 45 minutes, then prick the dough again to release any trapped air. Bake for 15 to 30 minutes more, or until the edges are light golden brown and the center feels just firm to the touch.

The shortbread will set to a very firm biscuit as it cools, so it must be cut while still warm. Cool the pan on a wire rack for 7 to 8 minutes, then run a sharp paring knife around the outside of the shortbread to loosen the edges. Cut the shortbread into thirds lengthwise, dividing it evenly into three long rectangles. Then cut the rectangles crosswise into about $3/4$-inch fingers, wiping the knife on a clean kitchen towel between each cut, since it gets sticky and can pull and tear at the cooling shortbread. Leave the shortbread to cool completely in the pan, then recut and serve or transfer to airtight tins.

cook's notes

- The quality of the butter makes a difference in this recipe; be sure yours is as fresh as possible.
- This shortbread can be frozen before or after it is baked. Freeze the raw dough pressed into the prepared pan, well wrapped with plastic and aluminum foil. Thaw overnight in the refrigerator, without disturbing the wrapping. Unwrap and bake directly from the refrigerator. The baking time may have to be increased by a few minutes to compensate for the chilled dough. To freeze after baking, freeze the cooled fingers in airtight bags or containers, layering between sheets of waxed or parchment paper and wrapping the whole tin or container with aluminum foil. Thaw the entire package, without removing the wrapping, at room temperature for 6 to 8 hours.
- Fruit sugar, also labeled as fructose, is sold in some supermarkets and natural food stores. It has a finer granule, much like superfine sugar, and thus makes a smoother dough. If unavailable, spin granulated sugar in a food processor until it is finely ground.
- If you use a glass baking pan, expect the shortbread to cook a bit more quickly.

SOURCE: *Sweet Seasons* by Richard Leach
COOK: Richard Leach

coconut-basil macaroons

THE COMBINATION OF BASIL AND COCONUT is one that we've grown to love in many Thai dishes, so when we saw this recipe for coconut-basil macaroons, we couldn't resist. Sure, it's a little odd, but that doesn't stop it from being delicious. Basil is, after all, a close cousin to mint, and we think it has just as big a claim to appear in sweet things.

We probably don't need to add that these chewy macaroons are a great finish to an Asian meal.

makes 30 macaroons

5$\frac{1}{2}$ cups unsweetened coconut, finely chopped

$\frac{3}{4}$ cup corn syrup

$\frac{1}{2}$ cup sugar

9 large egg whites (about 1$\frac{1}{2}$ cups)

$\frac{1}{2}$ cup all-purpose flour

8–12 basil leaves, finely chopped

In a large bowl, combine 3$\frac{1}{2}$ cups of the coconut, the corn syrup, sugar, 3 of the egg whites, and the flour. Mix until well blended. Add the basil and mix just enough to incorporate. Form the mixture into 1-inch balls and place in the freezer to harden. The mixture will be very sticky. If you have trouble shaping them into perfect balls, it's no problem to reshape them once they are well chilled.

Preheat the oven to 300 degrees. Line a baking sheet with parchment paper. Coat the balls lightly with the remaining 6 egg whites and dredge in the remaining 2 cups coconut. Place on the prepared baking sheet. Bake the macaroons until very light golden brown, about 20 minutes. Cool on a rack and serve.

cook's notes

- When baking at lower temperatures, such as the 300 degrees in this recipe, you may find that your oven bakes quite a bit faster than you expect it to — it's hard for some ovens to hold a low temperature. Check the macaroons at about 18 minutes, but don't be surprised if they take a full 30 minutes to become golden.
- It's a good idea to have a little extra coconut on hand, because depending on how heavily you dredge the macaroons, you may find that you need a bit more than called for.

SOURCE: *BayWolf Restaurant Cookbook*
by Michael Wild and Lauren Lyle
COOK: G. Earl Darny

almond crisps

THESE AREN'T REALLY COOKIES, but stacks of slivered almonds glued together with crunchy sugar and toasted to a lovely golden brown. We've never seen anything quite like them, but if we had, we think it would have been in Paris. You can easily imagine them on the cookie plate that arrives at the end of a French restaurant meal — a crisp, lightly sweet tidbit with the savory goodness of toasted almonds. They're elegant and insouciant and easy as pie — easier, actually — to make.

They are a good addition to any cookie plate, and they'd also work with sweetmeats, those delectable little delicacies to be enjoyed with coffee and perhaps an after-dinner drink.

makes 10 crisps

1 cup slivered blanched almonds
$\frac{1}{2}$ cup plus 1 tablespoon sugar

Preheat the oven to 350 degrees. Line a baking sheet with parchment paper. In a small bowl, mix the almonds with 1 tablespoon water. Add the $\frac{1}{2}$ cup sugar and mix well. Pile the sugar-coated almonds in little mounds on the prepared baking sheet. They will not spread, so don't worry about spacing them closely. Sprinkle with the remaining 1 tablespoon sugar. Bake for 10 to 12 minutes, or until they just stick together and are golden in color. Lift the parchment to a rack to cool. Serve at room temperature.

SOURCE: *Williams-Sonoma Taste*
COOK: Deborah Madison

pecan brittle with black pepper

VEGETARIAN SUPERSTAR COOK Deborah Madison is passionate about sweetmeats, those intriguing little tidbits that have finished a good meal for centuries. She thinks they're as appropriate at the contemporary table as they were at the ancient banquet table, and we think she's right. We love restaurant meals that end with a little plate of treats from the kitchen, but it's rare to find them served at home.

Along with the predictable (but nonetheless wonderful) candied citrus peels and bits of chocolate and nuts, sweetmeats can be so interesting they knock your socks off. That's what we're talking about here, a sophisticated adult candy so enticing you can't stop eating it. It's nothing more complicated than pecans in caramel, but there's a secret ingredient: black pepper. The pepper, the crackle of the caramel, and the perfect complement of a toasty sweet nut make this brittle divine, and it's very simple to make.

This is a wonderful gift to bring along to any holiday dinner.

makes about ³/₄ pound

1 cup pecan halves
1 cup sugar
¹/₂ cup corn syrup
¹/₂ teaspoon salt

¹/₂–1 teaspoon freshly ground black pepper
1¹/₂ tablespoons unsalted butter, cut into small pieces

Preheat the oven to 350 degrees. On a baking sheet, toast the pecans until fragrant and starting to darken, 5 to 7 minutes. Lightly butter a rimmed baking sheet. Spread the pecans in a single close layer on the sheet.

In a medium saucepan, combine the sugar, corn syrup, and ¹/₂ cup water over medium heat. Cook, swirling the pan, until the sugar is completely dissolved. Cover and cook for 1 minute more. Uncover and cook, without stirring, until the syrup turns medium amber and reaches 295 degrees (hard-ball stage) on a candy thermometer.

Remove from the heat and stir in the salt and pepper, then the butter. The mixture will foam up. Pour it over the nuts while it's still foamy, spreading it out a little. When the brittle is cool, break it into pieces and store in an airtight container.

cook's note

- If the caramel doesn't turn color at 295 degrees, let it go just a little higher, until it does. Remove from the heat immediately.

- When you arrange the pecans on the baking sheet, don't expect them to cover the entire pan. Rather, they should be clustered together in a single, close layer in the center of the pan so that when you pour on the caramel, it can spread easily.

SOURCE: *Los Angeles Times*
COOK: **Marcy Goldman**

matzo buttercrunch

WE WERE SKEPTICAL — but this recipe really works and is really delicious. It has great crunch, a rich buttery flavor, and chocolate on top. It's much like standard buttercrunch or butter-toffee bark, but the matzo adds a little something extra — like having bread with chocolate, the matzo is a good counterpoint to the richness of the toffee and chocolate.

Serve this as a dessert or treat, or even pack it into tins to give as gifts at the holidays. In a tight container, it keeps for days.

We like the unusual technique here, too. Instead of cooking the butter-sugar mixture on the stovetop all the way, you pour it over the single layer of matzo and let it bubble away in the oven for 15 minutes. It works like a charm.

The only downside we've found to this recipe (aside from its addictive qualities) is that we haven't figured out how to make it if you have a side-by-side freezer, since you really need to be able to slide the rimmed baking sheet into the freezer. You could probably just chill it in the refrigerator for a longer time; for that matter, it would eventually set up at room temperature, too.

serves 6 to 8

4–6 unsalted matzos (preferably regular, but you can use egg)

16 tablespoons (2 sticks) unsalted butter or Passover margarine

1 cup firmly packed brown sugar

¾ cup coarsely chopped semisweet chocolate or chocolate chips

Toasted slivered almonds, for garnish (optional)

Preheat the oven to 350 degrees. Stack 2 rimmed baking sheets together (this will insulate the buttercrunch so it won't burn in the oven). Line the top sheet with aluminum foil, then with a sheet of parchment paper. Arrange the matzos as evenly as possible in a single layer on the baking sheet, cutting the squares into pieces as needed to fill any gaps. Set aside.

In a medium heavy saucepan, heat the butter or margarine and brown sugar, whisking to combine, and bring to a medium boil for 2 to 4 minutes. Remove from the heat and pour over the matzos. Pour as evenly as possible, but if you miss any spots, use a spatula to spread the butter-sugar mixture to cover all the matzos.

Bake for about 15 minutes. Remove from the oven and sprinkle the chocolate over the top. Let stand for 5 minutes, then smear the top with a metal spatula to spread the chocolate evenly. Sprinkle on the slivered almonds, if using. Slide the entire baking sheet into the freezer and freeze until firm, 1 hour or less. Break the buttercrunch into pieces, squares or odd shapes, and serve.

cook's notes

- Although the cook says the toasted almonds are optional, we can't imagine making this without them.
- During baking, keep an eye out for any bits of exposed matzo to be sure they don't burn.
- A 6-ounce bag of chocolate chips will give you the $3/4$ cup you need.
- Use a light touch when you smear the chocolate so that you don't mess up the buttercrunch layer, which has not set completely yet.
- Be careful when you freeze the buttercrunch not to let any ice or freezer frost drip onto it — any water will cause it to weep and melt.

desserts

SOURCE: *Mom's Big Book of Baking*
by Lauren Chattman
COOK: Lauren Chattman

coconut-ginger blondies

HERE IS AN UPDATED VERSION of an old favorite, butterscotch blondies. These dense and chewy bars turn tropical with crystallized ginger, flaked coconut, and a splash of rum. They're just as quick to make as a batch of brownies, and they offer a nice change from chocolate. Better yet, everything gets mixed together in a saucepan — no mixing bowl needed — and the foil-lined pan makes cleanup a nonissue.

makes 16 blondies

1 cup all-purpose flour
1 teaspoon baking powder
1 teaspoon ground ginger
1/4 teaspoon salt
8 tablespoons (1 stick) unsalted butter
1 cup firmly packed light brown sugar

1 large egg
2 tablespoons dark rum (optional)
1 teaspoon pure vanilla extract
3/4 cup sweetened flaked coconut
1/2 cup chopped unsalted cashews (optional)
1/4 cup finely chopped crystallized ginger

Preheat the oven to 350 degrees. Line an 8-inch-square baking pan with heavy-duty aluminum foil, making sure that the foil is tucked into all the corners and that there is at least 1 inch overhanging the edge of the pan on all sides.

In a small bowl, combine the flour, baking powder, ground ginger, and salt; set aside.

In a medium saucepan, melt the butter over low heat. Remove from the heat and, with a wooden spoon, stir in the brown sugar until it is dissolved. Let the mixture cool just a bit, then quickly whisk in the egg, rum (if using), and vanilla. Stir in the flour mixture until just incorporated. Stir in the coconut, cashews (if using), and crystallized ginger.

Pour the batter into the prepared pan. Bake the blondies until they are just set in the center, 25 to 30 minutes. Let them cool completely on a wire rack. Grasping the overhanging foil on either side of the pan, lift out the blondies and place them on a cutting board. Cut into 16 squares and serve.

cook's notes

- Work quickly when whisking the egg into the warm butter-sugar mixture, lest you end up scrambling it.
- Don't overbake these — they should be just barely set in the center — or they will be overly chewy.
- These blondies will keep at room temperature in an airtight container for up to 3 days.

SOURCE: *Barefoot Contessa Parties!* by Ina Garten
COOK: Ina Garten

lemon pound cake

THIS LEMONY POUND CAKE is very much like our all-time favorite, Maida Heatter's Lemon Cake — though Ina Garten has managed to get even more lemon into it. It's a perfectly made cake with lemon syrup poured over to give it extra moisture and flavor, plus a lemon glaze. The glaze gives the cake a homespun look, but you could skip it. The lemon flavor is the point here, and it really sings.

The cake is a homey one that's so moist you can make it a day ahead and serve it for tea as well as dessert. It's delicious with berries and a dollop of lemon curd on the side. In theory, it should be a keeper cake, but frankly, we've never managed to have it around long enough to find out.

makes two 8-inch loaves

1 cup (2 sticks) unsalted butter	$1/2$ teaspoon baking soda
$2^1/2$ cups sugar	$3/4$ cup fresh lemon juice
4 extra-large eggs, at room temperature	$3/4$ cup buttermilk, at room temperature
$1/3$ cup grated fresh lemon zest (from 6–8 large lemons)	1 teaspoon pure vanilla extract
3 cups all-purpose flour	GLAZE
1 teaspoon kosher salt	2 cups powdered sugar
$1/2$ teaspoon baking powder	$3^1/2$ tablespoons fresh lemon juice

Preheat the oven to 350 degrees. Grease two $8^1/2$-x-$4^1/4$-inch loaf pans.

In the bowl of an electric mixer fitted with the paddle attachment, cream the butter and 2 cups of the sugar for about 5 minutes, or until light and fluffy. With the mixer on medium speed, add the eggs, one at a time, and the lemon zest.

Into a medium bowl, sift together the flour, salt, baking powder, and baking soda. In a small bowl, combine $1/4$ cup of the lemon juice, the buttermilk, and vanilla. Add the flour and buttermilk mixtures alternately to the butter mixture, beginning and ending with the flour. Divide the batter evenly between the prepared pans, smooth the tops, and bake for 45 to 60 minutes, or until a cake tester inserted in the middle of a loaf comes out clean.

In a small saucepan, combine the remaining $^1/_2$ cup sugar with the remaining $^1/_2$ cup lemon juice over low heat, and cook until the sugar dissolves.

When the cakes are done, let them cool for 10 minutes, then invert them onto a wire rack set over a tray and spoon the lemon syrup over the cakes. Let the cakes cool completely.

TO MAKE THE GLAZE:

In a medium bowl, combine the powdered sugar and lemon juice, mixing with a wire whisk until smooth. Pour the glaze over the top of the cakes and let it drip down the sides.

cook's notes

- When making the glaze, you may need more lemon juice to get the right consistency. The glaze should pour easily and drip down the sides of the cakes but still cover them.
- You can use metal or glass loaf pans; we prefer metal because the cake doesn't get as brown on the outside, so it stays more tender. Loaf cakes look homey, but for a more impressive cake, bake it in an 8-cup bundt pan. To dress it up further, press some candied lemon slices into the top of the glazed cake. (To make these, in a small saucepan, mix $^1/_4$ cup water with $^1/_4$ cup plus 2 tablespoons sugar, boil it, and add thin lemon slices. Cook them slowly for just a few minutes to absorb the sugar, then let them cool on a wire rack before arranging on the cake.)

tips

- It's important for the butter to be the right temperature for creaming (70 degrees) — otherwise, it won't hold the air. You should be able to pick up the stick of butter and bend it without melting it in your fingers, says Carolyn Weil in *Fine Cooking*.
- Lori Longbotham (*Luscious Lemon Desserts*) recommends double-sifting the flour for the finest crumb.
- Pat Willard (*Secrets of Saffron*) has the lovely idea of adding saffron to lemon cake. Add a large pinch of saffron threads to the buttermilk and let it steep for 20 minutes, or microwave for 1 minute.

desserts

SOURCE: *The Valentino Cookbook*
by Piero Selvaggio and Karen Stabiner
COOK: Piero Selvaggio

valentino's chocolate truffle cake

VALENTINO IS A LANDMARK RESTAURANT in Santa Monica, and this divine cake is one of its classics. It's dense, dark, and rich, not moist or cakey at all — more like a truffle. The fresh raspberries are just the right touch to garnish and brighten it.

Though it features the word "ganache" (French for chocolate filling or frosting), which may frighten some cooks away, this is actually an uncomplicated recipe. You can make the cake itself up to two days in advance and the ganache up to eight hours ahead.

This is the perfect romantic valentine gift for a chocoholic — a valentino?

serves 8 to 10

CAKE

10½ ounces bittersweet chocolate, chopped

10 tablespoons (1¼ sticks) butter, cut into small pieces

⅔ cup sugar

5 large eggs, separated

¼ cup plus 2 tablespoons all-purpose flour

GANACHE

6½ ounces bittersweet chocolate, chopped

¼ cup heavy cream

¼ cup brewed espresso

2 tablespoons butter, at room temperature

1 tablespoon Triple Sec or other orange-flavored liqueur

Fresh raspberries, for garnish

TO MAKE THE CAKE:

Preheat the oven to 350 degrees with a rack in the middle. Butter a 10-inch springform pan. In a double boiler or a metal bowl set over a saucepan of barely simmering water, melt the chocolate, butter, and sugar, stirring until smooth (the sugar will not dissolve). Remove from the heat and let cool to room temperature. Transfer the mixture to a large bowl.

Add the egg yolks, one at a time, to the chocolate mixture, whisking well after each addition. In the bowl of an electric mixer, beat the egg whites until they just hold soft peaks. Sift the flour over the chocolate mixture and, with a whisk, fold in the flour and half the egg whites. With a rubber spatula, fold in the remaining eggs whites gently but thoroughly. Pour the batter into the prepared pan, smooth the top, and bake for 40 to 45 minutes, or until a tester inserted in the center comes out with moist crumbs adhering. Cool the cake completely in the pan on a wire rack. (If you're making the cake a day or two ahead, keep it in an airtight container at room temperature.)

TO MAKE THE GANACHE:

In a double boiler or a metal bowl set over a saucepan of barely simmering water, melt the chocolate, stirring frequently until smooth. Remove from the heat.

Meanwhile, in a small saucepan, bring the cream just to a simmer and add the espresso. Add the cream mixture to the melted chocolate, along with the butter and liqueur. Stir until smooth.

TO ASSEMBLE THE CAKE:

Remove the side of the springform pan. Invert the cake onto a large wire rack set over a shallow baking pan. Pour enough warm ganache over the cake to coat it, and let it stand for 5 minutes. Scrape the excess ganache from the baking pan and pour it over the cake a second time. Let stand at room temperature until the ganache is set, at least 1 hour and up to 6 hours.

Just before serving, garnish the top of the cake with raspberries.

cook's notes

- This cake is all about the chocolate, so use the best you can find.
- Use a flat cake spatula to spread the ganache over the cake.
- When you scrape up the excess ganache, you may need to give it a little blast in the microwave or water bath to soften just enough to pour — don't let it get melty or the butter will turn oily — you just want to warm it enough so that it will pour.

tip

Shouldn't you use cake flour for a cake? In *The Baker's Dozen Cookbook,* a collective of professional bakers and passionate amateurs tested cakes both ways and concluded they preferred the all-purpose flour. Cake flour does indeed give a finer crumb and may be the flour of choice for a fancy European-style cake — but for flavor and good texture, all-purpose is the way to go, and preferably organic.

desserts

SOURCE: *The Buttercup Bake Shop Cookbook*
by Jennifer Appel
COOK: Jennifer Appel

new year's honey cake

THIS HEIRLOOM HONEY CAKE has been in Jennifer Appel's family for a long time, traditionally served for the Jewish New Year. But it's such a lovely, old-fashioned cake that we think it should be an option for all holidays. It's golden brown, as a proper honey cake should be, and pretty with scattered sliced almonds on top. As it bakes, there's a delightful scent of spice, almond, and vanilla.

Together the honey and oil produce a cake with a wonderfully moist texture and very tender crumb. We're not quite sure what the cup of strong tea adds, but this cake is so perfect that we wouldn't dream of tampering with it, so don't leave it out.

And what a joy to bake a cake that doesn't require a frosting!

makes one 10-inch cake; serves 12 to 14

3½ cups cake flour
1 tablespoon baking powder
½ teaspoon salt
1 tablespoon ground cinnamon
½ teaspoon ground cloves
¼ teaspoon ground nutmeg
1 cup vegetable oil
1 cup honey
1½ cups sugar
½ cup firmly packed light brown sugar
3 large eggs, lightly beaten
1 teaspoon pure vanilla extract
¼ teaspoon almond extract
1 cup brewed strong tea, cooled
½ cup orange juice
3 tablespoons brandy
½ cup sliced blanched almonds

Preheat the oven to 350 degrees. Lightly grease a 10-inch tube pan.

In a large bowl, whisk together the flour, baking powder, salt, and spices. Make a well in the center and add the remaining ingredients, in the order in which they are listed, with the exception of the almonds. Mix with an electric mixer on low speed, making sure all the ingredients are thoroughly incorporated.

Pour the batter into the prepared pan. Sprinkle the top evenly with the almonds. Bake for 60 to 70 minutes, or until a cake tester inserted in the center of the cake comes out clean. Let cool in the pan for 20 minutes. Remove from the pan and cool completely on a wire rack.

cook's notes

❦ This cake can also be made in 2 loaf pans — which makes a nice holiday gift because it keeps for a few days.

❦ When you turn the cake out of the pan, you want to invert it so that the almond-sprinkled side ends up on top.

tip

If you forget to take the cake out of the pan once it's cooled, all is not lost, says Regan Daley, author of *In the Sweet Kitchen*. Put it back in the oven at 325 or 350 degrees for 3 to 5 minutes, remove it, run a thin-bladed knife around the edges of the cake, then invert it onto a serving platter.

SOURCE: *Mrs. Wilkes' Boardinghouse Cookbook*
by Sema Wilkes
COOK: Sema Wilkes

pecan whiskey cake

THERE WERE THREE ENTIRE COOKBOOKS this year devoted to the food of Savannah — and for good reason; these folks can cook. One of them was from Mrs. Wilkes, the legendary 93-year-old proprietor of an eponymous Savannah boardinghouse where eager diners have lined up every day for well over half a century now to eat her very good Southern home cooking. The food is served boardinghouse style, in big bowls passed from hand to hand and returned for seconds and thirds.

Mrs. Wilkes makes this wonderful cake for Christmas and describes it as "an indulgence beyond compare." We'd have to agree. This is big cake, much better than most fruit cakes. It's chockablock with pecans and raisins and heady with the scent of whiskey. Serve it for a festive breakfast or brunch, or on any buffet table. It would be lovely with afternoon tea as well.

makes 2 loaves or 1 large bundt cake

1 cup (2 sticks) butter, at room temperature
2 cups sugar
6 large eggs, well beaten
4 cups sifted cake flour
4 teaspoons baking powder
2 teaspoons ground nutmeg
2/3 teaspoon salt
1 cup good aged whiskey
3 cups golden raisins
4 cups broken pecans

Preheat the oven to 350 degrees. Line two 10-x-4-inch loaf pans with buttered waxed paper or butter and flour a large (12-cup) bundt pan.

In a large bowl, cream the butter. Gradually add the sugar and cream until fluffy. Gradually add the eggs and continue beating until well combined.

Into a separate large bowl, sift together 3¹/₂ cups of the flour, the baking powder, nutmeg, and salt. Alternate adding the flour mixture and the whiskey to the butter-sugar mixture.

In a medium bowl, dredge the raisins and pecans in the remaining ¹/₂ cup flour. Stir these into the batter, mixing well. Scrape the batter into the prepared pan(s). Bake until a tester inserted in the center comes out clean and the top springs back lightly when pressed, about 1 hour. Let cool on a wire rack before slicing and serving.

cook's notes

❦ Use an electric mixer to make quick work of creaming the butter and sugar. Proper creaming is essential to get the texture of the cake right. Continue with the electric mixer when adding the eggs. But when it comes time to add the flour and whiskey and so on, use a strong wooden spoon and stir just enough to combine in order to avoid toughening the cake.

❦ To make the pecan pieces, pulse the nuts a few times in a food processor. It's neater and faster than chopping. Just don't go overboard and grind them to a powder.

❦ If you are using metal loaf pans, it may take an extra 5 to 10 minutes of baking time to cook through. Glass cooks a bit more quickly.

SOURCE: Epicurious.com
COOK: Faith Heller Willinger

anarchy cake

FAITH WILLINGER IMPROVISED this unusual cake when she had a rather empty larder and company coming for dinner. It was immediately christened Anarchy Cake because, she writes, "With recipes, as with so many things, Italians are basically anarchists." You might think the anarchy is in putting salad dressing ingredients — olive oil and balsamic vinegar — in the cake, but it goes beyond that. The idea is that you act like an Italian, which is to say you pretty much do whatever you want and it will still come out beautifully — the sign of a really good recipe.

What we love about it is that it doesn't require any fancy ingredients, and you can add just about any fruit (or even chunks of chocolate) that you happen to have on hand. To see how far you can take it, read what one cook wrote in to the website (see note). We've found that when you use fruit, the cake comes out like a cross between a torte and a cobbler. With chocolate bits, it's a bit like a large, fluffy chocolate chip cookie. Either way, it's a tender low-profile cake that's golden brown, delicately cakey, a little crisp on the outside, and not too sweet. It's a great emergency dessert that also works for teatime.

serves 6 to 8

1½ cups fruit, sliced if using peaches, apricots, or plums (neatness does not count); if using cherries, pit them; or 4 ounces chopped bittersweet chocolate

½ cup plus an additional 1 or 2 tablespoons superfine sugar

¾ cup cake flour or pastry flour (all-purpose flour works in a pinch)

¾ teaspoon baking powder

Pinch of salt

1 large egg

¼ teaspoon finely grated fresh lemon zest

¼ cup extra-virgin olive oil

¼ cup milk

½ teaspoon balsamic vinegar

Preheat the oven to 350 degrees. Line the bottom of a 10-inch springform pan with parchment paper, brush with oil, and lightly flour.

In a medium bowl, gently toss the fruit with 1 tablespoon of the sugar and set aside. (If using chocolate, do not toss it with the sugar, just set aside until needed.) In a small bowl, combine the flour, baking powder, and salt and set aside.

Using an electric mixer, beat the egg with the ½ cup sugar and the lemon zest until light, fluffy, and pale in color. This could take as long as 5 minutes. Add the oil, then the milk and balsamic vinegar, beating until fully combined. Using a rubber spatula, fold in the flour mixture. Pour the batter into the prepared pan and drop the fruit or chocolate over the top. Sprinkle with the remaining 1 tablespoon sugar. Bake for 50 minutes, or until the top is a beautiful golden brown and a knife blade inserted in the center comes out clean. Cool on a wire rack for about 5 minutes, then remove the sides of the pan. Serve warm or at room temperature.

cook's notes

- The cake is best eaten the day it is made.
- A cook from Seattle posted this message on the Epicurious site: "This cake/torte totally exceeded my expectations. I used several fruits and much more than called for (true to the anarchist form) . . . I used cake flour and stuck to the rest of the recipe. It came out beautifully *Italian*-looking, and delicious. Not too sweet but very flavorful, with the cake bubbling up around the fruit, which gives it a tortelike look. I'll make this again and again. Powdered sugar on top makes this little baby party-worthy, for sure."

SOURCE: **Palace Market flyer, Point Reyes, California**
COOK: **Gloria Pedilla**

intense chocolate torte

THIS IS ONE OF THOSE SENSATIONAL recipes that travel quickly from hand to hand by e-mail, fax, and scribbled note. Part of the reason it's so over-the-top delicious is an entire pound of chocolate and a cup of cream barely held together by eggs and the tiniest amount of flour. But that's just the filling; there's a pecan–graham cracker crust to give it a homey crunch. Cooks also love this torte because it's so easy to make — even a tenderfoot in the kitchen will have no problems.

This dessert is so rich that you should serve only skinny slices, with espresso if possible.

serves 16

CRUST

1 cup pecans, toasted and coarsely chopped
1 cup graham cracker crumbs (about 10 double crackers)
2 tablespoons sugar
4 tablespoons (1/2 stick) unsalted butter, melted, plus more if needed

FILLING

1 pound semisweet chocolate, chopped
1 cup whipping cream
6 large eggs, beaten
3/4 cup sugar
1/3 cup all-purpose flour

TO MAKE THE CRUST:

Preheat the oven to 325 degrees. In a medium bowl, combine the crust ingredients, using more melted butter, if needed, to make the crust stick together. Press the mixture onto the bottom and 1 1/2 inches up the sides of a 9-inch springform pan.

TO MAKE THE FILLING:

In a medium saucepan, heat the chocolate and cream over low heat until the chocolate melts. Remove from the heat and set aside. In an electric mixer or large bowl, combine the eggs, sugar, and flour. Beat for 10 minutes (or less if you're beating by hand), or until thick and lemon-colored. Fold one quarter of the egg mixture into the chocolate mixture, then fold the chocolate mixture into the remaining egg mixture.

Pour the filling into the crust. Bake for about 45 minutes, or until puffed around the edges halfway to the center. Let cool on a wire rack for 20 minutes, then remove the side. Let cool for 4 hours before serving.

cook's notes

- Obviously, the better the chocolate, the better the torte — but this recipe also works with plain old chocolate chips from the supermarket.
- You may get a few cracks on top of the torte after it bakes, but don't worry; it will still be delicious.

SOURCE: *Luscious Lemon Desserts*
by Lori Longbotham
COOK: Lori Longbotham

lemon and goat cheese cheesecake

LORI LONGBOTHAM LOVES CHEESECAKE, but if it doesn't have lemon in it, she says, she's not interested. In some ways, this seems like a standard cheesecake: a graham-cracker crust with a lemony rich cheesecake filling. But using mild goat cheese has a startling effect here; this cheesecake is much lighter, very smooth, and has a slight tang that perfectly balances the sweet tang of lemon. It's a sophisticated dessert, but one we'll make again and again.

It's best made a day ahead because it needs at least eight hours to firm and settle in the refrigerator.

serves 10

1½ cups graham-cracker crumbs
6 tablespoons (¾ stick) unsalted butter, melted
2 cups sugar
¼ cup finely grated fresh lemon zest (from about 4 large lemons)

1½ pounds soft mild fresh goat cheese, such as Montrachet
1 8-ounce package cream cheese, at room temperature
½ cup fresh lemon juice
8 large eggs

Preheat the oven to 350 degrees with a rack in the middle. Butter the bottom and side of a 9-inch springform pan. Have a roasting pan ready. Boil water for a water bath.

In a medium bowl, stir the graham-cracker crumbs and butter with a fork until combined. Press the mixture into the bottom of the prepared pan. Bake for 8 to 10 minutes, or until the crust is set. Cool on a wire rack. Reduce the oven temperature to 325 degrees.

In a food processor, blend the sugar and lemon zest until the zest is finely ground.

In a medium bowl, beat the goat cheese and cream cheese with an electric mixer, beginning on low speed and increasing to medium-high, until light and fluffy. Reduce the speed to medium, add the sugar mixture and lemon juice, and beat until smooth, scraping the side of the bowl. Add the eggs, one at a time, beating well after each addition.

Wrap the outside of the springform pan with heavy-duty aluminum foil. Pour the filling into the pan and set it in the roasting pan. Place it in the oven, and carefully pour enough boiling water into the roasting pan to reach halfway up the side of the springform pan.

Bake for about 1¹/₂ hours, or until the center is almost set but still slightly jiggly. Do not overbake; the cheesecake will firm as it cools. Remove the roasting pan from the oven and let the cheesecake cool in the water bath for 15 minutes. Remove from the bath and cool on a wire rack. Remove the foil and refrigerate the cheesecake in the pan, loosely covered, for at least 8 hours or overnight.

Run a table knife around the inside edge of the pan and remove the pan's side. Let the cheesecake stand at room temperature for 20 minutes before serving.

cook's note

🐐 Be sure your goat cheese is mild and fresh or you'll have goaty-tasting cheesecake.

SOURCE: **MexGrocer.com**
COOK: **Unknown**

capirotada (mexican bread pudding)

CAPIROTADA IS A MEXICAN holiday bread pudding traditionally served on Christmas Eve, following La Misa del Gallo (the Mass of the Cock), and on El Dia de los Tres Reyes (the Day of the Three Kings), according to MexGrocer.com. *Gourmet* magazine says that it's eaten during Lent. Either way, this is not the soft, custardy bread pudding that most of us are used to. For one thing, it includes farmer's cheese and shredded Jack cheese, which melt and blend into the pudding as it bakes, giving it a richer, heartier texture than simple egg-and-cream custards. The aromatics here — cinnamon, cloves, orange zest, and lemon zest — provide a good balance of spicy, sweet flavor.

But it's the way this delicious pudding is made that accounts for its exceptional flavor and texture. First the bread is tossed with oil and melted butter and toasted. Then the pudding is assembled without its custard and briefly baked to caramelize the sugar and toast the nuts and bread even more. After the custard is poured into the pan and the pudding is baked, it emerges from the oven a deep caramel color, all bubbling and smelling delectable, with its nutty crunch intact. Don't forgo the whipped cream, which really elevates the whole thing.

makes one 9-x-13-inch pudding

1 pound stale white bread, torn into bite-sized pieces

8 tablespoons (1 stick) unsalted butter, melted

3 tablespoons canola oil

2 cups light brown sugar

1 3-inch cinnamon stick

1 cup chopped pecans, toasted

1 cup raisins

1/2 cup farmer's cheese

1/3 cup shredded Monterey Jack cheese

1 tablespoon grated fresh orange zest

1 1/2 teaspoons grated fresh lemon zest

1 teaspoon ground cinnamon

1/2 teaspoon ground cloves

3 large egg yolks

4 cups whole milk

2 teaspoons pure vanilla extract

1 cup whipping cream, for topping (optional)

Preheat the broiler. Generously butter a 9-x-13-inch baking dish. Put the pieces of bread into a large bowl. In a small bowl, combine 4 tablespoons of the butter and 2 tablespoons of the oil and drizzle over the bread, tossing to mix thoroughly. Spread the bread on a baking sheet and broil until lightly toasted, turning as needed to brown evenly. Remove and set aside. Set the oven temperature to 350 degrees.

In a medium saucepan, combine 1 cup water, the brown sugar, and cinnamon stick. Bring to a boil and boil until caramel-colored and syrupy, about 5 minutes. Remove from the heat and set aside.

In a large bowl, mix together the toasted bread pieces, pecans, raisins, and cheeses. Sprinkle with orange zest, lemon zest, cinnamon, and cloves. Mix to combine and transfer to the prepared baking dish. Whisk the remaining 4 tablespoons butter and 1 tablespoon oil into the sugar syrup (discard the cinnamon stick) and drizzle this mixture over the ingredients in the baking dish. Bake for 30 minutes. Remove from the oven.

In a large mixing bowl, beat the egg yolks until thick and lemon-colored. Gradually beat in the milk and vanilla. Pour the custard over the baked bread, and return to the oven for 40 minutes, or until the top is golden brown.

Whip the cream until stiff, if using. Serve the pudding warm, topping each serving with a bit of whipped cream, if you wish.

cook's notes

- Be sure to toast the pecans only lightly, since they get toasted again during baking.
- Save the bowl that you use for tossing the bread with the butter mixture, and use it again for assembling the pudding — no need to wash in between.

SOURCE: *Food & Wine*
COOK: Nick Malgieri

ginger puddings
with bittersweet chocolate sauce
and ginger caramel crunch

THIS IS A SENSATIONALLY GOOD DESSERT your guests won't be able to forget. Although there are three different elements to this recipe and it requires a set of ramekins, those cute little ovenproof dishes, we promise it's worth every bit of work it requires. The delicate individual ginger puddings contain not only ground ginger and molasses but also lemon zest and candied ginger; they'd be great on their own, but here they're embellished with a bittersweet chocolate sauce that's just right with the ginger, plus shards of ginger caramel crunch. That's the clincher; reminiscent of honeycomb (the British candy crunch) and coffee crunch, this delectable caramel also includes pecans.

You can, of course, use a good-quality store-bought bittersweet chocolate sauce to save yourself a bit of work, but this one is very tasty and can be made weeks ahead of time.

serves 6

¹/₄ cup all-purpose flour

2 teaspoons ground ginger

¹/₂ teaspoon baking powder

¹/₄ teaspoon salt

¹/₄ cup finely chopped crystallized ginger (2 ounces)

3 large eggs, at room temperature

3 large egg yolks, at room temperature

¹/₂ cup sugar

1 teaspoon finely grated fresh lemon zest

¹/₃ cup unsulfured molasses

6 tablespoons (³/₄ stick) unsalted butter, melted and cooled slightly

Bittersweet Chocolate Sauce (recipe follows)

Ginger Caramel Crunch (recipe follows)

Preheat the oven to 400 degrees. Butter and flour six ¹/₂-cup ramekins. Tap out the excess flour and set the ramekins on a heavy rimmed baking sheet. In a small bowl, whisk the flour, ground ginger, baking powder, and salt. Stir in the crystallized ginger. In a medium bowl, whisk the eggs, egg yolks, sugar, lemon zest, and molasses. Add the butter and whisk until smooth. Gently fold in the dry ingredients. Pour the batter into the prepared ramekins and bake for about

20 minutes, or until the puddings have risen and a toothpick inserted in the center of one comes out with a few moist crumbs attached. Let the puddings cool for 10 minutes.

Run a thin knife around the edge of each ramekin to loosen the pudding, then cover with a dessert plate and carefully turn over to unmold the pudding. Repeat with the remaining puddings. Drizzle the puddings with the Bittersweet Chocolate Sauce, garnish with the Ginger Caramel Crunch, and serve.

The baked puddings can be refrigerated overnight. Bring to room temperature before rewarming, loosely covered with foil, in a 300-degree oven for 10 minutes.

bittersweet chocolate sauce

makes 2¹/₂ cups

1 cup heavy cream
¹/₃ cup light corn syrup
¹/₃ cup sugar

³/₄ pound bittersweet or semisweet chocolate, chopped
2 teaspoons pure vanilla extract
Pinch of salt

In a medium saucepan, combine the cream, corn syrup, and sugar over low heat. Cook, stirring, just until the sugar dissolves. Bring to a boil, then remove from the heat. Add the chocolate and let stand for 3 minutes. Add the vanilla and salt and stir until the chocolate is melted and the sauce is smooth.

The sauce can be refrigerated for up to 3 weeks. Rewarm before serving.

ginger caramel crunch

makes about 1¹/₂ cups

¹/₂ teaspoon ground ginger
¹/₂ teaspoon baking soda
¹/₂ cup sugar

1¹/₂ tablespoons light corn syrup
¹/₂ cup toasted pecan pieces

desserts

Line a large baking sheet with aluminum foil and butter the foil well. Into a small bowl, sift together the ginger and baking soda.

In a medium heavy saucepan, combine the sugar, corn syrup, and 2 tablespoons water over medium heat and stir until the sugar dissolves. Bring to a boil and cook until the syrup is a pale honey color and registers 310 degrees (hard-crack stage) on a candy thermometer. Remove from the heat.

Using a long-handled wooden spoon, stir in the pecans, then carefully stir in the ginger mixture. Immediately pour the caramel onto the prepared baking sheet and evenly spread out the nuts on top. Let cool completely, then crack into long shards.

Ginger Caramel Crunch can be stored in an airtight container for up to 3 days.

SOURCE: *New York* magazine
COOK: Tom Valenti

crème fraîche panna cotta with berry puree

CHEF TOM VALENTI FROM OUEST in New York City came up with this dessert as a good example of something to make for a casual summer weekend in the country. We love every panna cotta (which simply means "cooked cream") we've ever met, but this vanilla-bean-flecked one is distinctive because it contains not only buttermilk but also crème fraîche, that darling of chefs and cooks everywhere this year. It's a brilliant touch that brings a complex slight tartness to the very rich cream. In fact, this panna cotta reminds us a bit of Swedish cream, one of our all-time favorites to serve with summer berries.

The crème fraîche panna cotta is so intensely rich that we like it best not as large single servings but served in a bowl with lots of berries alongside, so guests can help themselves and choose either just a couple of spoonfuls with their berries or a more generous portion.

serves 6 to 12

PANNA COTTA
- 1½ cups heavy cream
- 1 cup milk
- ½ cup buttermilk
- ½ cup sugar
- 1 vanilla bean, split
- 1 cup crème fraîche
- 1 envelope gelatin

STRAWBERRY PUREE
- 1 pint strawberries, hulled (or raspberries, peaches, or blueberries)
- 1 tablespoon sugar, or more to taste
- 1 teaspoon fresh lemon juice, or more to taste

TO MAKE THE PANNA COTTA:

In a medium saucepan, combine the cream, milk, buttermilk, sugar, and vanilla bean and bring to a simmer over high heat. Remove from the heat and whisk in the crème fraîche. Scrape the vanilla bean to remove the seeds. Pour the cream mixture through a strainer into a medium bowl and add the gelatin, stirring until it has dissolved.

desserts

Pour evenly into 6 molds or martini glasses or a 1-quart soufflé dish. Chill for at least 3 hours to set.

TO MAKE THE BERRY PUREE:

In a food processor, puree two thirds of the berries until smooth. Add 1 tablespoon sugar and 1 teaspoon lemon juice, puree again, and depending on the ripeness of the fruit, adjust the sugar and lemon juice to taste. Strain through a fine sieve into a medium bowl to remove seeds, if you like.

Unmold each panna cotta onto a plate or spoon out individual servings and pour about 2 tablespoons berry puree around each serving. Garnish with the remaining strawberries and serve.

cook's notes

- If you can't find a vanilla bean, use 1 teaspoon pure vanilla extract instead.
- If you can't find crème fraîche, use the same amount of sour cream.
- Sometimes the gelatin doesn't dissolve completely, so you may need to strain the mixture again before pouring it into the molds. Or sprinkle the powdered gelatin over 2 tablespoons cool water and let it stand for about 2 minutes before mixing it into the cream. The extra water won't be noticeable.

SOURCE: *Yankee* magazine
COOK: Irene S. Young

cranberry puff-up

IN 1947, *YANKEE* sponsored one of its first recipe contests, and Mrs. Irene S. Young of Melrose, Massachusetts, won first prize ($3) for her cranberry dessert. Homey and elegant, it holds up very well more than 50 years later.

You can play with the recipe a bit by adding some orange zest or other favorite cranberry-friendly flavorings, but don't omit the puff of whipped cream when you serve it, or the dessert could be a little too tart.

serves 6

2 cups fresh or frozen cranberries	1¹/₂ teaspoons baking powder
1¹/₂ cups sugar	¹/₄ teaspoon salt
4 tablespoons (¹/₂ stick) butter, at room temperature	¹/₃ cup milk
	¹/₂ teaspoon pure vanilla extract
1 large egg	
1 cup all-purpose flour	Whipped cream, for serving

In a medium saucepan, combine the cranberries, 1 cup of the sugar, and ¹/₂ cup water. Mix well, bring to a boil, and cook over low heat for 10 minutes, or until most of the berries have popped. Remove from the heat, cover, and let stand for 20 minutes. Spoon half of the berry mixture into 6 greased custard cups, using about 2 tablespoons per cup. Set aside to cool.

Preheat the oven to 350 degrees. In a medium bowl, cream the butter and the remaining ¹/₂ cup sugar. Add the egg and beat well.

In a small bowl, whisk together the flour, baking powder, and salt. Add to the creamed mixture alternately with the milk. Stir in the vanilla, then spoon the batter evenly onto the berries in the cups.

Bake until the tops are lightly browned, 25 to 30 minutes. Cool for 10 minutes. Run a knife around the edge of each cup and turn out the puff-ups onto dessert plates. Serve with whipped cream and the remaining cranberry sauce.

cook's note

☙ Put the custard cups on a heavy rimmed baking sheet to transfer them easily to and from the oven.

desserts

SOURCE: *Fine Cooking*
COOK: Carolyn Weil

double-crust jumble berry pie

THE FIRST TIME WE MADE THIS PIE (featured on our book jacket), it was deemed "the best pie I ever tasted" by some pretty jaded friends, so we made it again and again. There's something about the summery combination of the not-too-sweet berry filling and the very flaky, American-style piecrust that sings. This is the ultimate double-crusted pie, made with a tasty jumble of raspberries, blueberries, blackberries, and a few strawberries.

The pastry technique here is a little unusual and much more convenient than the usual directions. You make the dough in a mixer — making sure that it stays cold and never gets oily — and then roll it out *before* chilling. Carolyn Weil says chilling before rolling it out will actually make the crust tougher, since you have to wrestle with cold dough. After it's rolled out, you assemble and fill the pie and chill the entire pie before baking. Keep in mind, though, that if at any time the pastry starts to get too warm or oily, you need to slide it onto a tray and into the refrigerator. Melting will ruin the pastry.

Another smart idea is the combination of tapioca and cornstarch, which really works — one thickens the juices and one adds texture without making the filling opaque or gummy.

You're not limited to berries for this pie; use these same measurements for sliced or chunked stone fruit, such as peaches, nectarines, or plums.

makes one 9-inch pie

CRUST
1 cup (2 sticks) cold unsalted butter
2 cups all-purpose unbleached flour
1/4 cup sugar
1/4 teaspoon salt
1/4 cup cold water

FILLING
1 cup sugar
2 tablespoons cornstarch

2 tablespoons quick-cooking tapioca
1/4 teaspoon salt
6 cups washed and well-dried mix of blackberries, blueberries, raspberries, and quartered strawberries
1 tablespoon unsalted butter, cut into small pieces

TO MAKE THE CRUST:

Cut the butter into ¹/₂-inch cubes. In a stand mixer fitted with the paddle attachment (or in a large bowl, if mixing the dough by hand), combine the flour, sugar, and salt. Mix for a second or two to blend. Add the butter and, on low speed (or by hand with two knives or a pastry cutter), work the mixture until it's crumbly and the largest pieces of butter are no bigger than a pea (about ¹/₄ inch). The butter should remain cold and firm. To test it, pick up some butter and pinch it between the thumbs and forefingers of both hands to form a little cube. If the butter holds together as a cube and your fingers are not greasy, then the butter is still cold enough. If your fingers look greasy, put the bowl in the refrigerator for 15 minutes to firm up the butter before proceeding. On low speed (or tossing with a fork, if mixing by hand), sprinkle ¹/₄ cup cold water evenly over the flour mixture. Work the dough until it just pulls together in a shaggy mass.

Cut the dough in half and pat each piece into a thick flattened ball. Lightly flour a work surface and tap one of the dough balls down with four or five taps of a rolling pin. Begin rolling from the center of the dough outward. Stop the pressure ¹/₄ inch from the edge of the dough. Lift the dough and turn by a quarter and repeat the rolling until the dough is at least 12 inches in diameter. Be sure to re-flour the work surface if the dough is sticking.

Using a pot lid or a circle of cardboard as a template, trim the dough to form a 12-inch round (this should give you a 1¹/₂-inch margin all around a 9-inch pie pan). Fold the dough in half, slide the outspread fingers of both hands under the dough, and gently lift it and transfer it to a 9-inch pie pan. Unfold and ease the dough round into the bottom of the pie pan without stretching it.

Roll out the other dough ball and cut a second 12-inch round to be used as the top crust.

TO MAKE THE FILLING:

In a large bowl, mix together the sugar, cornstarch, tapioca, and salt. Add the berries and toss with your hands until the berries are evenly coated. Pile the berries into the dough-lined pie pan, sprinkling any remaining dry ingredients on top. Dot the surface with the butter, cover the berry mixture with the top crust and seal the edges by fluting. Cut 5 or 6 slits in the top crust to let steam escape during cooking.

Preheat the oven to 400 degrees while you chill the pie in the refrigerator for 15 to 20 minutes.

Put the pie on a baking sheet to catch any drips and bake for 15 minutes. Reduce the oven temperature to 350 degrees and continue baking until the crust is golden and the filling juices that are bubbling through the vents and edges are thick, glossy, and slow, 50 to 60 minutes more.

For the best texture for serving, cool the pie completely (which may take up to 5 hours), and then just slightly reheat slices or the whole pie before serving. (Cooling completely allows the filling juices to firm up, while a quick reheat makes the pastry nice and flaky.) You can serve the pie while it's still warm, but the filling will be slightly liquid; definitely don't serve the pie hot from the oven, since the juices will be too fluid.

cook's notes

- Use high-quality butter and keep it very cold.
- Be gentle when washing the berries; just rinse them and let them air-dry on paper towels. Only the strawberries really need rinsing.
- Don't leave out the strawberries in the berry mix. They add a wonderful floral perfume without becoming overpowering. Even if you don't like cooked strawberries, a few really help here.
- Don't overfill the pie. The 6 cups may not look like the heaping mound of filling that you're used to, but it is enough, and it actually makes for a prettier pie.
- And finally, probably the hardest tip of all is to let the pie cool before you slice it. If you want a warm slice, you can warm it in the oven (once it's cooled and sliced).

tip

You wouldn't want to use a store-bought piecrust for this pie, because it has a double crust, and the pastry is a big part of the pleasure here. But for a single-crust pie, why not? The *Gourmet* magazine staff tested some store-boughts and found they generally performed well. The favorite was Pillsbury's refrigerated piecrust. Other options include Pillsbury's Frozen Pet-Ritz Pie Crust, which was a little sweeter, and Oronoque Orchards flaky piecrust. If it's a question of pie or no pie, we say go for it.

SOURCE: *Washington Post*
COOK: Anne Willan

ported rhubarb

AMERICANS DON'T HAVE A HISTORY of cooking with port, as the British do, but Anne Willan opened our eyes to its great possibilities this year. This baked rhubarb dish is just amazing: the rhubarb holds its shape instead of dissolving into damp strings, and the port and orange zest add a complexity that is almost unbelievable in such a simple dish. It's wonderful served over vanilla or strawberry ice cream, but it's also a tasty relish for turkey or ham — all this for less than five minutes of work.

The right port for this dish is ruby port, the youngest and sweetest of the ports. If your rhubarb isn't very sour, you'll need much less sugar, since the port itself is quite sweet.

serves 4 to 6

1½ pounds rhubarb, cut into 2-inch pieces

¾–1 cup sugar

¾ cup ruby port

Zest of 1 orange

Preheat the oven to 350 degrees. Arrange the rhubarb in a baking dish large enough to hold it in a single layer. Sprinkle with the sugar to taste. In a small bowl, mix the port and orange zest and drizzle over the rhubarb.

Bake until the rhubarb is just tender when pierced with a knife, about 20 to 30 minutes. Serve chilled.

cook's note

℞ The rhubarb will look prettier if you cut it at an angle.

tip

If you're looking for a savory use for port, Anne Willan recommends a great homemade Stilton cheese spread: crumble ½ pound Stilton into a bowl, beat in 1 cup softened butter and ½ cup port. Not only is this more delicious than the Stilton spread sold in crocks, but it's a fraction of the price.

SOURCE: *A New Way to Cook* by Sally Schneider
COOK: Sally Schneider after Paula Wolfert

roasted apricots with cardamom

IN THE MIDDLE OF WINTER, there's nothing quite so reviving as a dish of roasted apricots, which seem to bring sunshine itself to the table. The classic Elizabeth David treatment flavors the apricots with vanilla bean; Paula Wolfert's version takes it to another dimension with cardamom. Now Sally Schneider puts these two approaches together and adds a little lemon juice to spark the flavors. It's a gorgeous, wonderfully fragrant dish that makes a fine end to a meal — just add crème fraîche, thick yogurt, whipped cream, or even ice cream.

We especially love these apricots for breakfast with yogurt, but they'd be wonderful on a brunch table also. And if you can manage to keep dried apricots on hand, this is a good emergency dessert, since everything in it is a kitchen staple. Dried apricots and cardamom pods last virtually forever, and vanilla beans are also long-lived.

serves 4

8 ounces large California dried apricot halves (about 30)

2 tablespoons plus 2 teaspoons sugar

½ vanilla bean

3 cardamom pods

2 teaspoons fresh lemon juice

In a small bowl, combine the apricots and 2 cups water. Let soak for at least 6 hours or overnight.

Preheat the oven to 400 degrees. Drain the apricots, reserving ½ cup of the soaking liquid. Arrange the apricots skin side down in a baking dish.

Place the sugar in a small bowl. With a sharp paring knife, split the vanilla bean half lengthwise in half. Scrape out the seeds and stir them into the sugar. (Place the pod in a jar of sugar to make vanilla sugar for another use, if you like.) Crush the cardamom pods and stir the black seeds into the sugar; discard the pods.

Sprinkle 2 tablespoons of the vanilla sugar over the apricots. Reserve the rest. Drizzle 6 tablespoons of the reserved soaking liquid and the lemon juice over the fruit; reserve the rest.

Roast the apricots until they are tender, about 30 minutes, spooning the juices over them twice. (If the juices are evaporating too quickly, add some of the reserved soaking liquid to the dish.)

Sprinkle the apricots with the remaining 2 teaspoons vanilla sugar and roast for 10 minutes more, or until the apricots are well glazed and tinged with brown and almost all the liquid has evaporated. Serve warm or at room temperature.

You can roast the apricots up to 5 hours before serving. To serve warm, reheat gently in a shallow pan on the stovetop.

cook's notes

- The recipe specifies California apricots, and that's an important direction — they're much tastier.
- We're not fond of biting into cardamom seeds, which are intensely flavored, so we suggest grinding the seeds. Or use ¼ teaspoon ground cardamom instead.

SOURCE: *The Last Course* by Claudia Fleming
COOK: Claudia Fleming

pear crisp with dried sour cherries

CLAUDIA FLEMING, THE CELEBRATED pastry chef at Manhattan's Gramercy Tavern, has made a specialty of upgrading homey desserts into something extraordinary. This wonderful fall dessert has a lovely, golden brown crisp topping over bubbling burgundy-colored juices. It's fragrant with wine, cherries, pears, and spices. The fruit has a rich, subtle flavor and a perfect level of sweetness — the tartness of the sour cherries in concert with the sweet pears. Whipped crème fraîche would be just the thing for a topping.

Be sure to plan ahead for this dessert, since you need to soak the cherries for at least eight hours.

serves 8

1 cup dried sour cherries
Water and/or fruity red wine, such as Zinfandel, to cover

2½ pounds ripe pears (about 8 medium), peeled, cored, and sliced (5 cups)

½ cup sugar

1¼ cups all-purpose flour

⅓ cup plus 1 tablespoon coarsely ground almonds, toasted

¼ cup firmly packed dark brown sugar

¼ teaspoon ground cinnamon

⅛ teaspoon ground nutmeg

8 tablespoons (1 stick) unsalted butter, melted and cooled to room temperature

The day before you make the crisp, in a small saucepan over medium heat, combine the dried cherries with enough water and/or wine to cover them by 2 inches. Bring the mixture to a simmer, then remove from the heat and let cool. Let the cherries soak overnight or for at least 8 hours in the refrigerator, or until plump and soft. Drain the cherries, reserving the juices.

In a large bowl, combine the pears, drained cherries, and ¼ cup of the granulated sugar and toss well. Mix in ½ cup of the cherry soaking liquid (or whatever cherry soaking liquid is left plus enough water to make ½ cup). Let stand for 30 minutes.

Meanwhile, preheat the oven to 375 degrees. In a large bowl, whisk together the remaining ¼ cup of granulated sugar, the flour, almonds, brown sugar, cinnamon, and nutmeg. Slowly drizzle in the butter and stir with a fork until the mixture is crumbly and all the flour is incorporated. Do not let the mixture come together in a ball. Break up any large crumbs with your fingers. The crumbs should be smaller than 1 inch (otherwise, they won't cook all the way through).

Spoon the fruit mixture into eight 8-ounce ramekins and place them on a baking sheet (to bake one large crisp, see note). Evenly sprinkle the crumbs on top of the fruit. Bake until the fruit is bubbling and the topping is browned, about 40 minutes. Serve hot or warm.

cook's notes

- If you don't want to bake this in individual 8-ounce ramekins, use a 2-quart baking or gratin dish instead, and bake for 45 to 50 minutes. It works beautifully and still serves 8.
- Although the fruit cooks down a bit, it holds its shape really nicely.
- If you make this crisp with water and not wine, you'll still get the deep burgundy color from the cherries, but you'll lose a bit of the complexity of flavor.

tip

To deal with hardened brown sugar, according to Robert L. Wolke, the kitchen science guy who solves cooking conundrums for the *Washington Post* food section, you need to rehydrate the molasses that makes it brown. To do that, place a layer of plastic wrap over the brown sugar, add a damp paper towel, and seal tightly. Leave overnight — or all day — then remove the paper towel. The sugar should be soft and will stay that way for a while, unlike the highly touted microwave method, which just warms the molasses for a few minutes, long enough to measure the brown sugar, which then hardens up again right away.

SOURCE: *Central Market Foodie*
(newsletter for Central Market, Austin, Texas)
COOK: Unknown

apple-chile cobbler

IF WE HAD TO SETTLE FOR shopping at a single market for the rest of our lives, it would be Austin's Central Market. Once you've wandered through its magical aisles, other markets seem to be two-dimensional, photographed in black and white. It's Texas-huge, spilling over with fabulous produce you don't see anywhere else, and brimming with new ideas for the curious cook. The market is such a hit that it has spawned almost identical outposts in San Antonio, Dallas, Fort Worth, and Houston. So we were ripe for the picking with this amazing cobbler. Apples and chile? Anywhere else in America, we'd probably say no thanks, but in Texas it seems like a great idea. Chiles are good in everything, right? And the recipe calls for Hatch chiles, which come from a little town in New Mexico and have a distinctive flavor with moderate heat. We had to try it.

Once again, Texas is right: roasted green chiles and a splash of cider vinegar give this dessert a delicious edge that we love. If you're serving this to skeptics, don't even tell them what's in it — chances are, they won't guess but will clean their plates. The lemony crumble topping is crisp and lovely. We especially like this cobbler with a scoop of vanilla or cinnamon ice cream.

serves 8 to 10

FRUIT FILLING

5–6 Granny Smith or Gala apples, peeled, cored, and sliced
²/₃ cup packed brown sugar (see note)
¹/₂ cup chopped roasted and peeled green Hatch or New Mexico chiles (see note)
1 teaspoon cider vinegar
¹/₄ teaspoon ground cinnamon
¹/₄ teaspoon salt
¹/₈ teaspoon ground allspice
¹/₈ teaspoon ground nutmeg

CRUMB TOPPING

1¹/₄ cups all-purpose flour
1 cup sugar
Zest of 2 lemons
¹/₈ teaspoon salt
¹/₈ teaspoon ground cinnamon
¹/₈ teaspoon ground nutmeg
12 tablespoons (1¹/₂ sticks) cold unsalted butter
2 tablespoons heavy cream

Preheat the oven to 375 degrees and butter a 9-inch-square baking pan.

TO MAKE THE FRUIT FILLING:

In a large bowl, combine the apples, brown sugar, chiles, vinegar, cinnamon, salt, allspice, and nutmeg and toss to mix. Spoon into the prepared baking dish.

TO MAKE THE CRUMB TOPPING:

In a medium bowl, combine the flour, sugar, lemon zest, salt, cinnamon, and nutmeg and mix well. Cut the butter into small pieces and add it to the bowl. Work in the butter using a pastry cutter, two knives, or a fork until the mixture looks crumbly. Stir in the cream.

Spoon the topping over the filling and press down firmly. Bake until brown and bubbly, 45 to 50 minutes. Serve warm.

cook's notes

- For the chiles, look for small cans of whole green chiles. A 4-ounce can, drained, gives you exactly the ½ cup of chopped chiles you need here. Don't buy the already chopped canned chiles; they're impossible to drain and have a floppier texture.
- Use light or dark brown sugar in the filling.

tip

If you want to roast your own green chiles (Anaheims would be a good choice), here's how the *Central Market Foodie* says to do it: Place the fresh chiles on a baking pan 8 to 10 inches below the broiler. Broil the chiles, turning with tongs to cook all sides, until the skin is blackened overall. Transfer the blackened chiles to a paper bag, close tightly, and let cool for 15 minutes. Then slip off the peels with a small knife and remove the seeds before chopping to use in this recipe. If you have extra roasted chiles, freeze them with their skins on for extra flavor.

SOURCE: *Saveur Cooks Authentic Italian*
by the editors of *Saveur* magazine
COOK: Giovanni Stancampiano

pistachio gelato

GELATO IS JUST THE ITALIAN WORD for ice cream, and yet it's another thing entirely. Intensely flavored, smooth and elegant, somehow refreshing instead of satiating, gelato is ice cream taken to its highest power. There's no cream to coat your tongue and dull the taste — the richness usually comes from eggs, not butterfat — and although it's sweet, it's never overly sweet.

This sensationally good Sicilian gelato doesn't even include eggs and takes only about 15 minutes to put together. We're amazed at how simple it is to make something so celestial — in fact, we've never tasted a gelato this brilliant on our side of the pond. If you don't own an ice-cream maker, it's worth getting an inexpensive one just to make this great dessert.

Note that you need to start making the ice cream a day ahead.

serves 6 to 8

4 cups milk
1 cup sugar
3 tablespoons cornstarch

2 cups shelled unsalted pistachios, finely ground

The day before you plan to serve the gelato, in a medium heavy saucepan, heat 3 cups of the milk over medium heat until bubbles appear around the edge and the milk seems about to boil. Meanwhile, in a small bowl, combine the remaining 1 cup milk, the sugar, and cornstarch. Stir until well combined; set aside.

When the milk is ready, remove it from the heat and stir in the cornstarch mixture. Return the pan to the heat and cook, stirring frequently, until the sugar dissolves and the mixture thickens slightly, 8 to 10 minutes.

In a large bowl, stir together the pistachios and hot milk mixture. Let cool, stirring often. Cover with plastic wrap and refrigerate overnight.

Strain the pistachio-milk mixture through a fine sieve into a medium bowl, pressing the pistachios with the back of a wooden spoon to extract as much of the flavor as possible. Discard the pistachios.

Pour the strained milk mixture into an ice-cream maker and process according to the manufacturer's directions.

cook's notes

- If you're not serving the gelato right away, spoon it into a container, cover the surface with plastic wrap, seal, and store in the freezer. Let it soften slightly before serving.

- You can grind the nuts in a food processor, using the pulse method. If you let them go too long, however, they'll turn into an oily mess.

- The pistachios don't give up quite all their flavor, and the discarded pistachios are delicious blended into a vanilla milk shake.

tip

Rinsing the saucepan with water before heating milk or cream will make the pan easier to clean afterwards, according to Roy Finamore and Molly Stevens (*One Potato, Two Potato*), and they're right. You don't end up with that stubborn film of cooked-on milk solids that typically appears.

SOURCE: *Nuts* by Tina Salter
COOK: Gary Danko

spiced almond powder

SAN FRANCISCO CHEF GARY DANKO calls this "magic dust," and we quite agree. It was originally devised to stir into a rich custard base for home-made ice cream, but once you have some on hand, you'll no doubt find many uses for it. We certainly did.

The flavor is hauntingly delicious — sweet, nutty, spicy, lemony, and underlined with a hint of salt. Stir it into some softened store-bought vanilla ice cream (about ³/₄ cup per pint), or just sprinkle it on top. Use it in place of cinnamon-sugar on morning toast. Try it on hot cereal or French toast. Stir it into pudding or whipped cream. Sprinkle it on cookies, muffins, coffee cakes, and so on, before baking.

makes about ³/₄ cup

¼ cup whole almonds
⅓ cup sugar
½ teaspoon grated fresh lemon zest

½ teaspoon ground cardamom
⅛ teaspoon salt

Preheat the oven to 350 degrees. Spread the almonds on a baking sheet or in a shallow pan. Bake, stirring once or twice, until lightly browned and fragrant, 10 to 12 minutes. Let cool.

In a food processor, combine the almonds and the remaining ingredients. Process, pulsing on and off, until the almonds are chopped from coarse to very fine, depending on your preference. Use at once, or store in an airtight container.

cook's note

℞ You can use blanched almonds or almonds still in their skins. Either will do, although we prefer the added flavor, color, and texture of skin-on almonds.

SOURCE: *Chocolate Desserts by Pierre Hermé*
written by Dorie Greenspan
COOK: Pierre Hermé

cinnamon-caramel hot chocolate

THIS IS HOT CHOCOLATE LIKE no other, with an unmistakable French accent. It's rich, deep, dark, and decadent, with a caramelized sugar base. It makes a lovely dessert on its own, served in little coffee cups. As with every recipe we tried from Pierre Hermé's book, this is a serious chocolate fix. Unless you're a hardcore chocolate freak, you may find that this makes more than enough for two servings. Some may prefer smaller demitasse-sized portions. (The recipe counts a serving as an opulent 10 ounces.)

The whipping at the end — which you do with an immersion blender or in a bar blender — is essential to give this drink a thick, luxurious consistency to match its taste. For a grown-up treat, add a shot of dark rum or Grand Marnier to each cup. That would warm anyone up.

serves 2

2¹/₂ cups whole milk
¹/₃ cup sugar
1 cinnamon stick

4 ounces bittersweet chocolate, melted (see notes)

In a medium saucepan, combine the milk and ¹/₄ cup water. Bring to a boil and immediately remove from the heat.

Meanwhile, in a separate medium heavy saucepan, heat the sugar and cinnamon stick over medium heat. Cook, undisturbed, until the sugar starts to melt and color. As soon as you see the sugar start coloring around the edges, start stirring with a wooden spoon. Continue to cook and stir, making sure that the cinnamon stick is submerged and cooking along with the sugar, until the sugar is a deep amber color.

Still stirring, pour the hot milk mixture over the caramel. Don't be concerned if the caramel seizes and clumps — keep heating and stirring it, and it will liquefy again. When the mixture is smooth, whisk in the chocolate. Continue to whisk and heat the mixture until one bubble pops on the surface. Remove from the heat and discard the cinnamon stick. Whip the hot chocolate for about 1 minute with an immersion blender or in a regular blender. Serve immediately in large

desserts

cups, or pour into a medium bowl to cool. (The hot chocolate can be made up to 2 days ahead and kept tightly covered in the refrigerator.)

Reheat the chilled chocolate in a medium saucepan over low heat, whisking gently, just until the first bubble pops. Remove from the heat, whip the chocolate for 1 minute with the immersion blender or in a regular blender, and serve.

cook's notes

- When caramelizing the sugar, don't worry if small bits crystallize and stick to the wooden spoon. You can scrape these back into the pan once you've added the milk and water, and they will dissolve.
- The original recipe suggests using a French chocolate (but of course!) known as Valrhona Noir Gastronomie. If you're a chocophile, you'll be glad to know it's 61 percent cocoa. For the rest of us, any good-quality dark chocolate will be fine.
- Never let the hot chocolate boil or it may separate. Once that first bubble breaks the surface, remove it from the heat.

drinks

SOURCE: *Real Simple* magazine
COOK: *Real Simple* staff

real simple lemonade

IN THE SAME WAY THAT LEMONS were everywhere this year, lemonade was too — and made all different kinds of ways. Some people make a sugar syrup; others boil the zest with some sugar and water before adding the juice; *Cook's Illustrated* likes the old Amish way of pounding lemon slices and sugar with a potato masher for about 4 minutes until the sugar dissolves and the zest gives up its tasty oils. This one (a high-tech variation on the Amish method) is our favorite, because it has all the flavor of the lemon zest and it's child's play to make it.

It's real, real simple.

serves 6

3 large lemons, scrubbed and cut into eighths
1½ cups sugar (see note)
1 cup water plus 6 to 7 cups additional water

In a blender, process the lemons, sugar and 1 cup water until the lemons are coarsely chopped. Pour the slush through a fine sieve into a pitcher. Add 6 to 7 cups water to taste. Stir and serve in tall glasses over ice.

cook's note

This lemonade may be a little sweet for some palates. If you like your lemonade on the tart side, start with 1 cup of sugar and taste the end result; you can always add more.

tip

Michele Urvater, host of the Television Food Network's *Cooking Monday to Friday*, makes lemonade ice cubes so the lemonade doesn't get diluted by watery ice.

SOURCE: *Saveur*

COOK: **Niloufer Ichaporia King**

watermelon punch

IN MEXICO, THIS PUNCH IS KNOWN as agua de sandia (watermelon water), and it's one of those endless numbers of refreshing light drinks that Mexicans adore. All there is to this drink is some pureed watermelon, a lot of squeezed lime quarters, a little sugar, and lots of water. Add some ice, and you've got it. Add cachaça, the heady Brazilian sugar cane liquor, or white rum or vodka, and you've got something even better. At a party, you can have the bottles sitting next to the big jug or bowl of watermelon punch and let those who'd like to fortify their punch do it themselves.

makes 1 gallon

1 8-to-10-pound watermelon, preferably yellow

3–5 limes, scrubbed and quartered, seeds removed

¼–½ cup sugar

Cachaça, white rum, or vodka (optional)

Seed the watermelon and cut it into chunks. Puree it in a blender, then strain it into a large wide-mouth jar to catch any stray seeds.

Squeeze the quartered limes into the puree, adding the rinds. Add the ¼ to ½ cup sugar and 6 to 8 cups water to taste and mix well. Adjust the flavor with more sugar or limes, if you like. Add plenty of ice, then ladle into tall glasses. Let drinkers add liquor to their own glasses, if they like.

cook's note

℞ Of course you can use several smaller melons and it's fine to use seedless ones as well.

tip

From *Gourmet's Casual Entertaining:* To choose a good watermelon, says Ed Kee, a cooperative extension specialist at the University of Delaware, look for the place on the rind where the melon touched the ground as it grew. A creamy white rind means the melon isn't ripe; you want a yellowish orange cast to the rind for the best melon.

SOURCE: *Williams-Sonoma Taste*
COOK: Andy Harris

rum-cranberry fizz

THIS REFRESHING, ZIPPY DRINK is not only great in summer but works during the holidays in the same way ginger ale does, to counteract the richness of holiday fare. You could substitute vodka for the rum, but rum has a warming, tropical element that works magically here.

serves 1

¼ cup white rum
¼ cup cranberry juice

¼ cup grapefruit juice
Soda water

In a shaker, combine the rum, juices and 4 or 5 ice cubes. Shake well and strain into a cocktail glass. Top up with a splash of soda.

SOURCE: *New York Times*
COOK: **The Red Cat**

fragolas
(sparkling strawberry cocktails)

THIS WAS THE YEAR PROSECCO, a light sparkling wine from a small area north of Venice, got a lot of attention from bartenders across the country. Lighter than Champagne (and much cheaper), with smaller beads of sparkle, it's also lighter in alcohol, which means it's a good companion for fruity drinks like this one. Prosecco is what's in the famous Bellini served at Harry's Bar in Venice, mixed with an ethereal white peach juice.

This charming summer cocktail from the Red Cat restaurant in Manhattan takes a similar approach with strawberries. The berries need a couple of hours to release their flavor, then you add Prosecco just before serving.

This pretty, festive drink would be lovely to serve arriving guests at an outdoor wedding.

serves 4

½ cup plus 2 tablespoons sliced ripe sweet strawberries
1 teaspoon sugar, or more to taste
1 750-ml bottle Prosecco, chilled

In a small bowl, combine the strawberries and sugar. Using a fork, crush the strawberries to a rough pulp. Taste, and if the strawberries aren't sweet, add a touch more sugar; the mixture shouldn't be too sweet. Cover and refrigerate for 2 hours.

To serve, divide the strawberry mixture among 4 Champagne glasses. Pour chilled Prosecco on top and serve.

SOURCE: *Ismail Merchant's Passionate Meals*
COOK: **Ismail Merchant**

minted vodka tonic

THE FILM PRODUCER AND DIRECTOR Ismail Merchant is also known as a fabulous cook. If his vodka tonic with mint is a fair example, the man is a genius. This long tall drink is not only a stunner (it's made with 100-proof vodka) but also a knockout in taste, with a bit of the thrill of a mint julep.

Merchant advises potential tipplers to enjoy this drink in a hammock, with no thought of any postprandial navigating. Good plan.

serves 1

2 ounces 100-proof vodka
8–10 fresh mint leaves
       Tonic water, club soda, or seltzer water

Fill a large wine goblet with ice cubes and add the vodka. Add the mint leaves, stir vigorously, fill the glass with tonic water, club soda, or seltzer, and serve.

cook's note

❧ We love David Rosengarten's idea (in the *Rosengarten Report*) of making the ice cubes themselves out of tonic water so as not to dilute the drinks. Rosengarten feels that only Schweppes will do — and we agree.

SOURCE: *Dallas Morning News*
COOK: **Jean Andrews after Mark Miller**

serrano bloody marys

THE SERRANO CHILE is just the beginning of what's different about this terrific bloody Mary — it's the entire bunch of cilantro tossed in and the tequila and lime juice that make all the difference. This is a whole new taste. If you like cilantro, you'll love it.

Don't worry that the serranos will take your head off. Using three produces a drink that's no more peppery than a standard Bloody Mary; five will give you a very spicy hit. Non-imbibers will find this much more interesting than a Virgin Mary, so you might want to bring the tequila to the table and let people add their own, as they like.

The finished drink will have a dark rusty look, not the bright tomato-red you may be expecting — that's all the cilantro muddying the red.

This isn't a lot of tequila per person; it's a rather mild drink, which makes it useful for brunch.

serves 12

⅓ cup fresh lime juice
3–5 serrano chiles, stemmed and seeded
1 bunch cilantro, stemmed and chopped (reserve some sprigs for garnish)

1 46-ounce can tomato juice
¾ cup tequila, chilled
Salt and freshly ground black pepper

In a blender, blend the lime juice, chiles, and cilantro. Mix in the tomato juice and tequila and strain into a pitcher. (You may want to strain it twice.) Serve over ice. Garnish with salt and pepper to taste and a sprig of cilantro.

cook's notes

꿩 Taste the drink before you add any salt; some brands of tomato juice are very salty.

꿩 A thin circle of lime is another good garnish idea, since some people may want a little more lime in their drink.

tip

Chile expert Jean Andrews is quoted on her cure for chile mouth burn: "Try using vodka as a mouthwash and gargle, then spit it out . . . Cheap vodka works just as well!" Ms. Andrews is a fifth-generation Texan.

drinks

SOURCE: *Bobby Flay Cooks American*
by Bobby Flay
COOK: Bobby Flay

cranberry martinis

HOMEMADE FLAVORED VODKAS were everywhere this year, made with everything from raspberries (see tip) to candied ginger. It's a great idea, since it takes no time at all, just a little forethought, as the infusing takes several days, and it makes a huge splash at any party. This cranberry martini is especially tasty and gorgeous, perfect for Thanksgiving or Christmas revels. It tastes a little like a Cosmopolitan, but it's a lot easier to make.

If you can boil sugar and water together, you can astound your friends with this delicious, beautiful drink. And of course it also makes a really good holiday hostess gift.

The martini may seem a little overwhelming for some guests, who might prefer the cranberry vodka diluted a bit with sparkling water over ice. Just add a lime wedge.

serves 8

2 cups sugar

2 cups fresh or frozen cranberries
   (thawed), plus extra for garnish

1 fifth (1 liter) vodka

1 lime, cut into 8 wedges

At least 3 days before serving, in a medium saucepan, bring the sugar and 1 cup water to a boil. Cook, swirling the pan occasionally, until the sugar is completely dissolved and the mixture is slightly thickened. Remove from the heat, stir in the cranberries, and let stand at room temperature for 2 hours.

Pour the vodka into a large bowl (save the bottle) and add the cooled cranberry mixture. Cover the bowl or not, as you like. Let stand at room temperature for at least 2 days, stirring occasionally. Strain the vodka into the vodka bottle and chill overnight.

To serve, fill chilled martini glasses with the vodka. Add a few cranberries to each glass and garnish with a lime wedge.

- Probably some of the sugar will fall out of the mixture and settle on the bottom of the bowl in a hard layer. Just ignore it; the vodka will still be plenty sweet.
- Store any leftover cranberry vodka in the refrigerator.

tip

- In *Beard House* magazine, we found this raspberry vodka recipe, the work of Ari Nieminen at Manhattan's FireBird restaurant. It's a Russian restaurant, so presumably Nieminen knows his vodka. He takes 2 pints of raspberries and crushes them slightly, then mixes them with a liter of premium vodka in a large glass jar, seals it tightly, and leaves it at room temperature.

The next day he takes a taste — is the raspberry flavor intense enough? He tastes for three more days, and if there's any vodka left by the time it's fully infused, he strains it into the original vodka bottle, chills it and serves it neat.

SOURCE: *New York Times*
COOK: **Regina Schrambling**

high-octane glogg

SWEDEN'S FAMOUS SPICED HOT PUNCH is just the thing for a holiday party or a convivial after-ski evening. That's the point, actually; it's a convivial drink, and people rarely have just one cup. Glogg makes a party all by itself. This version is also particularly potent, so if a lot of guests are driving, it's not a good idea to serve glogg.

This glogg is a freewheeling invention based on the classic, with twice as much red wine and a bottle of ruby port thrown in to complicate the flavor. Regina Schrambling always serves it hot right out of the pot. Guests are encouraged to scoop the almonds and raisins out of the bottom of their cups with their fingers.

makes 1 gallon

2 750-ml bottles inexpensive dry red wine
1 bottle ruby port
4 cups aquavit
5 tablespoons sugar
4 cardamom pods
12 whole cloves
12 allspice berries
1 cinnamon stick
1 cup blanched slivered almonds
1 cup golden raisins

In a large enamel or stainless-steel pot, combine all the ingredients except the almonds and raisins. Bring slowly to a simmer, stirring to dissolve the sugar, and heat just until the glogg starts to steam, about 10 minutes. To serve, place a couple of almonds and raisins in each small cup and ladle the glogg over.

CREDITS

INDEX

credits

Spicy Maple Walnuts by Barbara J. Witt. Copyright © 2001 by Barbara J. Witt. First published in *Fine Cooking* magazine. Reprinted by permission of Barbara J. Witt.

Edamame with Szechwan Pepper-Salt by Jennifer Cox in *Asian Vegetables* by Sara Deseran copyright © 2001. Reprinted by permission of Chronicle Books, LLC, San Francisco.

Spicy Margarita Raisins by Robert Del Grande. Copyright © 2001 by The California Raisin Marketing Board. First published on www.calraisins.org. Reprinted by permission of The California Raisin Marketing Board.

Bacon-Wrapped Dates with Almonds by Marimar Torres. Copyright © 2001 by John Brown Publishing, Inc. First published in *Taste* magazine. Reprinted by permission of John Brown Publishing, Inc.

Vodka-Spiked Cherry Tomatoes with Pepper-Salt by Katy Massam. Copyright © 2001 by Condé Nast. First published in *Gourmet* magazine. Reprinted by permission of Condé Nast Publications. All rights reserved.

Almond Cheese Straws by Marian Burros after Ann Amernick. Copyright © 2001 by The New York Times Company. First published in *The New York Times*. Reprinted by permission of The New York Times Company.

Party Cheese Crackers by Karyl Bannister. Copyright © 2001 by Karyl Bannister. First published in *Cook & Tell*. Reprinted by permission of Houghton Mifflin Company.

Curried Almond Shortbread by Victoria Spencer. Copyright © 2001 by Victoria Spencer. First published in *Metropolitan Home* magazine. Reprinted by permission of Victoria Spencer.

Porcini Mushroom and Red Onion Tart by Tamasin Day-Lewis. Copyright © 2001 by Tamasin Day-Lewis. First published in *The Art of the Tart*, published by The Orion Publishing Group.

Beef Tenderloin Tapas by Alex Duran. Copyright © 2001 by Alex Duran. First published in *Santé* magazine. Reprinted by permission of Alex Duran.

Garlicky Sun-Dried Tomato Spread by Vivian Beatrice. Copyright © 2001 by Vivian Beatrice. First published on the Cody Creek Farm garlic package. Reprinted by permission of Vivian Beatrice.

Bacon, Scallion, and Caramelized Onion Dip by Julia Colin. Copyright © 2001 by Boston Common Press. First published in *Cook's*

lishing Co., Inc., New York. All rights reserved.

Zesty Cole Slaw with Peanuts by Sujata Halarnkar. Copyright © 2001 by Sujata Halarnkar. First published on the REI Web site, www.rei.com. Reprinted by permission of Sujata Halarnkar.

Chickpea Salad with Four-Minute Eggs by Gabrielle Hamilton. Copyright © 2001 by Gabrielle Hamilton. First published in *Food & Wine* magazine. Reprinted by permission of Gabrielle Hamilton.

Heirloom Tomato and Watermelon Salad by Geoffrey Zakarian. Copyright © 2001 by Geoffrey Zakarian. First published in *New York* magazine. Reprinted by permission of Geoffrey Zakarian.

Broccoli Salad with Creamy Mustard Dressing by Ken Haedrich. Copyright © 2001 by Ken Haedrich. First published in *Soup Makes the Meal*. Reprinted by permission of Harvard Common Press.

Georgian Bean Salad Reprinted with the permission of Simon & Schuster, Inc., from *The Joy of Cooking. All About Salads and Dressings* by Irma S. Rombauer, Marion Rombauer Becker and Ethan Becker. Copyright © 2001 by Simon & Schuster, Inc., The Joy of Cooking Trust, and The MRB Revocable Trust.

Sugar Snap Pea and Prosciutto Salad by Joanne Weir. Copyright © 2001 by Joanne Weir. First published in *Food & Wine* magazine. Reprinted by permission of Joanne Weir.

German Potato Salad by Corby Kummer. Copyright © 2001 by Corby Kummer. First published in *The Atlantic Monthly*. Reprinted by permission of Corby Kummer.

Fattoush (Middle Eastern Bread Salad) by Seta Keshishian. Copyright © 2001 by Seta Keshishian. First published in *The Boston Globe*. Reprinted by permission of Seta Keshishian.

"Squash and Smash" Tomato-Olive Salad from *The Naked Chef Takes Off* by Jamie Oliver. Copyright © 2001 by Jamie Oliver. Reprinted by permission of Hyperion.

Sicilian Slow-Roasted Onion Salad by Paula Wolfert. Copyright © 2001 by Paula Wolfert. First published in *Food & Wine* magazine. Reprinted by permission of Paula Wolfert.

Fiesolana by Stefano Lascialfari. Copyright © 2001 by Stefano Lascialfari. First published in *The New York Times Magazine*. Reprinted by permission of Stefano Lascialfari.

Sesame-Orange Granola. From *Back to the Table: The Reunion of Food and Family* by Art Smith. Copyright © 2001 by Art Smith. Reprinted by permission of Hyperion.

Lemon-Raisin Breakfast Bars by Dorcas Miller. Copyright © 2001 by *Backpacker Magazine*. First published in *Backpacker Magazine*. Reprinted by permission of *Backpacker Magazine*.

Double-Boiler Scrambled Eggs by Marcelle Bienvenu. Copyright © 2001 by Marcelle Bienvenu. First published in *The New Orleans Times-Picayne*. Reprinted by permission of Marcelle Bienvenu.

Sausage Links with Apricot-Mustard Glaze by Betty Rosbottom. Copyright © 2001 by Betty Rosbottom. First published in *Bon Appétit* magazine. Reprinted by permission of Betty Rosbottom.

Three-Cheese Baked Egg Puff with Roasted Peppers and Sweet Spicy Bacon by Amy Mastrangelo. Copyright © 2001 by Condé Nast. First published in *Gourmet* magazine. Reprinted by permission of Condé Nast Publications. All rights reserved.

Light Crisp Waffles by Pamela Anderson. Copyright © 2001 by Pamela Anderson. First published in *Fine Cooking* magazine and *CookSmart* (Houghton Mifflin). Reprinted by permission of Pamela Anderson.

Sow's Ear Baked Apple Pancake. Copyright © 2001 by *The Los Angeles Times*. First published in *The Los Angeles Times*. Reprinted by permission of The Los Angeles Times Syndicate.

Morning Bread Pudding by Rhonda Hesser. Copyright © 2001 by The New York Times Co. First published in *The New York Times*. Reprinted by permission of The New York Times Co.

Blueberry Muffin Topping Tip from *Cook's Illustrated* magazine. Copyright © 2001 by Boston Common Press.

Apricot–Cream Cheese Scones. Copyright © 2001 by The King Arthur Flour Company. First published on www.KingArthurFlour.com. Reprinted by permission of The King Arthur Flour Company.

Cherry-Almond Twist Pastry. Copyright © 2001 by Dierbergs Markets, Inc. First published in *Everybody Cooks* newsletter. Reprinted by permission of Dierbergs Markets, Inc.

Orange-Caramel Monkey Bread. Reprinted with permission from *Caprial's Desserts* by Caprial Pence and Melissa Carey. Copyright © 2001 by Caprial Pence and Melissa Carey, Ten Speed Press, Berkeley, Calif., www.tenspeed.com.

Baked Eggplant Parmesan from *Enoteca* by Joyce Goldstein copyright © 2001. Reprinted by permission of Chronicle Books, LLC, San Francisco.

Chile-Cheese Supper Dish by Marion Cunningham. Copyright © 2001 by *The Los Angeles Times*. First published in *The Los Angeles Times*. Reprinted by permission of The Los Angeles Times Syndicate.

Roasted Tomato, Basil, and Parmesan Pie. Reprinted with permission from Simon & Schuster from *Fearless Baking* by Elinor Klivans. Copyright © 2001 by Elinor Klivans.

Potato Cake Filled with Mozzarella and Prosciutto by Anna del Conte. Copyright © 2001 by Anna del Conte. First published in *The Gastronomy of Italy*, published by Friedman/Fairfax, a division of Sterling Publishing Co., Inc.

Moroccan Root Vegetable Stew with Charmoula by Robin Davis and Tara Duggan. Copyright © 2001 by *The San Francisco Chronicle*. First published in *The San Francisco Chronicle*. Reprinted by permission of The San Francisco Chronicle.

Danny's Lemon Pasta from *Comfort Me with Apples* by Ruth Reichl, copyright © 2001 by Ruth Reichl. Used by permission of Random House, Inc.

Pasta with Born-Again Zucchini and Pesto by John Thorne and Matt Lewis Thorne. Copyright © 2001 by John Thorne and Matt Lewis Thorne. First published in *Simple Cooking*. Reprinted by permission of John Thorne and Matt Lewis Thorne.

Spaghetti with Fried Eggs and Roasted Red Peppers from *Naples at Table: Cooking in Campania* by Arthur Schwartz. Copyright © 1998 by Arthur Schwartz. Reprinted by permission of HarperCollins Publishers, Inc.

Rigatoni with Sausage and Cannellini Beans by Barbara Lynch. Copyright © 2001 by Barbara Lynch. First published in *The Boston*

2001 by *The Atlanta Journal-Constitution*. First published in *The Atlanta Journal-Constitution*. Reprinted by permission.

Boulevard's Staff Turkey Breast by Nancy Oakes in *The San Francisco Chronicle Cookbook,* Volume II by Michael Bauer and Fran Irwin copyright © 2001. Reprinted by permission of Chronicle Books, LLC, San Francisco.

Spice-Rubbed Turkey with Sage Gravy and Wild Mushroom Stuffing by Tom Douglas. Copyright © 2001 by Tom Douglas. First published in *Food & Wine* magazine. Reprinted by permission of Tom Douglas.

Upperline Roast Duck with Ginger-Peach Sauce from The Upperline, New Orleans. Copyright © 2001 by JoAnn Clevenger. First published in *Chile Pepper Magazine*. Reprinted by permission of *Chile Pepper Magazine* and JoAnn Clevenger.

Blue Plate Meat Loaf. Copyright © 2001 by Weldon Owen Inc. and Williams-Sonoma Inc. Recipes by Beth Dooley. Photographs by Leigh Beisch. First published in *The Heartland* (Williams-Sonoma New American Cooking Series). Reprinted by permission of Weldon Owen.

New York Spiedies by Patrick Kennedy. Copyright © 2001 by Patrick Kennedy. First published in *The Washington Post*.

Chicken-Fried Steak with Chipotle Gravy. Copyright © 2001 by Weldon Owen Inc. and Williams-Sonoma Inc. Recipes by Kathi Long. Photographs by Leigh Beisch. First published in *The Southwest* (Williams-Sonoma New American Cooking Series). Reprinted by permission of Weldon Owen.

Barbecued Brisket by Eileen Weinberg. Copyright © 2001 by Eileen Weinberg. First published in Macy's DeGustibus Cooking

School handout. Reprinted by permission of Eileen Weinberg.

Italian Beef Stew from *Second Helpings from Union Square Café* by Danny Meyer and Michael Romano. Copyright © 2001 by Danny Meyer and Michael Romano. Reprinted by permission of HarperCollins Publishers, Inc.

Braised Short Ribs of Beef from *The Elements of Taste* by Gray Kunz and Peter Kaminsky. Copyright © 2001 by Gray Kunz and Peter Kaminsky. By permission of Little, Brown and Company, Inc.

Individual Beef Wellingtons with Mushroom, Spinach, and Blue Cheese Filling by Ris Lacoste. Copyright © 2001 by Ris Lacoste. First published in *Fine Cooking* magazine. Reprinted by permission of Ris Lacoste.

Pork Chops Adobado by Sarah Fritschner. Copyright © 2001 by Sarah Fritschner. First published in *The Courier-Journal* (Louisville). Reprinted by permission of Sarah Fritschner.

Pork Stew with Leeks, Orange and Mint from *The Glorious Foods of Greece* by Diane Kochilas. Copyright © 2001 by Diane Kochilas. Reprinted by permission of HarperCollins Publishers Inc., William Morrow.

Portuguese Pork Sausage and Clams with Saffron. From *Secrets of Saffron* by Pat Willard. Copyright © 2001 by Pat Willard. Reprinted by permission of Pat Willard and Beacon Press, Boston.

Honey-Bourbon Ham Steak by Cheryl Alters Jamison and Bill Jamison. Copyright © 2001 by Cheryl Alters Jamison and Bill Jamison. First published in *Born to Grill*.

Reprinted by permission of Harper-Collins Publishers Inc.

Cabbage Gratin with Red Pepper and Tomato from *The Best Vegetarian Recipes* by Martha Rose Shulman. Copyright © 2001 by Martha Rose Shulman. Reprinted by permission of HarperCollins Publishers Inc., William Morrow.

Cherry Tomato Gratin. Copyright © 2001 by Hearst Communications, Inc. First published in *The All New Good Housekeeping Cookbook*. Reprinted by permission of Hearst Books, a division of Sterling Publishing Co., Inc.

Scallion Noodles from *Pleasures of the Vietnamese Table* by Mai Pham. Copyright © 2001 by Mai Pham. Reprinted by permission of HarperCollins Publishers Inc.

Persian Rice with Dill and Pistachios by Bruce Feiler. Copyright © 2001 by Condé Nast. First published in *Gourmet* magazine. Reprinted by permission of Condé Nast Publications.

Green Pea Risotto from *How to Eat: The Pleasures and Principles of Good Food* by Nigella Lawson. Copyright © 2001 by Nigella Lawson. This material is used by permission of John Wiley & Sons, Inc.

Sardinian Old Bread and Tomato Casserole from *Lidia's Italian-American Kitchen* by Lidia Matticchio Bastianich, copyright © 2001 by A La Carte Communications and Tutti a Tavola, LLC. Photographs copyright © 2001 by Christopher Hirsheimer. Used by permission of Alfred A. Knopf, a division of Random House, Inc.

Bacon Bread Pudding by Jan Curry. Copyright © 2001 by Jan Curry. First published in *Fine Cooking* magazine. Reprinted by permission of Jan Curry.

Double Corn Polenta by Johanne Killeen and George Germon. Copyright © 2001 by Jo-hanne Killeen and George Germon. First published on www.marthastewartliving.com. Reprinted by permission of Johanne Killeen and George Germon.

Sweet Potato Spoon Bread. Copyright © 2001 by Le Zinc. First published in *Time Out New York*. Reprinted by permission of Le Zinc.

Cumin Apple Chips by Katy Massam. Copyright © 2001 by Condé Nast. First published in *Gourmet* magazine. Reprinted by permission of Condé Nast Publications.

Grape Salsa by Jacqueline Higuera McMahan. Copyright © 2001 by *The San Francisco Chronicle*. First published in *The San Francisco Chronicle*. Reprinted by permission.

Cranberry and Dried Cherry Relish by Rozanne Gold. Copyright © 2001 by Rozanne Gold. First published in *Bon Appétit* magazine. Reprinted by permission of Rozanne Gold.

Nadine's Onion and Black Pepper Rolls from *River Run Cookbook* by Jimmy and Maya Kennedy and Marialisa Calta. Copyright © 2001 by Jimmy and Maya Kennedy, and Marialisa Calta. Foreword copyright © 2001 by David Mamet. Afterword copyright © 2001 by Howard Norman. Reprinted by permission of HarperCollins Publishers Inc.

Hoosier Ham and Cheese Biscuits by Judith M. Fertig. Copyright © 2001 by Judith M. Fertig. First published in *Prairie Home Breads*. Reprinted by permission of Harvard Common Press.

Green Onion Buttermilk Biscuits by Debbie Day's grandmother. Copyright © 2001 by Day Kerr. Reprinted by permission of Day Kerr.

Lemon-Thyme Biscuits from *Moosewood Restaurant New Classics* by Moosewood Collec-

Buttercup Bake Shop Cookbook by Jennifer Appel. Copyright © 2001 by Jennifer Appel.

Pecan Whiskey Cake. Reprinted with permission from *Mrs. Wilkes' Boardinghouse Cookbook: Recipes and Recollections from Her Savannah Table* by Sema Wilkes. Copyright © 2001 by Marcia Thompson and Sema Wilkes, Ten Speed Press, Berkeley, Calif., www.tenspeed.com.

Anarchy Cake by Faith Willinger. Copyright © 2001 by Faith Willinger. First published on www.Epicurious.com. Reprinted by permission of Faith Willinger.

Intense Chocolate Torte by Gloria Pedilla. Copyright © 2001 by Unified Grocers/Palace Market. First published in a Palace Market advertisement. Reprinted by permission of Gloria Pedilla.

Lemon and Goat Cheese Cheesecake from *Luscious Lemon Desserts* by Lori Longbotham copyright © 2001. Reprinted by permission of Chronicle Books, LLC, San Francisco.

Capirotada. Copyright © 2001 by MexGrocer.com, LLC. First published on www.MexGrocer.com. Reprinted by permission of MexGrocer.com, LLC.

Ginger Puddings with Bittersweet Chocolate Sauce and Ginger Caramel Crunch by Nick Malgieri. Copyright © 2001 by Nick Malgieri. First published in *Food & Wine* magazine. Reprinted by permission of Nick Malgieri.

Crème Fraîche Panna Cotta with Berry Puree by Tom Valenti. Copyright © 2001 by Tom Valenti. First published in *New York* magazine. Reprinted by permission of Tom Valenti.

Cranberry Puff-Up by Irene Young. Copyright © 2001 by *Yankee* magazine. First published

in *Yankee* magazine. Reprinted by permission of *Yankee* magazine.

Double-Crust Jumble Berry Pie by Carolyn Weil. Copyright © 2001 by Carolyn Weil. First published in *Fine Cooking* magazine. Reprinted by permission of Carolyn Weil.

Ported Rhubarb by Anne Willan. Copyright © 2001 by Anne Willan, Inc. First published in *The Washington Post*. Reprinted by permission of Anne Willan.

Roasted Apricots with Cardamom by Sally Schneider. Copyright © 2001 by Sally Schneider. First published in *A New Way to Cook* (Workman/Artisan). Reprinted by permission of Sally Schneider.

Pear Crisp with Dried Sour Cherries from *The Last Course* by Claudia Fleming. Copyright © 2001 by Claudia Fleming. Used by permission of Random House, Inc.

Apple-Chile Cobbler. Copyright © 2001 by Central Market. First published in *Central Market Foodie*. Reprinted by permission of Central Market.

Pistachio Gelato from *Saveur Cooks Authentic Italian* by World Publications, Inc. copyright © 2001. Reprinted by permission of Chronicle Books, LLC, San Francisco.

Spiced Almond Powder by Gary Danko. Reprinted with permission from *Nuts: Sweet and Savory Recipes* by Tina Salter. Copyright © 2001 by Diamond of California, Ten Speed Press, Berkeley, Calif., www.tenspeed.com.

Cinnamon-Caramel Hot Chocolate from *Chocolate Desserts* by Pierre Herme. Copyright © 2001 by SOCREPA and Dorie Greenspan. By permission of Little, Brown and Company, Inc.

Real Simple Lemonade. First published in *Real Simple* magazine. Copyright © 2001 by

index

index

index

index

index

V

Valenti, Tom, 279
Valentino's Chocolate Truffle Cake, 262–63
Vatapa (Brazilian Fish Soup), 44–45
Vegetable(s). *See also specific vegetables*
    Root, Stew with Charmoula, Moroccan, 106–8
    Root, Whipped, 205
Vodka
    Cranberry Martinis, 304
    homemade raspberry, 305
    -Spiked Cherry Tomatoes with Pepper-Salt, 6–7
    Tonic, Minted, 302

W

waffle irons, buying, 81
Waffles, Cornmeal, 81
Waffles, Cranberry-Orange, 81
Waffles, Light Crisp, 80–81
Walker, Reagan, 146
Walnuts
    Lemon-Raisin Breakfast Bars, 74
    Spiced Spinach with Yogurt, 208
    Spicy Maple, 1
Watercress Salad, Baby, with Smoked Salmon Croque Monsieur, 134–135
Watermelon
    and Heirloom Tomato Salad, 56–57
    Punch, 299
    ripe, buying, 299
Weil, Carolyn, 261, 282

Weinberg, Eileen, 164
Weir, Joanne, 48, 61
Whiskey
    Beef Tenderloin Tapas, 17–18
    Pecan Cake, 266–67
Wilcox, Kip, 235
Wild, Michael, 40
Wild Mushroom Stuffing, 152–53
Wilkes, Sema, 266
Willan, Anne, 285
Willard, Pat, 180
Willinger, Faith Heller, 261, 268
wine, leftover, freezing, 115
Wiseman, Shelton, 27
Witt, Barbara J., 1
Wolfert, Paula, 66
Wondra flour, for coating fish, 129
Wright, Clifford A., 208

Y

Yogurt, Spiced Spinach with, 208
Yosses, Bill, 242
Young, Irene S., 281

Z

Zakarian, Geoffrey, 56
zesters, 93, 235
Zesty Coleslaw with Peanuts, 53
Zucchini
    Born-Again, and Pesto, Pasta with, 110–11
    Fresh, Almonds, Curry, and Mint, 209
    Laksa (Malaysian Noodle Soup), 32–33

THE B·E·S·T AMERICAN SERIES ™

THE BEST AMERICAN SHORT STORIES® 2002
Sue Miller, guest editor
Katrina Kenison, series editor

"Story for story, readers can't beat *The Best American Short Stories* series" (*Chicago Tribune*). This year's most beloved short fiction anthology is edited by the best-selling novelist Sue Miller and includes stories by Edwidge Danticat, Jill McCorkle, E. L. Doctorow, Arthur Miller, and Akhil Sharma, among others.

0-618-13173-6 PA $13.00 / 0-618-11749-0 CL $27.50
0-618-13172-8 CASS $26.00 / 0-618-25816-7 CD $35.00

THE BEST AMERICAN ESSAYS® 2002
Stephen Jay Gould, guest editor
Robert Atwan, series editor

Since 1986, the *Best American Essays* series has gathered the best nonfiction writing of the year and established itself as the best anthology of its kind. Edited by Stephen Jay Gould, the eminent scientist and distinguished writer, this year's volume features writing by Jonathan Franzen, Sebastian Junger, Gore Vidal, Mario Vargas Llosa, and others.

0-618-04932-0 PA $13.00 / 0-618-21388-0 CL $27.50

THE BEST AMERICAN MYSTERY STORIES™ 2002
James Ellroy, guest editor
Otto Penzler, series editor

Our perennially popular anthology is a favorite of mystery buffs and general readers alike. This year's volume is edited by the internationally acclaimed author James Ellroy and offers pieces by Robert B. Parker, Joyce Carol Oates, Michael Connelly, Stuart M. Kaminsky, and others.

0-618-12493-4 PA $13.00 / 0-618-12494-2 CL $27.50
0-618-25807-8 CASS $26.00 / 0-618-25806-X CD $35.00

THE BEST AMERICAN SPORTS WRITING™ 2002
Rick Reilly, guest editor
Glenn Stout, series editor

This series has garnered wide acclaim for its stellar sports writing and topnotch editors. Now Rick Reilly, the best-selling author and "Life of Reilly" columnist for *Sports Illustrated*, continues that tradition with pieces by Frank Deford, Steve Ruskin, Jeanne Marie Laskas, Mark Kram, Jr., and others.

0-618-08628-5 PA $13.00 / 0-618-08627-7 CL $27.50

THE BEST AMERICAN TRAVEL WRITING 2002

Frances Mayes, editor

Jason Wilson, series editor

The Best American Travel Writing 2002 is edited by Frances Mayes, the author of the enormously popular *Under the Tuscan Sun* and *Bella Tuscany*. Giving new life to armchair travel for 2002 are David Sedaris, Kate Wheeler, André Aciman, and many others.

0-618-11880-2 PA $13.00 / 0-618-11879-9 CL $27.50
0-618-19719-2 CASS $26.00 / 0-618-19720-6 CD $35.00

THE BEST AMERICAN SCIENCE AND NATURE WRITING 2002

Natalie Angier, guest editor

Tim Folger, series editor

This year's edition promises to be another "eclectic, provocative collection" (*Entertainment Weekly*). Edited by Natalie Angier, the Pulitzer Prize–winning author of *Woman: An Intimate Geography*, it features work by Malcolm Galdwell, Joy Williams, Barbara Ehrenreich, Dennis Overbye, and others.

0-618-13478-6 PA $13.00 / 0-618-08297-2 CL $27.50

THE BEST AMERICAN RECIPES 2002–2003

Edited by Fran McCullough with Molly Stevens
Foreword by Anthony Bourdain

"The cream of the crop . . . McCullough's selections form an eclectic, unfussy mix."—*People*

Offering the very best of what America is cooking, as well as the latest trends, time-saving tips, and techniques, this year's edition includes a foreword by Anthony Bourdain, the best-selling author of *Kitchen Confidential* and *A Cook's Tour*.

0-618-19137-2 CL $26.00

THE BEST AMERICAN NONREQUIRED READING 2002

Dave Eggers, guest editor

Michael Cart, series editor

The Best American Nonrequired Reading is the newest addition to the series—and the first annual of its kind for readers fifteen and up. Edited by Dave Eggers, the author of the phenomenal bestseller *A Heartbreaking Work of Staggering Genius*, this genre-busting inaugural volume draws from mainstream and alternative American periodicals and features writing by Eric Schlosser, David Sedaris, Sam Lipsyte, Michael Finkel, and others.

0-618-24694-0 $13.00 PA / 0-618-24693-2 $27.50 CL
0-618-25810-8 $35.00 CD

 HOUGHTON MIFFLIN COMPANY / www.houghtonmifflinbooks.com

132-3
136
216-17